ELECTORAL REFORM IN WAR AND
PEACE 1906-18

ELECTORAL REFORM IN WAR AND PEACE 1906-18

MARTIN PUGH

ROUTLEDGE & KEGAN PAUL
London, Henley and Boston

First published in 1978
by Routledge & Kegan Paul Ltd
39 Store Street,
London WC1E 7DD,
Broadway House,
Newtown Road,
Henley-on-Thames,
Oxon RG9 1EN and
9 Park Street,
Boston, Mass. 02108, USA
Printed in Great Britain by
Thomson Litho, East Kilbride, Scotland

British Library Cataloguing in Publication Data

Pugh, Martin
Electoral reform in war and peace, 1906-18.
1. Elections - Great Britain - History - 20th century
I. Title
324'.21'0941   JN955   78-40275

ISBN O 7100 8792 6

For Fran

CONTENTS

PREFACE

The Fourth Parliamentary Reform Act of 1918, in some ways the greatest of the series, has been unaccountably neglected by historians.
Perhaps this book will initiate a discussion on the subject.   Because the 1918 Act, unlike the earlier reform measures, occurred
during a war it has often been claimed or dismissed as a product of
that situation.   This is especially the case with those who study
war without also studying the periods before and between wars.
Seen in perspective, however, the Great War provided the occasion
rather than the cause of the Reform Act; it was unfinished business.   This is emphasised by the fact that in 1917-18 one finds
Parliament involved in a prolonged controversy not over the major
changes in the franchise, but solely over the reform of the electoral system by proportional representation and the alternative vote.
That debate grew directly out of the conditions of Edwardian politics; its outcome was the result of the special relationship between the Liberal and Labour Parties; and the achievement in 1918
of a democratic franchise in combination with an unreformed electoral system proved to be the most significant decision of the war,
for it produced a Conservative hegemony in British Government that
lasted until 1945.

In the course of writing this book I have incurred many debts.
I would like to thank several historians for making useful criti-
cisms of earlier drafts of the work, particularly Mr Neal Blewett,
Dr P.F. Clarke, Mr Edward David, Dr Henry Pelling and Professor J.R.
Vincent who first suggested the topic to me.   Among the many people
who have assisted me with material for the book at various stages I
would like to record my gratitude to Mr G. Awdry, Librarian of the
National Liberal Club, Mr Geoffrey Block, OBE, of the Conservative
Research Centre, Miss Enid Lakeman and the staff of the Electoral
Reform Society and Mr and Mrs John MacCallum Scott.

Martin Pugh

ACKNOWLEDGMENTS

I would like to express my sincere gratitude to the following indi-
viduals and institutions who have given me permission to quote from
papers in their possession: Mr Mark Bonham-Carter, the British
Library, the Hon. Mrs Vera Butler, the Carlisle Record Office, the
Department of Palaeography and Diplomatic (Durham University), the
Earl of Derby, Lord Dickinson of Painswick, Miss Anne Holt, the
House of Lords Record Office, Viscount Long of Wraxall, Mr J.H. Mac-
Callum Scott, the Marquess of Salisbury, Viscount Scarsdale, Mr L.P.
Scott, the Earl of Selborne, Mrs G. Stafford, Viscount Ullswater
and the Warden and Fellows of New College, Oxford.

                                                          M.D.P.

LIST OF ABBREVIATIONS

BLP   Bonar Law Papers
ERS   Electoral Reform Society Papers
FLP   Fawcett Library Papers
LGP   Lloyd George Papers
HC Deb. House of Commons Debates
HL Deb. House of Lords Debates

Part one

Chapter 1

THE PARTIES AND THE SYSTEM 1906-14

Now that something like universal suffrage has been introduced
... the franchise is little discussed, and much more is said
about the constituencies ... it was formerly assumed that the
interests of the mass of the people were fundamentally identical;
and hence the mode in which the electors were grouped was comparatively unimportant.... We have now learned that the formation of the constituencies offers a distinct problem with grave
practical effects. (A.L. Lowell, 'The Government of England',
1908)

For all their interest in constitutional controversies the Edwar-
dians refused to allow the parliamentary franchise to dominate politics. No doubt the suffragettes filled many columns of newsprint,
but, unfortunately, in becoming a great entertainment they could not
prevent the press from trivialising and obscuring the issues they
sought to raise. Indeed they allowed themselves to be provoked
into imitating both the Ulster Unionists, who displaced them from
the headlines, and the great nineteenth century campaigns for parliamentary reform; thus, if 1832 had been illuminated by Nottingham
Castle, ablaze for the franchise, so 1912 was lit by the modest glow
of Lloyd George's mansion at Churt.
    Many circumstances in fact conspired, as we shall see, to prevent
the vote, for women and for men, developing into the central issue
it had often been in the nineteenth century; we may note, at the
start, simply two. The first is that the Edwardian electorate was
already a fairly democratic one, and was regarded as such even by
those who wished to reform it. Until the early 1960s historians
were apt to assume that manhood suffrage had virtually been achieved
by 1900, a gross exaggeration which has collapsed in the face of the
evidence that only some 60 per cent of adult males were on the parliamentary register before the First World War. (1) However, there
is a danger of going to the other extreme and underplaying the democratic quality of the system. (2) For although the electoral body
was rather more representative of middle class than of working class
people, a substantial majority of the eight million Edwardian voters
were, none the less, working class. Moreover, among the four and a
half million men who were not on the Register at any one time only

one and a half million were expressly excluded in law from the franchise; (3) the majority enjoyed one of the seven franchise qualifications allowed by the Act of 1884, usually as householders or lodgers, but failed to be registered owing to the complexity of the registration system and particularly to the need for twelve months' continuous residence.   A man could thus move back and forth between voting and non-voting, and the dividing line between the enfranchised and the unenfranchised was therefore much less significant than the gross numbers would suggest.   This is reflected in the attitude of Liberal and Labour democrats of the time who, though they advocated reform, especially of the half a million plural voting element, did not find an intolerable grievance in a system which gave eight million men the vote.   In contrast to 1832, 1867 and 1884 when distinct sections of the people had awaited enfranchisement, the Reforms Bills of 1912 and 1917 did not define new and hitherto deprived classes in the community. (4)   The system undoubtedly seemed to many too complex and cumbersome, too weighted towards property, but for all that it was roughly representative.

There existed, however, a second general reason that tended to deprive the franchise of a pre-eminent place in the attention of reformers.   Since 1885 when the majority of constituencies had become single-member ones for the first time, interest had begun to centre less upon the number of voters and more upon means of grouping them and the methods of polling them.   In 1885 single-member seats had been seen partly as a way of checking the development of caucus politics which had sprung up since 1867 particularly in the three-member boroughs such as Birmingham created by the second Reform Act; a single-member system had seemed a simpler method of allowing minority representation.   The arrangement proved to be especially to the advantage of the Conservative Party in larger boroughs where middle class suburbs and business communities could often be grouped into single, homogeneous constituencies; (5) Liberals too came to see the virtues of a system which provided them with safe seats in the form of County Divisions designed to include all the miners. Thus, when boundaries were drawn in accordance with the 'pursuits of the people' the modern constituency pattern grew up in which professional politicians trained in hopeless seats and graduated to safe ones.

This development, taken with the swollen electorate and the growth of the party organisations in the last quarter of the nineteenth century, produced a variety of critical reactions by the Edwardian period.   For example, the backbench Member of Parliament was held to have surrendered much of his independence locally and at Westminster through his need for the party ticket; (6) doubts were cast upon the virtue of a mass electorate by Ostrogorski and Graham Wallas; (7) and the Cabinet was regarded as an élite of professional politicians growing steadily less responsible to the House of Commons, a trend which attracted the satire and criticism of a generation of observers from W.S. Gilbert and Rudyard Kipling to Hilaire Belloc and G.K. Chesterton as well as more objective observers like A.L. Lowell, the American academic. (8)   Moreover, the system of elections had not produced representative results for minorities or majorities.   Groups like the Conservative Free Traders and Gladstonian Liberals tended to be squeezed out; and the overall results of General Elections in this period bore only an indirect and erratic relationship to the votes cast. (9)   In 1885, 1886, 1895, 1900, 1906 and 1910 the majority of the victorious party was inflated far beyond its true proportions; it was even possible, as in 1900, for the Unionists to gain *votes* over the previous General Election but suffer a loss of *seats*.   However erratic in its working, the electoral system in this period assisted the Unionists on the whole, especially in 1895 and 1900 when their huge victories masked what was a rather slight lead in votes provided by the plural voters. (10)' 'Each party in turn has ruled by a false mandate', the radical 'Nation' summed it up in 1910. (11)

By the early twentieth century many Liberals felt, with some reason, that the system was weighted against them; the complexity of registration, plural voting, the expenses involved in becoming and remaining an MP and the electoral system itself seemed to have conspired to deprive them of the fruits of the popular franchise since the third Reform Act.   It was not until after the passage of the Parliament Act of 1911 that they had the opportunity to remedy this situation; yet they also had good reason, in view of the emergence of the Labour Party, to think carefully about the consequences of altering either the franchise itself or the system of voting.

It was to concentrate attention upon the need for electoral, as distinct from merely franchise, reform that the Proportional Representation Society was refounded in 1905 under the chairmanship of Leonard, later Lord, Courtney.   The revival of this society, which had last been active in the 1880s, was very much a sign of the times.   In the wide-ranging Edwardian debate on constitutional issues Proportional Representation marched along with the Second Ballot and the Alternative Vote, the Referendum, reform of the Second Chamber, Federalism or Home-Rule-All-Round and Governments of National Efficiency, all of which were treated with a seriousness that reflected not only immediate political crises but also an underlying dissatisfaction with the system of representative democracy as it had evolved in Britain since the late nineteenth century.

Of course there is something in the view that interest in electoral reform typified only the defeated, the frustrated or the faddists and incurable crossbenchers among politicians.   Electoral reform had long been associated with demands for the representation of minority or sectional interests which the experiments with cumulative voting in School Board Elections and the limited vote in three-member boroughs had been designed to satisfy.   Proportional Representation provided a natural panacea for those who no longer found a place within the rigid framework of parties, and it was sometimes advocated as a means of demolishing huge party majorities and loosening the bonds of party discipline.

However, in the Edwardian period Proportional Representation became far more than a stick with which to beat the party establishments.   Reform of the electoral system was forced upon the attention of even the most orthodox of partisans who normally detested anything that contributed to 'faddism'.   The basic reason for this was the increase in the number of parties.   Within the experience of Edwardian politicians several new parties had contrived to emerge with disturbing effects on the two-party system.   After 1874 the

Irish Home Rulers had managed to displace one of the major parties, the Liberals, by reason of the social-geographical concentration of their supporters. In the case of the Liberal Unionists from 1886 the rebels had been largely protected from the wrath of their old party by the willingness of the Conservatives to allow them a free run in their constituencies. Finally, from 1906 to 1914 the Labour Members were accommodated, if only imperfectly and temporarily, by means of the Gladstone-MacDonald Pact of 1903. Whether this Pact could endure was the fundamental question of Edwardian politics; if it did Labour would remain a stable minority party; if it lapsed the consequences would be disastrous for both the radical parties. Electoral reform, therefore, was by no means an academic question: it was one that had to be faced sooner rather than later.

This problem presented itself in a slightly different way to each of the political parties. The Unionist Party of 1914 was not simply the agent of uncompromising reaction and obstruction suggested by Lloyd George's colourful picture of the Peers. Its members were in fact driven partly by their repeated failure at elections and partly by their internal divisions to consider seriously all kinds of constitutional reforms. Thus by 1914 a staunch Unionist could be found advocating a panoply of reforms including a new Upper House, the Referendum, Proportional Representation, and a written Constitution with a judicial tribunal to interpret it and machinery to revise it. (12) Although 1906 had dealt the party a shattering blow it was a traditional type of disaster from which they could expect to make a recovery; they did so, but failed to return to office. The double defeat of 1910 was really more disturbing because the Unionists had no answer to the strategy which had foiled them; there is little doubt that they would have returned to office in 1910 but for the maintenance of the Liberal-Labour Pact which restricted the number of Labour candidates to seventy-eight and fifty-six in the two elections and thus kept the Liberal losses from split voting to a handful. (13) So long as the Pact held and a Liberal Government could tinker with the franchise to help itself by abolishing plural voting the Opposition's chances of ousting them actually declined. This is why the strategy adopted by the Unionists of fighting the Government all along the line, even to the point of bringing them down through a civil war in Ireland was so self-defeating; for it had the effect of polarising politics and compelling Labour in Parliament to sink its identity to a large extent in Liberalism. A more subtle policy would have exploited the latent conflict between the two radical parties.

It is interesting to find that the two representatives of Conservative Central Office, Sir John Boraston and Wilfred Gales, who gave evidence to the Royal Commission on Electoral Systems in 1910, approved the Alternative Vote, apparently in the belief that it would help the party in such areas as Lancashire where Labour votes were believed to be drawn as much from Unionists as from Liberals. (14) However, Unionist support for the Alternative Vote disappeared later when the proposal was actually before Parliament in 1917, due very largely to the confidence among Liberal and Labour Members that the system would assist the amalgamation of their votes at the expense of the Unionists. The evidence given in 1910 probably reflected the fact that at that stage the Alternative Vote had not been widely discussed in the party.

On the other hand Proportional Representation had a very strong
appeal for a distinct section of the Unionist Party.   The Free
Traders and Liberal Unionists, particularly Lord Hugh Cecil, John St
Loe Strachey, Lord Selborne and Lord Cromer, grasped at it as a way
out of their difficulties in the party.   When Joseph Chamberlain
launched the Tariff Reform Campaign in 1903 he had contrived to
retain control of the Liberal Unionist organisation at the expense
of the Duke of Devonshire, a Free Trader.   As a result Unionist
Free Traders looked hopefully to an electoral pact with the Liberals, but in vain, for by then the radicals were looking forward to
a victory in alliance with Labour.   There was to be no centre party
in Edwardian politics.   Apart from a few like Churchill, who chose
to fight Tariff Reform through official Liberalism, the Free Traders
stayed on to face a bleak future at the hands of a party machine
which crushed or cowed nearly all the dissidents.   'There is no
answer to the theoretical arguments in favour of proportional representation', Lord Hugh Cecil had written in 1905; (15)   the events
of the next few years amply convinced him of the feasibility and
necessity of the reform.   For at the 1906 elections a mere 3 per
cent of Unionist candidates openly advocated Free Trade in their
literature, a startling indication of the impact of the Chamberlain-
ites on the party. (16)   By 1907 there were hardly a dozen declared
Unionist Free Traders in the Commons.   Yet, as they claimed with
justification, the party's supporters were far more favourable to
Free Trade than were the candidates for whom they were obliged to
vote, unless they switched to the Liberal Party.   A Proportional
Representation system based on multi-member constituencies would
have left electors free to choose between Unionists of various
views, thereby saving Unionist Free Traders without necessarily
putting the party's seats at risk to the Liberals.   This possibility was in fact illustrated by the Model Elections conducted by the
Proportional Representation Society at this time. (17)   These suggested the existence of a substantial group of Conservative voters
who would vote for men like Hugh Cecil as first choice, but thereafter prefer a Free Trade Liberal to any Tariff Reform Conservative. (18)   This middle-of-the-road sentiment was echoed on the
Liberal side by such politicians as Harold Cox who had sat as Liberal Member for Preston from 1906 to 1910;   his complaint was that
each General Election squeezed out more 'moderates' and men adrift
of their Party on one issue.   How was an elector to vote if he disliked tariff reform as much as Lloyd Georgeian financial policy?
'Such is our political organisation that electors who hate both
these things are driven to vote for one or the other.   In effect
they are disfranchised.' (19)   Cox spoke for the Gladstonian Liberals as did the Cecils for Unionist Free Traders against the two-
party machines which limited the voters' choice increasingly to up-
holders of the current orthodoxy.   No wonder the Cecils toyed with
the idea of a Centre Party for which they tried to enlist men like
Rosebery and Cromer; (20)   their chance would come, according to
Hugh Cecil, (21) when the Parliamentary majority won by either party
was down to thirty: 'in such circumstances', he told Strachey,
'moderate people like you and I will begin to be appreciated at our
proper value.'   To this Strachey warmly assented: 'nothing could
suit us better than a small majority for the tariff reformers.   It

would entirely sterilise them and their schemes.' (22)   Such a situation was expected to become a normal condition under a system of
Proportional Representation.

In the same way Cox (23) looked to a new moderate party and advocated a revolt on the pattern of 1886 which would enable them to
hold the balance between the extreme partisans on either side.
However, the success of the Liberal Unionists had been due partly to
the ability of individual Members at that time to dominate their
local parties and hold their seats often without fighting both Gladstonian and Unionist candidates, and partly to the fact that Gladstone had not given the organisation enough time to put pressure on
the rebels.   Therefore 1886 marked the last of the successful
splits in British politics;   only with a Proportional Representation
system could an Edwardian breakaway group have survived an election.
Proportional Representation, moreover, would have greatly facilitated independent action within parliament by the rebel Members.   As
Professor Westlake observed, (24) a group of Unionist Free Traders
would 'not relax the energy of their resistance to both Home Rule
and Tariff Reform, but by voting against each they would tend to
defeat each'.   As a result a Government's control over legislation
would have been sharply reduced and much of the life that had departed from Commons' debates would have returned.   Westlake anticipated that splinter groups would both be more common and slower in returning to the parent party now that they could bargain with the
Government.   All this would not have made for radical, reforming
Parliaments, and the criticism that 'Proportional Representation
would prevent things being done is so far justified'. (25)

An interesting, if somewhat futile, debate took place in the
Labour Party over the reform of the electoral system before 1914.
In retrospect it appears, perhaps, that Labour was the one party in
whose interest it was to secure Proportional Representation, for, as
W.C. Anderson, MP, pointed out, every Socialist and Labour Party in
Europe at that time was a Proportional Representation party.   Apart
from Anderson, Philip Snowden and G.H. Roberts were its leading advocates in the movement.   The Chief Agent, Arthur Peters, wanted
Proportional Representation, the Independent Labour Party demanded
it at their 1913 Conference, the Trades Union Congress approved a
resolution for it in 1911 by three to one, in 1912 the National
Union of Railwaymen and the National Union of Clerks adopted it for
their internal elections, and H.G. Wells dubbed it 'sane voting'.
But the Labour Party remained uncommitted.   In part this reflected
the attitude of rank and file members who were, as one of them said,
'always suspicious of anything that came from the middle class movement'. (26)   In particular it was the persistent antagonism of
Ramsay MacDonald that influenced the Party's stand.

The question came to a head at the Lambeth Conference in January
1913 at which rival proposals for Proportional Representation and
the Alternative Vote were remitted to the National Executive who in
turn passed them to the Electoral Sub-Committee;   they could not
agree either, and merely decided to issue reports of the members'
views. (27)   The Executive then published the case against Proportional Representation by MacDonald and the rival view by Roberts and
Anderson in a pamphlet with an introduction by Arthur Henderson, (28) and decided in January 1914 to leave the Glasgow Con-

ference to a free debate on the issue. (29)   Conference discussed
the proposal for Proportional Representation solely in terms of
whether Labour would obtain more seats, (30) and rejected it by
1,387,000 to 704,000.   Moving on to the Alternative Vote plan which
MacDonald supported, they turned this down by a similar margin, thus
leaving the Party in the curious position of favouring the *status
quo*.   However, the parliamentary party seems to have supported Proportional Representation by at least three to two, and were unanimous for the Alternative Vote, judging by their voting record in
1917-18 on the Reform Bill.

What would have been the effect for Labour of Proportional Representation before the war?   Nothing less than 110 Members according to Snowden, (31) which 'it cannot get for a generation under the
present system'.   Roberts and Anderson (32) illustrated the point
by explaining that they would obtain a seat for every quota of
votes, which meant 8.4 per cent in an eleven-member Birmingham constituency or 9.1 per cent in a ten-member Liverpool seat.   This
prospect would naturally have acted as a spur to constituency parties presently idle, non-existent, or reduced to supporting Liberal
candidates, since the members would have known that their efforts
would have culminated in a contest without the danger of splitting
the radical vote.   Also, the Members thus elected would have enjoyed a 'closer political relationship' with their supporters because they would not have had to trim to keep reluctant Liberals
with them.   As things stood the Party Agent (33) had to urge local
workers to create an organisation, lack of which made it difficult
to fight by-elections, but not to adopt candidates until later on.
Even in some constituencies which returned Labour Members the party
was chronically deficient in electoral machinery, as in the case of
Enoch Edwards' old constituency at Hanley; (34) when he died it
was discovered that he had allowed the money contributed by the
miners to be used for registration purposes without bothering to set
up an independent Labour organisation.

By 1914 the case for Proportional Representation had become very
strong in the Labour Party.   This was partly because the existing
distribution of Members, a quarter of whom sat for north-western
constituencies, did not reflect the party's actual strength so much
as the weakness of the Lancashire Liberals before 1906;   conversely,
Liberal confidence and strength in Scotland and Yorkshire led them
to resist Labour encroachments rigidly.   Thus Labour had not been
able to make any significant advance over the ground conceded to
them in 1906, apart from the occasional victories like Anderson's in
West Fife in 1910.   The by-election gains early in the 1906 parliament had been lost where the Liberals contested the seats again;
the inclusion of the miners' Members in the party from 1909 represented no actual electoral advance;   and by 1913 the party had lost
four seats (Bow and Bromley, Hanley, Chesterfield and North-East
Derbyshire) and finished third in virtually every by-election they
had fought.   Not one of the remaining thirty-eight Members had won
against candidates of both other parties, so that, as one party
worker put it, 'to be a fighting organisation meant retaliation from
the Liberal Party, and that retaliation would probably mean the loss
of 50% of the seats now held'. (35)   Even the Alternative Vote
would have put these in jeopardy since sitting Labour Members could

not be sure of coming first or second on the first preference vote.
Thus the belligerence of the 'Labour Leader' contrasts markedly with
the energy of the National Executive Committee which devoted itself
to smothering many Labour candidatures in Liberal constituencies. (36)

Yet the attitude in the constituencies is clear from the sort of
dispute that occurred at Leicester in 1913 when the Liberal who sat
in harness with MacDonald died.   The Pact apparently carried no
weight with the local workers who demanded a fight for the Liberal
seat, and they gave a rude reception to Henderson and Roberts when
they went down to remonstrate with them. (37)   It was emphasised
that: (38)

> (1) the spirit and strength of the local Labour movement fully
> justified their fighting;   (2) the Labour Movement throughout the
> country was becoming disheartened because of a fear that Labour
> Party policy was too much influenced by consideration for the
> Liberal Government, and a fight at Leicester under present cir-
> cumstances was calculated to remove that fear;   (3) the local
> Labour Party were constantly being told that Mr. MacDonald held
> his seat by Liberal votes, and this was a good opportunity for
> disproving it.

However, the National Executive (39) did manage to prevent an official Labour candidature at Leicester, though by June 1914 the situation nationally was that 36 candidates had been adopted in Labour-
held seats, and had been sanctioned in 18 others;   22 had been 'selected', though not approved, elsewhere, and another 40 seats were
classed as 'uncertain'. (40)

What is the meaning of these figures?   Dr Ross McKibbin (41)
considers that at a 1914 General Election nearly all these 117 seats
would have been contested, possibly even 140;   he also argues that
the improvements in party organisation in the constituencies after
1910 prepared the way for this expansion.   Yet this number would
almost certainly have been cut back as in December 1910.   Indeed in
view of the Liberals' readiness to retaliate by attacking Labour
seats a cut-back was urgently necessary.   In the list of forty 'uncertain' seats a contest by Labour at Cockermouth, for instance,
would merely have guaranteed the loss of Whitehaven as in January
1910.   Nor is it appreciated that much of the extra Labour activity
in by-elections and in the adoption of candidates was the work of
the National Union of Women's Suffrage Societies (pp. 22-4).   This
is the case in at least seventeen of the constituencies on the
Labour Party list.   At by-elections the women's work had been concentrated and therefore significant, but in a General Election they
would be spread very thinly around.   Moreover, the NUWSS intended
to drop the electoral alliance with Labour just as soon as they
achieved their object, or when it seemed impolitic as it did during
the war.

What is most striking about the list of 117 possible Labour contests is the fact that such constituencies as Colne Valley, Hanley,
Chesterfield, Chester-le-Street, Holmfirth and Crewe were ranked as
'uncertain';   for not only had they all been contested recently, but
the first four had actually returned Labour Members.   In fact
Labour organisation in most cases was still chronically weak, almost
to the point of non-existence, and Ramsay MacDonald was understand-

ably anxious to stop hopeless candidatures whose only result would
be to destroy the chances of existing Members.

Ramsay MacDonald, in his report on Proportional Representation, (42) claimed that multi-Member seats would impose a bigger
financial burden on Labour than on the other parties.   In fact
Labour's existing expenditure had been quite lavish: £884 on
average for each of seventy-eight candidates in January 1910.   This
would hardly have been necessary under Proportional Representation
since the object would have been to poll the basic party vote not to
wheedle out reluctant Liberals to win an absolute majority.

MacDonald's next objection was that Proportional Representation
would confine Labour to a fixed number of seats - the very situation
they had reached - and denied that he and his colleagues sat by Liberal permission: 'we are elected because the strength of our Party
in the country compels the country to elect us, and forbids certain
parties opposing us.'   Though true this appeared to offer no alternative to the frustrating restrictions of the Pact now that the
Liberals would concede no further ground and Labour could not take
it.

He also contended that there was little point in electing Labour
Members independently of Liberals since they had to combine in Parliament; 'our political fights at present have to be conducted in
such a way as to compel people to face actual Parliamentary conditions, whereas Proportional Representation fights are more or less
in the air.'   Greater independence for Labour was therefore an illusion at present: 'nothing has hampered our Movement in the country more than this false idea of independence, that only Labour or
Socialist votes should be given to Labour or Socialist candidates.
It is humbug.'   Freer propaganda in the constituencies would have
widened the gulf with the Liberals.   Yet this was to overlook the
fact that under Proportional Representation Liberal and Labour
voters would have effected their own coalitions without the un-
pleasantness involved in the withdrawal or suppression of candidates.

MacDonald's remarks suggest that he took a pessimistic view of
Labour's immediate prospects and was reconciled to the position as
long as the Liberals remained in office; their fall would have
allowed and encouraged Labour to attack their constituencies.   Proportional Representation would not have helped Labour in the long
run to win office unless they could obtain a majority of votes: in
retrospect one can see that they have never done so.   Labour's
route to power involved nothing like a majority of votes or seats;
but the party was in fact well placed as a minority to take advantage of the single-member system by virtue of its social-geographical concentration.   Once Labour support began to grow again there
would come a point at which they would reap the benefits of the
system; the task, then, was to win a majority of the working class
majority under equal single-member seats rather than look for short-
term gains from Proportional Representation which would make Labour
a substantial minority party but never more than that.

The Edwardian Liberal Party, though it became understandably interested in electoral reform, was rather uncertain in its attitude
to Proportional Representation.   Part of the explanation for this
is chronological.   The Proportional Representation Society's cam-

paign only really got under way after the Liberals had returned to
power in 1906.   Thus it was the Unionists, with 157 seats instead
of the 244 that their poll entitled them to, who were more susceptible on grounds of short-term self-interest to the case for Proportional Representation.   In the glow of 1906 many Liberals were
disposed to look charitably upon the single-member system.   'I find
no zeal for Proportional Representation even among the Members who
consented to back our Bill and a large amount of deliberate opposition among Liberals', reported J.M. Robertson (43) in 1906; 'many
Liberals also avow that they want the system of large majorities,
which ever way the balance may go.   They hold that small majorities
would make weak ministries.'

This, however, was an attitude arising from the circumstances of
the 1906 election.   No Government was likely to initiate at that
stage schemes whose effect would be to cut their huge majority down
to a level proportionate to the 55 per cent of votes polled by the
Liberal and Labour Parties.   Yet it was not long before the huge
Liberal majority proved a broken reed against the House of Lords;
and by 1912 the possibility of Labour breaking out of the confines
of the electoral Pact made reform of the single-member system a
topic for serious consideration.   And so, after a slow start, the
campaign for Proportional Representation gained ground.   There was
a strong Liberal tradition stretching back through Lord Courtney to
John Stuart Mill in favour of Proportional Representation as a natural and necessary accompaniment to a full democratic franchise.
The minority must be given safeguards against the tyranny of the
majority, and Proportional Representation provided the means to this
end.   On grounds of justice and fairness of representation, then,
Proportional Representation claimed the allegiance of many radical
Liberal Members of both newer and traditional types; MPs like
Aneurin Williams, J.M. Robertson, H.G. Chancellor, John Gulland,
Thomas Burt, Alfred Mond, Richard Holt and E.T. John worked for the
Proportional Representation Society before 1914.   Among the neces-
sarily more cautious ministerial ranks the only two definite suppor-
ters appear to have been Sir John Simon and Lord Loreburn.

The opposing line of thought descended from Mr Gladstone who had
dismissed Proportional Representation as a *pons asinorum*; it was
natural that a reform which its advocates commended as a means of
ensuring accurate representation for each minority interest would
fail to appeal to party leaders struggling with faddism within the
Liberal ranks.   This attitude persisted among strict party men such
as J.A. Pease and Lewis Harcourt; the latter contemptuously rejected Proportional Representation elections for the Commons on the
grounds that 'almost every heresy gets a hearing in that
Assembly'. (44)   This was also the view of the party organisation.
J. Renwick Seager, Secretary of the Registration Department of the
Liberal Central Association, deplored the prospect of 'bores and
cranks' being introduced by Proportional Representation. (45)   The
'Liberal Agent' similarly made clear its disapproval of Proportional
Representation but none the less aired it along with alternative re-
forms from time to time.

One way of interesting Liberals in Proportional Representation
lay through local government and some effort was devoted to a Municipal Representation Bill which enabled local authorities to opt for

Proportional Representation in their own elections.   In London especially the elections frequently resulted in one Party taking every
seat in some boroughs owing to the return of Councillors in blocks
of 3, 6 or 9;   John Burns, when interviewed on the subject in 1907,
protested that there was no demand for the Bill, (46) but when the
Progressives lost control of the London County Council in 1909 attitudes began to change.   In March 1914 the London Liberal Federation
gave unanimous approval to Proportional Representation at their
General Council Meeting, (47) and when, in the summer of that year,
some 90 MPs put their names to a petition to Herbert Samuel asking
for an enquiry into London elections he agreed. (48)

Indeed the Government were by no means unwilling to accede to the
various requests of the Proportional Representation Members to col-
lect their own evidence on the operation of different electoral systems.   In 1906, after a plea from J.M. Robertson, the Government
sought information from their representatives abroad on the application of Proportional Representation in their areas, (49) and in 1908
they obtained a further set of reports on the use of the Second Ballot. (50)   The next step was for Courtney to win Asquith's agreement for a Royal Commission to investigate the applicability of
these schemes in Britain. (51)   Of the 29 witnesses called to give
evidence before the Commission (52) 18 spoke in support of the
Single Transferable Vote System of Proportional Representation,
while 9 were against it.   A somewhat mixed group of 10 witnesses
were willing to accept the Alternative Vote, though several of
these, such as J.M. Robertson, saw it as a step towards Proportional
Representation in that it would re-educate voters used to making a
single X on their ballot papers.   In their report (53) the Commissioners conceded much of the Proportional Representation case;   its
feasibility had been established by expert witnesses from Tasmania
and Belgium where it was in operation;   moreover the single-member
system 'actually promotes the return of the least popular candidate'.   However, they considered that the simplest remedy for the
problem of minority Members was the Alternative Vote which they
recommended for use in all single-member constituencies.

This was almost certainly the verdict the Government were looking
for at this time.   In 1910, when Aneurin Williams secured a debate
on Proportional Representation in the Commons, (54) John Burns
flatly condemned the idea;   in December 1911, when the Government's
new Franchise Bill was arousing interest, the Proportional Representation Society endeavoured to persuade the Master of Elibank and
J.A. Pease to agree to a debate on Proportional Representation without success. (55)   The difficulty was that Proportional Representation Conservatives such as Hugh Cecil saw the reform as an insurance
against the consequences of a one-man-one-vote system, (56) and his
advocacy of Proportional Representation would certainly have been
construed by Liberals as a wrecking tactic.   Asquith from time to
time received deputations from Proportional Representation supporters and dropped many favourable if general remarks on the subject
of fair representation, (57) but appeared to regard it in an academic light.   It is evident that he gave the matter some serious consideration for in 1912 he sketched out a scheme for an experiment
with Proportional Representation in 150 constituencies spread
throughout the country. (58)   There is no indication what conclu-

sions Asquith drew from this;   however, as his figures indicate,
Proportional Representation would have sharply raised Liberal representation in England, especially in the South, while reducing
their swollen majorities in Wales and Scotland, quite apart from
cutting down the Nationalist hold on Irish seats from five-sixths to
two-thirds.   Even a limited experiment, therefore, would almost
certainly have had to await the enactment of Home Rule.   The near-
est the Government got to approving Proportional Representation was
in agreeing to its use in elections to the Irish Senate under the
Home Rule Bill in 1914.

The central consideration was simply that the Parliamentary Liberal Party was weighted heavily towards the Celtic countries and the
North of England where they were vastly over-represented;   consequently a certain complacency over the system of constituencies grew
up especially in Wales;   even in 1906 the Conservatives polled a
third of the votes in the Principality, but the radicals monopolised
the seats.   In Scotland the Conservatives' meagre total of twelve
Members elected in 1906 actually fell to eleven in each of the 1910
elections despite two successive and substantial improvements in
their poll.   No wonder, then, that Sir George Younger (59) was re-
cruited for the cause of Proportional Representation, as also was
the Scottish Liberal John Gulland: (60)   'You can understand', wrote
Gulland, 'that I do not wish to emphasise unduly the disproportion
of Conservatives from Scotland.   I have been working all my life
to ensure that they shall be as few as possible.'   Liberals in
Birmingham, Liverpool or the Home Counties could not expect to represent their own areas, but the career politicians among them easily
acquired the habit of migrating to Yorkshire, Northumbria or even
Scotland to join the distinguished band of Liberal refugees holding
impregnable seats there.

In fact it is difficult to see how Liberals representing the
party's heartlands would have been stirred from their complacency (61) had it not been for the coincident rise of the Labour Party
in those regions.   After some dramatic growth around 1906-7 Labour
had been effectively reduced to a stagnant position by 1910, as Dr
Blewett (62) has convincingly argued, but appeared to be breaking
out in by-election contests again from 1912 to 1914.   Since a growing Labour Party meant splitting the radical vote and a return to
Conservative Government the parties were forced to give serious
attention to Proportional Representation and the variants of the
single-member system known as the Second Ballot and the Alternative
Vote.   (See Appendix 1.)   At the elections from 1885 to 1900 between five and thirteen Members were elected each time on a minority
vote and the Second Ballot would thus have had little application
and no chance of altering the overall results.   However, in 1906,
despite the existence of the Pact, thirty minority Members were returned;   in 1906 and 1910 the Second Ballot would only have had the
effect of giving the Liberals a handful of extra seats thereby increasing their already inflated majority.   This underlines the
fact that this system is quite different from Proportional Representation systems which would have had the effect of reducing the Government's majority in 1906 from 356 to 104 and in January 1910 from
124 to 56.   Indeed, in view of the Liberal Party's interest in Proportional Representation since 1918 it is worth stressing that while

many of its Members did advocate and work for Proportional Representation before 1914, the more common preference was for a simpler
Second Ballot scheme which would meet the immediate problem of split
voting.   Proportional Representation was 'excellent in theory',
Churchill admitted in 1905, but, 'at present I incline towards
single-member seats with 2nd Ballot'. (63)   J.M. Robertson complained in 1907 that 'there is not a touch of enthusiasm in the
House for P.R.', (64) though only a month earlier he had forecast,
'it only needs another three-cornered election or two to poke up
the smouldering feeling on the [Second Ballot]'. (65)
     Between 1906 and 1914 the Liberals lost 25 seats to the Unionists
at by-elections of which 10 could reasonably be ascribed to the intervention of Labour, Independent Labour or Socialist candidates; (66) 3 were lost directly to Labour (67) at Sheffield
Attercliffe, Jarrow and Colne Valley, some 16 seats held in three-
cornered contests, and 3 at Hanley and North East Derbyshire and
Chesterfield, lost by Labour through Liberal intervention.   Bitter
contests in radical seats undermined the electoral Pact; Labour
were outraged when the radical Liberal, R.L. Outhwaite, walked off
with their seat at Hanley in 1912, and when North East Derbyshire
fell to the Unionists in 1914 with Labour again at the bottom of the
poll (68) Philip Snowden wrote: (69)
     Political developments in this country are making P.R. inevit-
     able.   The circumstances of the by-election which is taking
     place today ... are intolerable, and whichever party gets the
     seat can have no satisfaction in holding it, for it will be won
     by a minority vote.
The immediate consequence of this contest was that Labour intervened at the Crewe by-election which the Liberals lost; and at the
Ipswich by-election Labour voters were thought to 'have compassed
the defeat of Mr Masterman ... by voting for the Conservative candidate'. (70)   Liberal losses as a result of split voting led to much
comment (71) on the need for a Second Ballot system in Britain, and
this solution was plainly preferred by the party organisation (72)
to Proportional Representation.
     It is evident from the papers of Joseph Pease that the Alterna-
tive Vote was considered a *desirable* reform by the Cabinet (73) and
was omitted from the 1912 Franchise Bill only because of the shortage of parliamentary time.   Now the question arises why did the
Liberals not find it *imperative* to protect themselves from the
menace of split voting?   The answer is two-fold.   In the first
place the Alternative Vote was not an unmitigated blessing;   it
would have given a definite stimulus to constituency Labour parties
to field more candidates which would have led to widespread conflict
between the two parties, thereby rendering co-operation at the parliamentary level more difficult.   In the second place the by-elections in the last three years before the war clarified the issue by
demonstrating the relative position of the two parties.   At this
time Labour was certainly making belligerent noises in the
press (74) and backing this up with candidates in by-elections in
Liberal strongholds such as Holmfirth and East Carmarthen in 1912,
Houghton-le-Spring and Keighley in 1913, and North West Durham in
1914.   In these contests Labour polled respectably but always finished bottom of the poll with the Liberals at the top.   In such

overwhelmingly working-class seats this was a poor performance and
shows how far Labour had slipped since the days of Jarrow and Colne
Valley in 1907.

Dr McKibbin (75) sees these results differently, pointing out
that the Labour vote at North East Lanark, Holmfirth, Crewe, Keighley and Leith Burghs represented an increase over the previous performance.   Though this is true it in no way suggests a pattern of
growth;   for in each case except Keighley (where there was practically no change) the last contest was at the General Election of
January 1910.   In the by-elections of 1911 to 1914 the conditions,
both politically and organisationally, were far better for the
Labour Party, and their inability to score then did not augur well
for the approaching General Election.   If the Liberals could hold
on to their industrial constituencies in three-cornered contests in
these years there was little hope that Labour, still lacking a dis-
tinctive political programme and with a sketchy organisation, could
gain ground.   As Dr P.F. Clarke has argued, (76) the Liberal Government seems to have passed through the same cycle of slump and
recovery from 1911 to 1914 as they had experienced between their
victories in 1906 and 1910.   The by-elections, in short, are no
guide to the next General Election.

On the other hand, some comparatively low Labour votes in by-
elections at Crewe, Midlothian and Leith Burghs were sufficient to
hand the seats over to the Unionists by narrow margins.   Again, at
a General Election the Liberals would have clawed back enough of the
Labour vote to regain these seats, and in view of the absence of
Labour organisation it was unlikely that candidates could have
stood without a great deal of outside help.   Thus, from the Liberal
point of view a withdrawal of Labour candidatures in the weaker constituencies was certainly to be anticipated, while in the solid
working-class seats in the North Labour and Liberalism could more
safely be left to fight it out.   This is why, though the Liberals
were, to a degree, pressed by their erstwhile electoral ally, the
pressure was nothing like enough to make the Alternative Vote an
urgent measure;   as the 'Labour Leader' retorted angrily in 1912,
the Government 'could have brought in such a reform as the transferable vote any time since 1906 ... if the Liberals think that by
leaving things as they are the progress of Labour can be retarded,
nothing will be done'. (77)   In other words until Labour began to
demonstrate much more strength in the constituencies the Liberals'
best tactic was to apply the logic of the split-vote argument so as
to squeeze the Labour vote.   The Liberals thus had to weigh the
danger of encouraging Labour by promoting the Alternative Vote
against the risk of losing seats to the Unionists without it.   The
number of Labour candidatures was not, therefore, the only factor;
only a real upsurge in the Labour vote would have upset the delicate
balance of this calculation.   Since there was no indication of a
Labour upsurge before 1914 the Alternative Vote did not become a
necessity.

Chapter 2

WOMAN SUFFRAGE 1906-14:
THE FRUITS OF MODERATION

The whole of the women's movement finds itself side-slipping,
almost unintentionally, into Labour and Socialist politics.
(Beatrice Webb, 'New Statesman', 14 February 1914)

The militant suffragettes did their best to impress upon history the
fact that they had essentially won their campaign by the time of the
outbreak of the Great War; it is one myth among many.   For the
members of the Women's Social and Political Union and its offshoots
were endeavouring through their members to continue their fight on
two fronts: first, the fight with Mr Asquith and, second, the
struggle with their rivals in the women's movement for the credit
for the political enfranchisement of women in 1918.   And the Pankhursts have largely succeeded in that they have drawn to themselves
a tradition of literature which shows no signs of drying up, (1)
despite the fact that nothing of material importance is added by
each new publication.   As a result writers in this field have concentrated excessively on the Edwardian campaigns and escapades of
the suffragettes and ignored the constitutional section of the movement in which lay the great majority of organised women suffragists;
more seriously the militants managed to divert attention from the
actual passage of woman suffrage legislation in 1918, an episode
which accords ill with the heroics of the pre-war period.   In short
the Pankhursts have led historians around the course for far too
long; to play the suffragette game has proved so absorbing that the
winning of the match has largely escaped our attention.
   The chief organ for the promotion of the woman suffrage cause in
Edwardian England was the NUWSS under the Presidency of Mrs Milli-
cent Garrett Fawcett, the wife of the former Liberal Minister Henry
Fawcett.   With up to 600 branches around the country the NUWSS
functioned like a normal pressure group; it was constitutional,
responsible, respectable - and dull; and it was consequently often
ignored.   Woman suffrage had been for years an issue that agitated
a number of middle-class ladies but left the great mass of women
comparatively unmoved.   Mrs Fawcett, who was nothing if not
patient, recognised that to overcome the apathy that was as big an
obstacle to the cause as male chauvinism would require a lengthy
campaign of persuasion by means of rational argument.

Not so the Pankhursts.   When they established the WSPU in 1903
they found themselves in much the same frustrating position for the
first two years.   At first it looked as though their organisation
might make a singular contribution by incorporating working-class
women into the suffrage movement, but this did not survive the move
from Manchester to London.   The Pankhursts never achieved the or-
ganisational efficiency of the NUWSS, partly because they were tem-
peramentally unsuited to the steady plod through committees,
minutes-of-the-last-meeting, resolutions and formation of branches;
but also because they simply never obtained the membership necessary
to generate such activity.   What the Pankhursts lacked in numbers
and efficiency they had to make up for by the spontaneous and dramatic quality of their interventions.   Their appearance at the public
meetings of leading Liberal politicians from 1905 quickly made woman
suffrage an issue and the Pankhursts themselves a household name.
Violence proved to be an overnight success;   in the era of the
'Daily Mail' it could hardly have been otherwise.

Once having embarked upon direct action the Pankhursts found that
the temptation to take it to ever greater extremes and thereby maintain their momentum proved irresistible.   As Andrew Rosen has shown
in his scholarly study of the WSPU, (2) the suspension of militant
tactics not only deprived the Pankhursts of headlines, but had the
further consequence of causing a sharp drop in financial contributions.   The return to violence and hunger strikes in the last years
of peace imposed a terrible physical and emotional strain upon the
women involved, so much so that they no doubt genuinely believed
that victory could not long elude them;   only Christabel from the
safe distance of Paris could coolly assess the real decline in the
militants' cause in these years.

What was their contribution to the suffrage?   The attempt at
persuasion plainly failed;   the WSPU fell back upon a prolonged campaign to coerce Asquith's Government partly by embarrassing them and
partly by contriving the defeat of Liberal candidates in by-elections.   Yet by claiming credit for the various Liberal losses the
Pankhursts merely succeeded in alienating the Liberal suffragist
politicians upon whom a woman suffrage Bill would, and in the end
did, primarily depend.   Lloyd George, though in despair at their
wrecking tactics, (3) continued to work for woman suffrage behind
the scenes with Sir Edward Grey.   But militancy fast reduced the
enthusiasm of politicians like Churchill who, despite the influence
of his suffragist wife, 'practically admitted that his present
wrecking tactics are the outcome of resentment at the treatment he
has received from the WSPU.' (4)   Asquith's attitude, however, was,
if anything, worse than this;   for the Prime Minister believed that
his party's by-election losses had nothing to do with woman suffrage;   he was inclined to ascribe them, quite reasonably, to factors
such as the unpopularity of the National Insurance Act. (5)   For
Asquith the suffragettes became a *law and order* problem rather than
a political problem to be decided on political grounds in the normal
way.   This is why it was mistaken tactics for the Pankhursts to
persist with militancy, for they enabled their opponents in the Government to switch the debate away from the merits of the issue.

The more the Pankhursts annoyed Ministers the more intransigent
Churchill and Asquith became, thereby giving Christabel the justifi-

cation she needed.   Even her allies considered that she 'envisaged
the whole suffrage movement in its present phase as a gigantic duel
between herself and Lloyd George whom she desired to destroy.   She
had lost all sense of proportion and honestly believed she could
force the Government to yield'. (6)   To have alienated the political friends of the suffrage cause would not have mattered so much if
the suffragettes had meanwhile been able to extract an undertaking
from the Unionists about their actions when returned to power.
Even the Labour Party were needlessly offended and alienated by the
Pankhursts' habit of ignoring their (invariably pro-suffrage) candidates at by-elections and helping instead the Unionists who were
frequently anti-suffragists.   The WSPU in fact went out of their
way to seek excuses for branding Labour as an enemy, which was not
easy since the Labour Party was clearly the most united party on the
women's cause even if enthusiasm for the franchise varied a great
deal.   Christabel demanded that the Labour Party vote against the
Government on every issue until they granted a woman suffrage Bill -
terms which allowed none but a Unionist to qualify as a friend of
the cause! (7)   Only Keir Hardie and George Lansbury whose relationship with the Labour Party was somewhat tenuous felt able to co-
operate with demands of this sort. (8)

There is no easy answer to the question, what was the public response to militancy and woman suffrage.   Despite the claims of the
Pankhursts there is no indication that electors switched votes because of their by-election campaigns;   some may have done so in
spite of their efforts.   Indeed on the one occasion when woman suffrage was put squarely to the electorate it was rejected.   This
was the by-election at Bow and Bromley in London in 1912 where
George Lansbury sat as Labour Member.   He resigned his seat in a
fit of temper with the Labour Party National Executive who declined
to try to compel the Government to legislate for woman suffrage.
On presenting himself before the electors seeking a new mandate on
woman suffrage Lansbury, who had enjoyed a comfortable victory in
December 1910, was well beaten in a straight fight with a Unionist
anti-suffragist.   Such evidence can hardly be reconciled with the
militants' notion that they had the people with them against the
Cabinet;   it suggests that the voters were being alienated as much
as the politicians.

Of course the crowds continued to attend the public functions of
the suffragettes, yet as a more candid WSPU member admitted, 'the
vast mass of people were simply curious - not sympathetic - not
opposed.   Simply indifferent'. (9)   There was no purpose in merely
gathering huge rallies if they did not give vent to a really widespread demand for the vote;   even among women themselves the attitude seemed very mixed - certainly members of the Government felt
that there was little demand for the vote from most women since
their needs were adequately met by Parliament as presently constituted.   Churchill summed it up: 'there is no great practical grievance'; (10)   it was for this reason that he welcomed the idea of a
referendum for he had no doubt that a popular vote would go against
woman suffrage. (11)   Moreover, the militants clearly stimulated
women anti-suffragists to campaign against them.   In their determination to demonstrate the unwillingness of their sex to undertake
the responsibility of the Parliamentary Franchise they canvassed the

women municipal electors. (12)   From reply-paid postcards they
found that more than two-thirds of these ladies were indeed opposed,
though only half of the electors responded; the results from a
door-to-door canvass were predictably even less favourable; majorities against woman suffrage were recorded everywhere except in some
of the Liverpool Divisions (West Derby, Scotland, West Toxteth and
Everton).

As for the public in general such evidence as there is suggests a
rapidly growing hostility towards the suffragettes, if not to the
suffrage itself.   Indeed since 1908 public response to militant
demonstrations had become steadily more unfriendly.   By early 1912
when Mrs Pankhurst was practising stone-throwing in the country,
WSPU speakers were being shouted down at meetings and their own win-
dows were being broken.   The immediate reaction of the WSPU to the
result of the Bow and Bromley by-election was to resort to the burning of letter boxes.   By October of that year public meetings had
become futile with the result that nearly two years before the war
the attempt to persuade people had come to an end.   This simple
truth is easily lost sight of amid the traditional accounts which
dwell upon the sufferings of the women on hunger strikes.   For the
Pankhursts' tactics had backfired badly and they were now the victims of violence and merciless barracking by the multitudes that
they had alienated.

By 1914 new ideas were in short supply for the embittered, militant section of the women's movement.   The aim for all the groups
was to make woman suffrage dominate the next General Election which
was expected in 1915.   This the cause had never done before, and,
in view of the Ulster crisis, it was most unlikely to do in the near
future.   The only hope lay in utterly humiliating the Government
and forcing the Home Secretary to such extremes as would disgust
Liberals in the country enough to disrupt morale before the election.   It must be said that Mrs Pankhurst had already gone some way
towards this by claiming credit for the attempt to blow up Lloyd
George's house at Churt in February 1912 and thereby earning a
three-year prison sentence.   The hunger strikes proved an excellent
means of breathing life into the cause since Liberal disapproval of
the force-feeding methods adopted by prison authorities led the Home
Secretary to introduce what became known as the 'Cat and Mouse Act'.
The succession of release and recapture of suffragettes under this
Act presented the victims with wonderful opportunities to play games
with the police and the pleasure of repeated martyrdom.   However,
nothing short of a suffragette death that could be ascribed to the
treatment meted out by the authorities would serve to upset the Government's position, and in view of the very obvious concern of the
Government to make a death of this sort impossible the chances of
success were slight.   For one woman had already made the ultimate
sacrifice.   In 1911 Emily Wilding Davison had attempted suicide in
prison; she explained afterwards to the medical officer that she
had done this because she 'had a feeling that a tragedy was wanted'.
Next year at Epsom Miss Davison provided that tragedy.   Yet the
significant thing about it is that it appeared to have no appreciable effect upon the Government.   The Cabinet showed no sign of
abandoning their intention of having a reform Bill on their own
terms which were, adult suffrage for men with no plural voting, and

an unspecified franchise for women if the House of Commons approved
on a free vote (see Chapter 3).   In the face of the Liberals' refusal to contemplate passing a Bill to enfranchise wealthy women -
the only type that the House of Lords was likely to accept - the
militants were making no progress at all.

From this deadlock no way out could be seen.   The Women's Freedom League, casting around for expedients, actually considered res-
urrecting a plan to threaten the Government with a campaign to
assist working-class women to limit the birth rate, but decided
against it. (13)   The problem was that continued failure only fur-
thered the disintegration of an already fragmented movement.   What
remained of the WSPU by 1914 was more than ever the personal tool of
Christabel Pankhurst.   The first breakaway group back in 1907 had
been the Women's Freedom League under Mrs Despard who endeavoured to
pursue a more intelligent form of militancy than was possible under
the Pankhursts' erratic and self-centred direction.   In particular
the WFL resented the Pankhursts' habit of ignoring democratic practice within the WSPU whenever they anticipated opposition to their
own policy.   Then in 1912 the Pethwick-Lawrences had been forced by
Christabel to sever their links with the WSPU;   as the 'United Suffragists' they continued to publish 'Votes for Women' while Christabel created the 'Suffragette'.   Finally Sylvia Pankhurst, much to
the fury of her sister, was operating under her East London Federation which campaigned for a comprehensive Socialist solution to
society's problems, of which the parliamentary franchise was only a
small part.

On the constitutional side of the woman suffrage spectrum stood
the Conservative and Unionist Women's Franchise Association presided
over by Lady Selborne and Lady Frances Balfour, who were working for
a measure along the lines of the Conciliation Bill.   Then there was
the Women's Liberal Federation, fast losing patience with Asquith,
who naturally favoured a wider franchise;   their leadership enjoyed
much personal contact with the NUWSS through such persons as Lady
Eleanor Acland.   The National Union itself, which since the onset
of militancy had been under great strain, attempted to break out of
the impasse into which the women's movement had fallen by concluding
an electoral pact with the Labour Party in 1912.   Though this in no
way affected their staunchly non-violent approach it did compromise
their position somewhat and led to the resignation of many Liberal
members.   'It is this alliance which bids fair to be the rock on
which the suffrage ship is going to be wrecked', commented the jub-
ilant 'Anti-Suffrage Review'. (14)   Certainly the pact with Labour
provided the main manifestation of the disintegrating process before
the war and left the women's movement stretched right across the
political spectrum from moderation to violence.   Even if their objective was a common one the women's groups disagreed on basic questions of tactics such as how many women voters would be acceptable,
whether a Government Bill or a private one should be adopted, and
whether the women should enjoy a separate Bill or form part of a
general franchise measure.

In so far as the WSPU had been the custodian of the women's cause
it had reached a sorry state by 1914;   for the militants, having
made the suffrage first a great spectacle and then a law and order
problem, had rather tended to drag the cause down with them so that

it became the province of an isolated, ineffectual caucus.   The
chief progress that was made particularly in the last three years of
the peace was achieved in the dull, worthy ranks of the moderate
groups.   The historian has to listen carefully for their more muted
voices amid the general uproar.

The NUWSS was not in obvious decline before the war.   On the
contrary by 1913 it was reporting an increase in membership of 1,000
per month;   it boasted 443 branches organised in sixteen Federations
and comprising 42,000 members.   Most importantly the National
Union's income had doubled in 1912 over 1911 to some £40,000.   Despite this, however, the National Union was deeply unhappy.   Most of
its leaders were Liberal-inclined politically, and this, plus their
adherence to non-violent methods, had led them to persist with the
attempt to persuade their friends in the Government to enact a
women's suffrage Bill.

It was a dismal strategy.   In June 1914 even the Women's Liberal
Federation at their Annual Conference debated a motion pledging all
women Liberals to refuse to work for the re-election of anti-suffragist Liberal candidates at the next election;   the motion was defeated by only 456 to 400 votes, and for the first time the Conference unanimously demanded a Government Bill on woman suffrage.   It
is clear that after the loss of the Government's own Franchise and
Registration Bill in 1913 (see Chapter 3) the attitude of the parliamentary Liberals drove women suffragists to despair.   The fact
that the Liberal Party and the moderate women's organisations to a
large extent enjoyed a common membership proved for some time a useful weapon for Asquith because most suffragist Liberal women gave
their first loyalty to the party leadership and accepted the need to
remove the obstacle the House of Lords presented to all Liberal reforms.   In the long run, however, it became dangerous for Asquith
to take the women's acquiescence for granted.   After the passage
of the Parliament Act in 1911 many Liberals looked for action on
political reform and the party workers were not to be denied it indefinitely.   Disgruntled rank and file Liberals stimulated schemes
such as the one in the Lancashire, Cheshire and North Wales Liberal
Federations in 1912 designed to obtain pledges from Liberal workers
and constituency officers refusing to work for the party if Parliament passed a franchise Bill which omitted women. (15)

One can understand the dilemma of the Liberal suffragist through
the case of Catherine Marshall, Chairman of the North-Western Federation of the NUWSS from 1910 and subsequently Parliamentary Secretary of the National Union. (16)   By the end of 1913 she reluctantly faced the fact that trying to work with the Government was
futile: (17)

I think the conviction has been growing that there is nothing to
hope for from the Liberal Party, even when Home Rule and Welsh
Disestablishment are out of the way;   and I am becoming rather
discredited as a false prophet because I have so often predicted
better things of Mr. Lloyd George than he has performed.

It was for this reason that Catherine Marshall had been willing
to acquiesce in the National Union's new strategy involving electoral co-operation with the Labour Party in 1912.   This policy was
carried out through a separate arm of the National Union, the Election Fighting Fund, which channelled money and workers into by-

elections in support of Labour candidates.   By 1914 the National
Union had intervened in eight by-elections in this way (18) and
assisted in the loss of four Liberal seats at Crewe, Midlothian,
Leith Burghs and South Lanark.   Since these losses were quite
narrow ones the National Union had some reason to claim that its
efforts had been instrumental particularly in view of the dependence
of the Labour candidates upon the women as organisers in places like
Crewe and Midlothian where the party organisation was practically
non-existent.

The National Union did not at first press itself too strongly
upon its new ally.   It worked with sensible restraint, bearing in
mind the suspicion with which Labour stalwarts were apt to regard
middle-class ladies who came among them.   It was a necessary qualification for EFF workers, as Catherine Marshall assured Arthur
Henderson, (19) that they should be sympathetic to Labour on other
issues, and not merely be fanatics for woman suffrage.   This indeed
was a lesson to be drawn by the London NUWSS from the WSPU's disastrous interventions on Lansbury's behalf at Bow and Bromley where
the tactless and hectoring militant ladies had alienated support in
a working-class constituency.   This fiasco revealed to the National
Union both the incredible weakness of the Labour Party's organisation and the need for the women's groups to argue their case by emphasising the common cause of working men and women.

The electoral pact coincided with the upsurge in Labour candidatures in Liberal held constituencies.   No doubt the National Union
did not create this new aggressive policy but they did a lot to make
the new candidatures effective and almost certainly extended the
range of practicable candidatures into hitherto hopeless seats.
The National Union witheld its support and encouragement only in
such cases as Keighley where the Liberal incumbent Sir Stanley Buckmaster was a staunch woman suffragist.   The EFF organisers clearly
felt that they had a real weapon at last, for as early as July 1912
they were claiming: (20)

Our enemies in the Liberal camp have uneasy doubts as to how much
we are concerned in the revolt of the Labour Party and what mis-
chief we may be up to next.   There is just that feeling of un-
easiness that we want to create both in the House of Commons and
in the Daily Press.

In July 1912 the money at the disposal of the EFF stood at only
£2,800, but the Committee planned for £10,000 by October of that
year; they decided to engage three organisers to build up the
Labour organisation in thirty constituencies represented by anti-
suffragist Liberals.   Once underway the scheme quickly gathered
momentum as is apparent from a letter from Catherine Marshall to
Henderson in which she offered terms for a longer term alliance. (21)   According to her the National Union would send its
workers to help defend every Labour constituency where the sitting
Member was firmly pro-suffragist; they would also make funds available to finance Labour Agents provided that the party in turn co-
operated in attacking certain Liberal seats.   For example the
Labour Members in Blackburn and Gorton would be assisted while
Labour candidatures were promoted in Liberal Rossendale and Accrington; similarly Leeds East and Bradford West would be defended while
the Liberal Leeds North and Bradford East were attacked.

The defensive aspect of this was straightforward enough; a list
was drawn up of the twenty-five Labour Members who were to be helped
prior to the General Election; the other fifteen were designated as
not to be helped either because their seats were considered by
Arthur Peters to be 'safe', or because of their hostility to woman
suffragists, usually summed up by the phrase 'hates rich women';
the chief source of this information was Philip Snowden.

However, an aggressive strategy was not to be adopted by Labour
simply at the behest of the women, and on the eve of war the
National Executive Committee had not finally decided whether to risk
abandoning the pact with the Liberals.   Meanwhile, however, the EFF
staff did their best to push Labour away from the Liberal pact by
creating local pressure for extra Labour candidatures.   The prime
targets for EFF activity in 1913 and 1914 were Rossendale, represented by Lewis Harcourt, East Bristol (Sir Charles Hobhouse), Rother-
ham (J.A. Pease), North Monmouth (Reginald McKenna), Ilkeston (Colonel Seely), Accrington (Harold Baker) and Glasgow Bridgeton
(J. MacCallum Scott) - all notorious anti-suffragists; they were
also active in South Shields, Gateshead, West Hull, Nuneaton, Gran-
tham and Ipswich.   In these seats the EFF freely offered money in
order to promote election contests.   Two organisers were placed in
North Monmouth constituency who ultimately obtained a joint committee for the Labour and Suffrage causes; they won the backing of the
local miners and railwaymen, and succeeded in getting women suffragists co-opted onto the local Trades Council.   The upshot was that
by 1914 the Labour Party in North Monmouth, hitherto content to be
represented by McKenna, had decided to run their own candidate at
the next election. (22)   A great deal of work also went into the
North-East, particularly into Barnard Castle, where Henderson was in
danger of being unseated by a Liberal candidate, Bishop Aukland,
Houghton-le-Spring, Chester-le-Street, Mid-Durham, Gateshead and
South Shields.   In all these constituencies registration work was
done for the Labour Party, and in one, Mid-Durham, the National
Union organiser even went into the Revision Court as the Labour
Agent.   In Rossendale three National Union branches sprang up; in
Accrington, where there had been no prospect of a Labour candidate,
a local Labour Party was organised by the women and the adoption of
a candidate went ahead during the early stages of the war.

Despite the admitted difficulties and the expense involved in
organising what were usually poor and geographically scattered constituencies the EFF staff felt it to be a more profitable exercise
than attempting to convert the middle-class Liberal to woman suffrage, for his attachment to his party was so strong that until
woman suffrage became part of the official programme it would remain
no more than a pious opinion with him.   But it was not so difficult
to persuade the working-class Liberal whose dissatisfaction with the
party leadership could more easily be turned into support for
Labour.

However, the EFF's attempts to disturb the Liberals by promoting
Labour candidatures was by no means the only part of their work in
this direction.   For the National Union appreciated that in spite
of the Parliamentary Labour Party's formal approval of woman suffrage the Labour movement encompassed a wide range of opinion on the
subject.   Much basic work had therefore to be done in converting

Labour and Trade Union members to the cause.   The virtue of the EFF
policy was that it brought the National Union into direct contact
with Trade Unionists in much more favourable circumstances than
would otherwise have been the case.   Even on formal occasions such
as rallies they were careful to use only speakers who 'had a grasp'
of Labour and Trade Union issues.   By November 1913 Catherine Marshall claimed much success in this work: (23)

> Witness the resolutions passed by the Annual Conference of the
> National Labour Party last January, the Annual Conference of the
> I.L.P. last Easter and the T.U.C. and Miners' Federation of Great
> Britain this autumn - and a vast number of resolutions which pour
> in every week from local branches of these bodies all over the
> country.

One may trace some of the effects of this process of conversion.
In 1912 the Labour Party Conference had adopted a demand for a Government Bill for woman suffrage by 919,000 votes to 686,000;   this
formidable anti-suffragist vote was swollen by the Miners' Federation.   In 1913 the Conference voted by 850,000 to 437,000 for
woman suffrage with the miners now neutral.   Continued propaganda
among the miners resulted in a decision to support women suffrage
which their representatives did at their own Conference at Scarbor-
ough in October 1914.

Building up pressure for woman suffrage on the left of the Liberal Government was only one part of the National Union's strategy.
The other aspect was the attempt to persuade the Government that the
Conservatives were thinking seriously about an 'equal terms' Bill
for women.   Catherine Marshall confided to Lady Selborne in 1913
that the Liberals were of the belief that such a measure would 'keep
them out of office for a generation'. (24)   There were sufficient
indications to keep the Liberals in some doubt as to the intentions
of a future Unionist Government on woman suffrage.   In 1911 the
National Union of Conservative and Unionist Associations used their
Annual Conference to give approval to both the Conciliation Bill and
a proposal for referring the matter to a vote of the people.   Balfour and Bonar Law were known to be sympathetic to the Conciliation
Bill, and in 1914 Balfour kept speculation going with his speech on
the Scottish Home Rule Bill in which he declared his support for
women voters under a Scottish parliament.   Lord Lytton and Lord
Robert Cecil actually approached Catherine Marshall to request a
confidential discussion of the women's question. (25)   The two Conservatives wanted to persuade their leaders to promise a Government
Bill on woman suffrage with a referendum clause attached if and when
they were returned to office: would the National Union consider
this an advance on the present position?   The ladies had no hesitation in saying that a Government Bill would represent an improvement
over Private Members Bills which they regarded as 'hostile' measures;   but they did not desire a referendum at all and there could
be no question of their supporting the Conservatives if they came
out with such a plan.   None the less Cecil and Selborne (26) did
their best to convince the party leaders of the wisdom of adopting
the referendum for the women's issue, but Curzon, the leading anti-
suffragist, always flatly rejected the proposal on the grounds that
it would effectively throw away the two-year period for which the
House of Lords could hold up any franchise Bill.   The only circum-

stances in which he could envisage the referendum being a useful
expedient was when the Liberals were forcing a Bill through under
the Parliament Act. (27)

Now although the Conservatives did not adopt a definite policy
over woman suffrage in the event of their return to power, it seems
clear that the party began to shift away from its traditional hostility to the cause.   Indeed the Conservative Party fought out its
own discreet battle on the issue just as the Liberals did.   The
Conservative and Unionist Women's Franchise Association, one of the
most moderate but most influential branches of the women's movement,
worked away with the help of Lord and Lady Selborne, Robert Cecil,
Lytton, and Ladies Frances and Betty Balfour to convert the party by
inches.   Here it was often a matter of persuading the women first
and their husbands later.   Lady Selborne, for one, was convinced
that the Unionist Peers were 'really quite well disposed to women,
but their own wives and sisters are mostly "anti" and they don't
realise that there are a vast number of respectable women who feel
that the vote would be a just safeguard'. (28)

While these ladies endeavoured to undo the effects of militancy
it remained true that the Conservative Party provided much of the
leadership for the League For Opposing Woman Suffrage particularly
in the form of Lords Curzon and Cromer (pp. 39-40).   Paradoxically
the League found real cause for alarm in the attitude among rank and
file Unionists.   From 1911 onwards Cromer was complaining of the
lack of interest in the anti-suffragist cause and of the absence of
new recruits especially on his own side of the House; and by 1912
he was writing: 'the apathy and want of intelligence amongst the
Unionists generally is past all belief.' (29)   He admitted that a
major source of the trouble was Bonar Law who 'considers he is
pledged to support the Conciliation Bill, and will vote for it if it
comes up in Parliament'. (30)   At the same time Walter Long and
Austen Chamberlain, both staunch anti-suffragists, were reluctant to
take an open stand for fear of provoking a split in the Party.
Cromer considered that the tacit approval given by Bonar Law and
Balfour for a moderate women's Bill had 'produced a very considerable effect upon the subordinate ranks and has more or less hypno-
tised the Unionist Agents ... they tell me that the Liberal Agents
are very helpful, give them lists of names and so on, but they can
get nothing done by the Unionist Agents'. (31)

One does not have to look very far to find the explanation for
this peculiar situation; the agents were willing to follow Bonar
Law's lead out of apprehension about the party's electoral prospects.   For in 1912 it seemed that nothing could stop the Government passing legislation in time for a General Election in 1915
which would deprive them of plural voters, University seats and the
restrictions of registration and the twelve-month residence qualification which excluded so many men from the Register.   Under these
circumstances the Liberals could hardly fail to improve their position, and many Unionists felt they were heading for a fourth successive electoral defeat.   However, the infusion of one million
women voters under the Conciliation Bill would have made this much
less likely (pp. 34-5);   hence the indifference and hostility shown
towards the League by the agents.

By 1913 Arnold Ward MP was prepared to admit privately that the

Conservative and Unionists Women's Franchise Association had made so
much progress in converting the party that it was feared that the
Unionists would adopt the Conciliation Bill as official policy. (32)
This interesting possibility may well have been a contributory
factor in encouraging Asquith to make concessions to the women in
1912 and 1913, for he could hardly risk allowing the Labour and Conservative Parties to monopolise suffragist support.   Doubts over
the Conservative intentions may also explain why Asquith continued
to take the full brunt of suffragette opposition for so long;   for
it must have been tempting to allow the Conciliation Bill through
the Commons to face rejection from the House of Lords.   He would
thus have forced the Pankhursts to face up to the fact that their
ultimate opponents were the Peers not the Liberal Party.   But could
the Peers be entirely depended upon to reject a Bill that was increasingly seen as one which would assist their own party electorally?   In 1914 they defeated Selborne's Bill by only forty-four
votes, which the Liberal 'Nation' interpreted as evidence of their
Lordships' growing appetite for woman suffrage. (33)   In 1918,
moreover, the Peers were indeed to give way very tamely over this
issue for all the belligerent noises from Curzon.   It was not a
risk Asquith wished to take.

    In this way the two-pronged strategy of moderate women suffra-
gists operated before 1914, mobilising support on the left and right
flanks of the Liberal Government.   By the end of 1913 Catherine
Marshall claimed: 'the result of this fear of an equal terms' bill
on the one hand, and pressure for an adult suffrage bill on the
other hand, is to make the Liberals more and more inclined to think
that the safest course would after all be to pass a bill on Dickinson lines.' (34)   This is a reference to the measure introduced by
a Liberal backbencher which would have enfranchised some five million women (p. 43).   However, the National Union's strategy was not
an unqualified success.   For one thing, the Government, if dis-
turbed, did not feel driven to drastic action by the Labour Party's
by-election performances which appeared more as an irritant than a
threat.   Also the EFF policy brought in its wake a large number of
resignations from members, as Catherine Marshall's correspondence
shows, with Liberal sympathies.   In fact by 1914 a demand had developed for a return to the original non-party basis of the National
Union.   Indeed Catherine Marshall still took the view that the
National Union was a non-party organisation and that they were not
pledged to work for *every* Labour candidate.   This was her response
to complaints that they had not assisted Labour in the Keighley by-
election in 1913. (35)   She felt genuinely torn between loyalty to
Liberalism and to woman suffrage, which is why she had never regarded the EFF policy as more than a temporary expedient and had endeavoured to avoid committing the National Union irretrievably to
the Labour alliance.   Towards the end of 1913 she warned Francis
Acland that their existing policy committed the National Union to
assisting particular sitting Labour Members and attacking certain
particularly hostile Liberals;   it was on their seats that the funds
were concentrated. (36)   But there was a new move, according to
Catherine Marshall, to increase the EFF's finances in preparation
for the General Election in which they would attack Liberals on a
much wider front, the main criteria now being simply the size of the

Liberal majority and the potential Labour vote in each constituency.
Yet she wished to avoid this threat to Liberal suffragists and to
keep open a line of retreat so that they might withdraw from Labour
as soon as the Liberal Party changed its mind on woman suffrage.
If the National Union went on as at present it would become very
difficult to leave Labour candidates in the lurch especially in the
North East where many joint Labour-Suffragist committees were now in
existence.

For this reason Catherine Marshall desired a meeting with Sir
Edward Grey to discover whether there was any basis for her attempt
to restrain the expansion of EFF activity.   Francis Acland (37)
told her on behalf of Grey that everything depended on the circumstances in which the next election was fought; if it centred on
Home Rule he could not offer much hope of concessions on woman suffrage, but if the Government's major Bills were out of the way and
'it was a question of fighting on a new programme [viz. land, etc.]
he could do a good deal'.   They were still invited to wait and see.

No doubt Catherine Marshall was trying to achieve maximum effect
for the cause while minimising the damage done to the Liberal Party.
Apart from this political hesitancy there were obvious financial
limitations on EFF policy.   When challenged by the anti-suffragist
Liberal William Pringle, MP for North West Lanark to justify neglec-
ting his seat while fighting those of pro-suffragists, Catherine
Marshall wrote confidentially to Mrs Acland that although Pringle's
seat had been under consideration, they preferred boroughs to county
seats and North West Lanark would be costly to work: 'we do not
think Mr. Pringle important enough to justify the expense.' (38)
Quite how far the National Union would have spread its resources at
a 1915 General Election and with what result must remain in doubt.
In fact after the outbreak of war the National Union came to believe that it was tied to a declining force in the Labour Party and
withdrew from the alliance.   The achievement of their strategy
before 1914 must be seen partly as the undermining of the Liberals
by helping Labour, not supporting the Unionists as the WSPU had
done; and also as the conversion of important sections of the working class to woman suffrage at a time when militancy was merely
alienating the people.   It is clear from Asquith's conciliatory
response to a delegation of working-class suffragists led by Sylvia
Pankhurst in 1914 (39) that he was now fully alive to the danger of
losing them to Liberalism.

Chapter 3

THE GOVERNMENT AND FRANCHISE REFORM 1906-14

> I think the Liberal Party ought to make up its mind as a whole
> that it will either have an extended franchise which puts the
> workingmen's wives on to the register as well as spinsters and
> widows, or that it will have no female franchise at all.
> (D. Lloyd George to the Master of Elibank, 5 September 1911)

Historians have established that four out of every ten Englishmen
were still deprived of the parliamentary suffrage, either through
failure to qualify under the law or through inability to register,
until 1918. (1)   What is not so clear is why this situation was not
remedied between 1906 and 1914; for, as Dr P.F. Clarke has observed, (2) the conspicuous failure of the Liberal Governments of this
period was in the field of political not social reform.   Why did
the fourth Reform Act have to wait until 1918?   In this chapter we
shall attempt to account for this flaw in the Liberal programme.

By the early twentieth century the franchise seems to have become
a politicians' issue rather than one that stirred the population at
large.   Although half the Liberal candidates in 1906 mentioned constitutional reforms in their election literature, (3) this does not
seem to have aroused any great interest at the time, which is not
surprising in view of the other issues of that election.   Again, in
1910 the franchise was crowded out by other questions. (4)   While
Edwardian England resounded to the claims of the women, the unenfranchised males seem to have raised little attention; as Philip
Snowden - no anti-suffragist - admitted, he had never been questioned about male suffrage in fifteen years of addressing public
meetings: 'the absence of any strong demand for the extension of
the vote proves that those who are outside the pale of the political
franchise care very little about the extension of the political
franchise.' (5)

Why was this?   One obvious reason in the post-1905 period was
that any popular interest in the franchise was somewhat qualified
and confused by popular prejudice against the women; they so dominated the debate as to leave the working man unsure whether he had a
common grievance with them as a *non-voter,* or whether he ought to
stand on his superior status as a *man.*   It was inevitable that,
under Christabel Pankhurst's assault on men and marriage, many would
take the latter position.

A second reason was that the unenfranchised men tended to include
the least organised, least politically conscious and least articu-
late sections of the population.   The Trade Union leadership was
largely absorbed with exploiting to the full the benefits which were
available through the political influence their members already
possessed.   Those outside the pale did not constitute a coherent
class within the community; as the 'Nation' observed of the 1912
Franchise and Registration Bill: 'it lacks the human and social
interest of·the three historical reform bills ... it emancipates no
subject class and raises the status of no body of men who labour
under the stigma of deliberate exclusion from the franchise.' (6)
These two factors help to explain the absence of popular agitation
following the fiasco over the Government's reform Bill in 1913.   On
past form this would have been the occasion for action, for the
popular agitation normally came as a *response* to a parliamentary
struggle or fiasco over reform as in 1832 and 1867; when, as in
1884 and 1918, the question was settled within the parliamentary
sphere relatively smoothly the prospect of mass action did not
arise.
    Another explanation for the absence of demand for the vote is
that many workers simply did not value the franchise sufficiently to
agitate for it, preferring to by-pass the parliamentary system and
the discredited Labour Party, and rely instead on the power of the
Trade Union movement to help the working class through syndicalism.
The syndicalist argument was almost certainly too sophisticated to
appeal to most unenfranchised men, and influenced only a small minority even among Union leaders. (7)   It may be true that Union
members were more concerned with practical industrial action at
times of full employment as around 1910 than with 'politics', though
this is not borne out by the extremely high turnout in the two
elections of that year.   Involvement in industrial action and
interest in parliamentary politics almost certainly went hand in
hand; a worker was either keen on both or on neither.   Some socialists undoubtedly lost patience with the Labour Party - if indeed
they had ever had any - and looked elsewhere for a theoretical base
for political action other than the opportunism and compromise of
parliamentary politics, but this was characteristically the dilemma
of middle-class intellectuals like the Webbs rather than of the
working man.
    Finally what of the Labour Party itself which one might expect to
have taken the initiative over franchise reform?   Although the
party was committed to adult suffrage it did not on the whole bring
the Government under pressure to legislate except in so far as its
position on the suffrage was an embarrassment to the Liberals.
This was largely a reflection of the NEC's preoccupation with the
task of maintaining and controlling its existing strongholds in the
constituencies; the party's immediate interest lay in the organised, politically aware sections of the working class already on the
parliamentary register; nothing was as yet to be expected from domestic servants living with their employers or labourers residing
with farmers who bulked large among the unenfranchised, or indeed
from many industrial workers in areas in which, in Ramsay Mac-
Donald's words, 'poverty and degradation are of the worst type'. (8)
    In the last resort action on the franchise depended on the atti-

tude of the Liberals after 1906.   There were a number of half-
hearted attempts to pass Bills dealing with aspects of the franchise
between 1906 and 1911, all doomed by the hostility of the House of
Lords.   However, Liberals on the backbenches and in the country
expected to see some indication that the Government intended to
reform the franchise, and the robust Party men in the Cabinet like
Lewis Harcourt were anxious to erase the old franchise system from
which the Unionists had profited for so long.   Thus before 1911
there were some sporadic attempts to reduce or abolish plural
voting; (9)   such Bills had the great merit of hurting the Unionists
without helping the Labour Party very much.   Historians are still
in doubt as to whether plural voters favoured the Unionists by as
much as four to one, (10) but contemporaries had no such doubts.
After the December 1910 election, for instance, the 'Westminster
Gazette' (11) listed the thirty English constituencies in which the
ownership vote exceeded the Unionist majority by five times or more;
this was the minimum advantage that the Liberals expected to gain
by abolishing the plural vote.

In 1906 Harcourt took responsibility for a simple abolition of
plural voting Bill, and a backbencher, A.J. Sherwell, drafted a One-
Day Polling Bill in 1910 which Churchill urged the Cabinet to adopt
as an alternative; (12) this would have had the practical effect of
reducing the opportunities for using widely scattered qualifications, but could also be defended on other grounds such as the need
to avoid prolonged disruption to business caused by the usual three-
week polling period.   The notorious case of London formed the subject of Bills by W.H. Dickinson in 1908 and Harcourt in 1909.   The
source of Liberal grievance here lay in the fact that London was
divided into twenty-eight separate parliamentary boroughs which
meant that an estimated 25,000 to 50,000 electors were annually deprived of their vote through loss of their twelve-month residence
qualification as a result of moving house.   At the same time 10 per
cent of the 600,000 electors in London had duplicate qualifications
in the city.   Making London a single borough for parliamentary purposes was therefore a simple remedy for both grievances.

In the repetitive debates on these abortive Bills the Liberals
had no difficulty in demonstrating the illogicality of the claim
that plural voting gave weight to property holders.   After all, a
man could have any number of interests in one constituency and yet
possess only one vote;   the owner of a house in the country and a
business in the town had a second vote only if the town happened to
be a parliamentary borough;   and if the owner of a business turned
it into a limited liability company he lost his vote;   thus money in
shares was unrepresented while wealth in the form of, say, a bar-
ber's shop carried an extra vote.   In short the concept of a 'stake
in the country' as the basis for representation merely provided a
spurious rationalisation for the increase in plural voting which
had been a by-product of the reforms of 1884 and 1885.

However, plural voting never provoked much emotion beyond the
confines of 21 Abingdon Street, where Liberal Party Organisation resided, and the Unionists privately took confidence in the belief
that 'there is no public demand for its abolition', (13) and hence
no risk in the House of Lords rejecting Bills on plural voting.
Liberal organisers professed much confidence in manhood suffrage

based on a short residence qualification and continuous registration, (14) and the party professionals took a lively interest in
simplifying the whole system.   In 1911 the Master of Elibank, then
Liberal Chief Whip, sought the views of all the Liberal Federations
on three questions: the effect of the existing registration law
on the Liberal Party, the value of a simple residential qualification, and the consequences of granting woman suffrage along the
lines of the Conciliation Bill.

A summary of the replies prepared for the Cabinet by J. Renwick
Seager, Head of the Party's Registration Department, revealed an
almost unanimous attitude in the constituencies on the first two
questions. (15)   The desirability of a residential franchise was
qualified only by the belief that since 'the Services mostly vote
Tory' a few constituencies would be adversely affected.   Winston
Churchill, much alarmed at the prospect of all the troops qualifying
by virtue of residence in barracks, warned the Cabinet (16) that
where men were grouped together the franchise would serve only to
stimulate a 'class campaign' for the improvement of soldiers' working conditions - an invincible Trade Union!   There were in fact
some 10,250 soldiers at present on the register (17) and according
to the War Office the maximum electorate of troops over twenty-one
years old would be 53,000, the largest concentration by far being
the 11,000 men at Aldershott.

Apart from this the extension of the male suffrage was considered
likely to swell the Labour vote in a few places, but not disastrously: (18)

> In Yorkshire it is estimated that in 38 constituencies it would
> be favourable to the Liberal Party, while in some industrial
> areas such as Bradford, Hull, Dewsbury and Shipley, it may tend
> to increase the Labour vote.   Only in three Divisions in York-
> shire is it suggested that the effect would be unfavourable, viz.
> Spen Valley, Colne Valley and Buckrose.   There the Extensive en-
> franchisement of young workers, it is thought, would give those
> seats to the Socialists.

It was only the Northern, Yorkshire and East Scotland Federations
that expected any increase in the Labour vote; the Midlands believed the new franchise would 'make the difference between winning
and losing' for the Liberals.   Overall there emerged an unequivocal
desire for one-man-one-vote, with a simplified registration system
and the Alternative Vote.   What little the party might lose to
Labour they would more than make up with gains from the Conservatives in rural seats.

In spite of this underlying confidence of the Liberal Party in
manhood suffrage it is clear that during the life of the 1906-10
Parliament electoral reform did not rank as a priority for the Government; measures for Wales, Scotland, Licensing and Education
filled the timetable, and there is no indication that a comprehensive measure for the franchise was prepared until 1911.   This is
understandable; basking in the glow of their victories and with a
seven-year term stretching ahead of them, the Liberals saw no urgency in the question.   Nor, in view of the apparent upsurge in Labour
support in 1906 and 1907 would they rashly extend the electorate.
In 1906 it cannot have been evident that Labour would lose the initiative to the Government, nor that they would be effectively con-

tained to fifty-odd constituencies.   The Liberal Federations' verdict in 1911 no doubt reflected a confidence based upon Labour's
poor performance in 1910.   What is certain is that in 1906 the
Liberals intended to leave the franchise until the next election
began to approach, and in the meantime Campbell-Bannerman thought
only of starting the process by means of a committee of enquiry into
electoral facts. (19)
    Thus although the Peers blocked the desultory attempts at partial
reform before 1910, one must not forget that they never had the
option of rejecting a manhood suffrage Bill.   They could always put
up an adequate argument against plural voting Bills on the grounds
that the worst plural voters were the Irish electors whose constituencies were half the size of the average English seat.   The connection between franchise and Home Rule via redistribution of seats
cannot be over-emphasised; the Government would not risk trying to
apply the principle of equal constituencies to Ireland until Home
Rule had been settled to the satisfaction of the Nationalists because the over-representation of Ireland as a whole plus the small
size of the Nationalist seats compared to the Unionist ones would
have resulted in a loss of approximately forty Government supporters
in the Commons.
    However, the main obstacle to franchise reform proved to be woman
suffrage, though it should not be forgotten that it also acted as a
stimulant at the same time.   Mrs Fawcett's dictum that the Liberals were an army without generals and that the Unionists had suffragist generals who lacked an army of supporters is still much
quoted, (20) though it is somewhat misleading.   The point is that a
majority of Unionists at all levels were unsympathetic to the suffragist cause, while a majority of Liberals at all levels including
the Cabinet were sympathetic by doctrine and by history, and could
not, indeed, afford to lose their title to the leadership of pro-
gressivism.   But doctrine was qualified by tactical considerations.
As on previous occasions in history the Unionists could afford to
play fast and loose with the franchise because the position of the
Liberals could be undermined in theory both by new women and new
working-class voters.   Bonar Law, an unlikely latter-day Disraeli,
always resisted suggestions that he should make more of these possibilities.
    In the Cabinet the anti-suffragist minority led by Asquith in-
cluded Harcourt, McKenna, Pease, Hobhouse and Samuel, while the most
definite among the suffragists were Sir Edward Grey, Lloyd George,
Sir John Simon, R.B. Haldane and Walter Runciman.   Some of the
'democrats' were easily discouraged; Churchill is an obvious
example; and C.P. Scott found Augustine Birrell 'dead against adult
suffrage' in 1911 just after having had his knee-cap painfully displaced by the suffragettes. (21)   What is certain is that the suffragist majority acquiesced in the Lloyd George-Churchill view that
it would be unwise to allow any Bill to pass that would assist the
Opposition electorally.   Lloyd George is often considered to have
been suspect as a suffragist on the grounds of his enthusiasm for
frustrating the Conciliation Bill, (22) but this seems unjustified.
He never took personal offence at the treatment he received from the
militants as other Ministers did, and, if C.P. Scott's many conver-
sations with him on the subject are anything to go by, he continued

to work for the cause as effectively as he could under an anti-suffragist Prime Minister.   It is possible that Lloyd George merely
humoured C.P. Scott, but this implies that Scott was easily gulled,
which, judging by his talks with other Ministers, was not the case.

The question then centred on what was and what was not damaging
to the Liberal Party?   Early in the life of the 1906 Parliament
woman suffrage, being more or less an academic issue in view of the
Peers' presumed hostility, was the subject of co-operation between
backbenchers of all parties;   yet this in no way altered the fact
that Liberal suffragists preferred an adult suffrage Bill to any restricted franchise for women, and any measure like Geoffrey Howard's
Adult Suffrage Bill in March 1909 immediately dissolved the non-
party strategy since most Conservatives would go no further than a
franchise for *propertied* women.   Asquith, from the start of his
Premiership, had made it clear that when the Government were ready
they would bring in a manhood suffrage Bill and allow the Commons to
introduce a women's clause if they wished, and this was the position
until 1913.

Thus the revival of the non-party strategy in the form of Lord
Lytton's Conciliation Committee after the January 1910 election was
doomed to failure.   The Conciliation Bill would have granted a vote
to women who possessed a household qualification or a £10 occupation
qualification.   It was to this that almost the whole Cabinet took
exception;   the Master of Elibank's enquiries of 1911 drew a chorus
of horror from the Party Federations when he consulted them about
the effect of the Conciliation Bill: 'suicidal to pass the bill.
Women six to one against us', wailed the Eastern Counties; 'would
wipe out Liberal representation', warned the Western Federation;
'Nobody wants it and [everybody] dreads its advent', declared
London. (23)

Behind all this lay the assumption that the proposed electorate
would comprise wealthy women of the sort already on the local government register;   it would also facilitate the creation of faggot
votes for the wives and daughters of property owners who already
exercised undue weight in the Conservative interest among the electorate.   However, this interpretation was disputed.   The Liberal
suffragist Willoughby Dickinson claimed that in his constituency,
St Pancras North, 60 per cent of the women on the Municipal Reigster
were working class, and the ILP put the figure at 82 per cent after
a survey conducted in 1904.   Of course the fact that ILP branches
were only to be found in strongly working-class districts explains
their figures.   The Conciliation Committee which held enquiries in
the constituencies of Churchill and Lloyd George, found that in
Dundee only 11 per cent of women municipal electors were middle
class, whereas in Bangor and Caernarvon it was 75 per cent. (24)

Obviously the figures reflected the general social character of
the constituencies, so that, as the East Scotland Liberal Federation
commented, they expected that women would be Liberal in the working-
class areas as the men were. (25)   Even so the Federations had very
mixed feelings about women as voters;   it was feared that 'religious
bigotry would find a ready response among the women', but on the
other hand, 'in matters of Social Reform, Peace, Temperance, the
impression is they would vote for these causes'.   If the Liberals
were right about women's support for Temperance - which was pre-

cisely what anti-suffragist men expected and feared if their women-
folk won the vote - they would have had a fine opportunity to turn
the traditional Liberal Temperance policy to advantage at last among
working-class wives who suffered heavy-drinking husbands.   However,
women as a whole were one thing, the million or so women covered by
the Conciliation Bill were taken to be potential Unionist votes,
rightly or wrongly, and this belief immensely strengthened Asquith's
hand as well as justifying Lloyd George's view that no Bill for
women was acceptable unless it was a really democratic one.   It was
also instrumental, as we have seen (pp. 25-7) in depressing anti-
suffragism in the Unionist Party.

Asquith could not prevaricate for ever over woman suffrage;   for
one thing he greatly irritated close colleagues like Grey and exposed the popular democrats like Lloyd George to the charge of hypo-
crisy;   and in the long run he risked losing the support of women
activists to the Labour Party (pp. 22-4).   Moreover, since it was
not possible to prevent debates on backbenchers Bills in the House,
he was frequently faced with what seemed to be a large suffragist
majority in his own party.   However, Asquith moved with typical
stubbornness and shrewdness;   it was not easy to say precisely what
Liberal Members wanted in the way of woman suffrage, nor how badly
they wanted it.   In 1910 the estimate made by the League for Opposing Woman Suffrage (see Appendix 2) showed 283 suffragists in the
whole House against 189 antis and 175 whose views were unknown.
The breakdown of Liberals showed 58 antis, 60 advocates of a limited
franchise, 77 who wanted the same terms for women as for men, 9 who
insisted on nothing less than adult suffrage and 46 whose views were
unknown.   The strength of Asquith's position lay not only in the
fact that the suffragist majority was divided over what was acceptable, but also in the Members' reluctance to give priority to the
issue in a situation in which parliamentary time was very precious.
As Dickinson put it retrospectively: (26)

From time to time the House protested its undying devotion by
voting in favour of the second reading of Bills that it knew
could make no further progress: but if you asked me to name a
dozen members who would have gone through fire and water for the
cause of Women's Suffrage I could not do it.   Now this does not
involve any reflection upon Members of Parliament because, as a
rule they are not the sort of persons who go through fire and
water for any political cause.

Thus the Cabinet were quite well aware that most of their supporters were less than enthusiastic about the Conciliation Bill regardless of the fact that many would vote for it out of principle.   As
a result, when the Cabinet discussed Lord Lytton's request for parliamentary time for the Bill in 1910 they decided only to offer a
Second Reading debate;   the surprising thing is that it took three
meetings on 8, 15 and 23 June to arrive at this decision. (27)   In
May 1911 the success of Sir George Kemp's Conciliation Bill on Second Reading caused the Cabinet to hold another heated debate in
which Grey, Runciman, Birrell and Haldane favoured allowing the
House a free vote on whether to proceed with the Bill or not; (28)
this was resisted by Lloyd George, McKenna and Loreburn as also by
'apparently a majority of the Cabinet' as Asquith put it. (29)

In fact a firm decision was postponed;   first it was announced

that one week would be made available in 1912 to debate the Bill,
but this was modified in a statement by Grey in which the Government
offered a free vote on whether sufficient time should be   permitted
to ensure the passage of the Bill.   The obvious muddle over the
problem and the absence of further discussions in Cabinet after 17
May 1911 suggest that Asquith was seeing his colleagues individually
in an effort to conciliate Grey and Lloyd George who were bent upon
obtaining a concession for the women.   This was precisely the
period in which Simon and Pease were working out a firm timetable
for a major franchise Bill;   to this extent then, the suffragettes'
claim that the object of the 1912 Franchise and Registration Bill
was simply to sabotage the Conciliation Bill is justified.   For it
was the determined pressure of some suffragist Ministers that led
the Government to undertake a comprehensive measure at a time when
they would not otherwise have done so for lack of parliamentary
time.
    It was not until November 1911 that a surprised delegation from
the People's Suffrage Federation led by Arthur Henderson, Walter
Rea, G.M. Trevelyan and Mrs Francis Acland heard of the Government's
proposed legislation.   The critical point was that the Bill was to
deal with male suffrage but could be amended to include the women.
This caused the WSPU to declare all-out war because they were being
denied their own separate Bill.   Looked at rationally they were
being invited to exchange a Private Member's Bill which would sooner
or later be buried,for a place in a Bill which the Government would
force through the House of Lords under the Parliament Act - a far
more reliable method.   The moderate societies saw this and welcomed
the new step. (30)
    Superficially, of course, it did appear that the Government had
acted purely to defeat the women;   for the majority of 167 for Sir
George Kemp's Bill in 1911 turned into a deficit of 26 when Sir
John Agg-Gardner introduced a similar measure in March 1912.   Yet
the 1911 Bill was simply not treated as a serious measure;   it had
been passed in a small House on the assumption that it would go no
further.   The number of Liberal Members voting against the Bill
jumped from 36 to 73 though even now more Liberals voted for it.
The Unionists who had approved the Bill in 1911 by 53 to 43 how
rejected it by 114 to 63.   Both parties were reacting against the
latest round of suffragette violence, but the Unionists had been
irretrievably divided from the Liberal and Labour suffragists now
that the Government had opened up the prospect of extending the vote
to working-class women and men.
    It is now possible to throw some light on how the Government
arrived at a decision to adopt their own Reform Bill.   The 1911
Parliament Act had opened up new and tempting legislative vistas for
the Cabinet.   Unhappily the parliamentary timetable now became
crowded with legislation among which the Bill for Irish Home Rule
had to have first place.   Early in 1911 Pease and Simon had been
thinking in terms of yet another measure for plural voting, (31)
but this was shelved in favour of a more comprehensive Bill for
franchise and registration which was to be the responsibility of
Pease, then President of the Board of Education, aided by Harcourt,
Simon and the parliamentary draftsman, Sir Arthur Thring.   Time
became the vital factor: the Bill had to pass into law in time to

allow for the preparation of a new parliamentary register to be used
at a 1915 General Election.   According to Simon (32) its timetable
hinged on a dissolution in January 1915, Royal Assent on 15 March
1914, and an initial Second Reading by 15 March 1912; he concluded,
'it would therefore have to be the *very first* legislative proposal
next year'.   This allowed them the summer and autumn of 1911 to
prepare the Bill and to consult the party in the country by means of
the enquiries made by the Master of Elibank.

By December Pease and Simon were ready to bring precise proposals before the Cabinet. (33)   Designed to be as simple as possible, the Bill provided a one-man-one-vote scheme for an anticipated nine and a half million male electors based on a six-month residence qualification and continuous registration; those with several 'residences' would be allowed to choose which one to use for
their qualification.   The main objections to this came from Sir
Charles Hobhouse (34) who pointed out that continuous registration
would encourage the transfer of 'swallow voters' to marginal seats
of which there were forty-four with majorities below 100.   He
therefore wanted a three-month qualifying period without continuous
registration even within parliamentary boroughs.

However, the chief obstacles remained the timetable and the
women's question; and it is evident from letters of Pease and Harcourt at the end of December that Asquith preferred to abandon a
comprehensive Reform Bill in favour of another Plural Voting
Bill. (35)   Pease readily conceded that abolition of plural voting
would suffice 'from the party point of view', but he reminded the
Prime Minister that he was in the position of having promised a week
of parliamentary time for the Conciliation Bill, which they both
deplored; that measure would be effectively 'snowed under' once a
major Reform Bill was before the House.   The strength of this argument rested on the assumption that the Commons would *not* add a
women's clause to the Government Bill, a step to which Pease was as
opposed as Asquith.   Yet if they did the situation would be very
awkward as Churchill pointed out: (36)

How can the P.M. honourably use the Parliament Act to force
[woman suffrage] upon the King, when he has himself declared it
to be a 'disastrous mistake'?   The King will say the constituencies have not been consulted upon it - and the Government itself
is not behind it.   Hence he will dismiss the Ministry....   If
Lloyd George and Grey go on working themselves up, they will have
to go, if female suffrage is knocked out.   And the P.M.'s position will become impossible if it is put in.   The only safe and
honest course is to have a referendum - first to the women to
know if they want it; and then to the men to know if they will
give it.   I am quite willing to abide by the result.

Yet it does seem that Asquith's immediate objection to Pease's
Bill was practical rather than political: (37)

I do not see how it is possible, without resort to quite inde-
fensible developments of the guillotine, to get through three
highly controversial bills [the Bills for Home Rule and Welsh
Church Disestablishment] without an autumn sitting.   We cannot,
I think, again deprive private members of their days *before*
Easter; and it is most important that the Budget should once
more be introduced at a normal date, and passed so as to antici-

pate, and not merely to ratify, the collection of the taxes which
it imposes.   Nor do I think there would be any advantage in
point of time in a Plural Voting Bill as compared with a Single
Qualification Bill.

This statement suggests that whichever Reform Bill were adopted it
would be unlikely to pass into law; by implication, therefore, its
merit lay in torpedoing the Conciliation Bill to which the Government had already offered time.

Consequently Pease, who took some trouble in preparing his case
for the Cabinet, (38) boldly threw out a reminder to his colleagues
that many Liberals, who were quite unmoved by the measures of Welsh,
Scottish and Irish interest, would rally around a Reform Bill.
Moreover, his Bill had the virtue of comparative simplicity; it
swept away some thirty existing Acts and deliberately omitted such
desirable changes as the Alternative Vote so as to minimise the time
used up in the Commons.   It also retained an occupation qualification for land or premises which, though likely to be unpopular with
the radicals, would save several business constituencies from being
denuded of electors; and this, Pease suggested, would lessen the
force of the case for a Redistribution Bill.   Assuming, however,
that the   Peers still held up the Bill for lack of a redistribution
of constituencies, it could come into force in November 1914 by
which time a redistribution scheme could have been prepared; thus
redistribution would be able to *follow* the Home Rule Bill into law,
and, taking into account the abolition of the University seats as
well, this would reduce the total membership of the House of Commons
by sixty-eight.   In this way Home Rule would clear the way for redistribution to accompany franchise reform; but in the event of a
failure to pass Home Rule there was a kind of insurance in the form
of the preserved business electorate; for this would serve to justify a decision by the Government to hold an election under the new
franchise but on the *old* constituencies.   On terms such as these
the Unionists would find it very difficult to win a majority.   On
the basis of franchise first and seats later the Cabinet went ahead
with Pease's Bill, (39) though, according to Pease, they decided to
make application of the new franchise contingent upon a scheme for
the constituencies. (40)

When the Bill received its Second Reading in July 1912 some radical Members, as anticipated, took a dim view of the retention of the
occupation qualification, (41) and after meeting the chiefs of the
Federations Pease failed to convince them that the Cabinet were
right. (42)   However, as Simon pointed out, there was no longer any
point in attempting to conciliate the House of Lords with the occupation qualification;   let the Bill be passed in two years and the
Peers would then 'have to decide whether they were prepared to
reject redistribution proposals when these are put forward in
1914'. (43)   In accordance with this programme John Burns at the
Local Government Board prepared several redistribution schemes which
the Cabinet inspected in January 1913; (44)   the occupation qualification was to be dropped from the Bill.

During 1912 the question revolved around the prospects of the
Commons producing a majority for a woman suffrage clause in the
Bill.   It looked increasingly doubtful.   Only the Labour Party was
likely to give a solid vote for such a clause.   But despite the

Party's pact with the NUWSS the National Executive expressly refused
to oppose the Government's Bill in the event of the women's clauses
being rejected. (45)   This was the cause of Lansbury's resignation
and the estrangement of Keir Hardie from his colleagues.   In 1913
the National Executive recommended that Labour Members should devote
their second place in the Ballot to a women's Bill, the first place
being reserved for the Right To Work Bill. (46)

On the other hand the Irish Nationalist Members swung sharply
against woman suffrage in 1912.   In general they could not be expected to welcome new legislation that competed with Home Rule for
parliamentary time, especially on a topic that did not agitate the
Irish electorate.   C.P. Scott, anxious to avoid the loss of woman
suffrage through Irish votes, interviewed Redmond (47) whose explanation was that since Asquith had given a pledge to accept a woman's
clause 'at all events he must be relieved from the necessity of ful-
filling it'.   Devlin and Dillon, apart from being somewhat alienated by militant tactics, considered that (48)

> two motives weighed with the Nationalists.   (1) Gratitude and
> loyalty to Mr. Asquith....   They would not willingly do anything
> to hurt or wound him.   (2) they felt that his personal position
> and authority was involved - that he had placed himself in an
> almost impossible position and that, as the maintenance of his
> personal credit and authority were vital to the prospects of Home
> Rule, it was clearly to their interest to rescue him from his
> difficulties.

The practical results of this feeling were very evident.   For
whereas in 1911 the Nationalist Members had voted for the Conciliation Bill by 31 to 9, in 1912 they rejected it by 35 to 3, and in
the following year they also rejected Dickinson's Bill by 34 to 13,
in both cases their votes were decisive in producing the anti-
suffragist margin.   Scott's intervention was therefore necessary
if, in the event, futile.

Manoeuvring between and within the political parties at this
critical time was the League For Opposing Woman Suffrage; the
League was the result of a merger, instigated by Lord Cromer and
aided by Lord Curzon, of the existing men's league with the women
anti-suffragists under Lady Jersey's leadership.   Despite the existence of this body only a fraction of the potential strength of
anti-suffragism was mobilised formally under its banner; for the
chief strength of the opposition to the women's cause lay in the
combination of inertia and prejudice among politicians absorbed with
other issues.   What Lords Curzon and Cromer accomplished fairly
successfully was the raising of money, though the reserve fund
which they created for a last ditch campaign became a fertile source
of conflict between Curzon and the Committee, chiefly because Curzon
would never accept that the time had come to spend the money.

In fact the correspondence of the two Peers illustrates the fact
that they were absorbed more with the internal problems of the
League than with combating suffragism.   It is punctuated with a
discussion of the difficulty of working with women.   First they had
to ensure that Lady Jersey was prevented from becoming either President or Chairman of the Committee without giving offence to the
women members; (49) then they had to find a Secretary - a man, naturally; Lady Jersey accepted that, other things being equal, a man

would be better, but made so bold as to insist that a first-class woman would have the edge over a second-class man! (50)   Then there were the personalities; Mrs Humphry Ward, for example, is variously referred to by Cromer as 'a rather disturbing element' and 'that most tiresome woman'.   Even the office work did not go smoothly, and poor Cromer was soon wishing he had not been so hasty in disbanding the men's league. (51)   Still, he admitted that the women were quite efficient workers, at a certain level, of course, and one had to make the best of it.   Women were allowed onto the Committee but, he consoled Curzon, 'it is very improbable they will all attend at once'. (52)

That women were denied the vote before the war was due less to the effectiveness of the League than to their allies in the Government.   'I am indeed one of your best assets', Lewis Harcourt told Curzon when donating £100 to the funds. (53)   Ministers like Harcourt naturally avoided being drawn into public controversy if possible, as did their wives; Mary Harcourt declined to serve on the Committee of the League for fear of provoking the wives of suffragist Ministers. (54)   In 1910 Cromer tried unsuccessfully to obtain a subscription from Asquith, (55) and in 1911 actually invited him to speak at an Albert Hall Rally, (56) an idea which the Prime Minister was apparently considering at the end of that year. (57) Similarly Grey and Haldane were turning down C.P. Scott's requests for public appearances in support of the women for the sake of maintaining what survived of Cabinet harmony. (58)   The chief reason for the failure of the anti-suffragists to mobilise their resources lay in their confidence in Asquith's ability to thwart the suffragists, and the information relayed to them by friendly Ministers. Thus early in 1912 Cromer consulted Hobhouse because he was worried about the possible passage of the Conciliation Bill, only to be reassured of the Cabinet's hostility to the Bill and to the idea of holding a referendum on it: 'You may depend upon it that Asquith and his friends will somehow or other find a method for not passing the Conciliation Bill into law', he told Curzon. (59)

Although the Unionists were bound to oppose the Franchise and Registration Bill as a whole it was a foregone conclusion that the Government would force it through under the Parliament Act.   The question for them, therefore, was what attitude to take on the women's clauses which were being prepared.   To some Unionists the Cabinet's division offered an opportunity which should be exploited; F.E. Smith was sure they could be wrecked over the issue. (60) Feelings certainly ran high in the Cabinet, and Asquith had agreed to allow the Bill to be amended in the Commons only because of severe pressure from his colleagues: 'I am clear that the Government as a Government, could not take any other course than we have taken.   The only alternative was for the minority among us to resign'. (61)   In any vote on woman suffrage the Labour Party would be cancelled out by the net anti-suffragist Nationalist vote of about forty.   On the basis of two divisions in 1912 and 1913 the pro-suffragist majority among the Liberals was likely to be narrowly exceeded by the anti-suffragist majority among the Unionists.   This was no doubt the outcome for which Asquith hoped.   Yet from the Unionists' point of view it was bad tactics to assist Asquith towards the male franchise Bill that would damage them most.   If, on

the other hand, the Unionist antis abstained in sufficient numbers
to allow an amendment on conciliation lines to get a majority the
reaction of the Liberals could be predicted.   If there had to be
votes for women the Liberal antis would insist on a more radical
franchise as being less harmful to their party;   for on the subject
of enfranchising joint householders, man and wife, 'even the Prime
Minister was prepared for it' according to Lloyd George. (62)   He
would no doubt have accepted this if driven to it, but the more
likely outcome, in view of the reaction of Members to militancy and
the pressure exerted by Asquith on the Nationalists, was that the
women's amendments would have been defeated.

In the event it was Bonar Law who contrived a major *coup* over the
Franchise and Registration Bill before the House had a chance to
vote on woman suffrage again.   After receiving its Second Reading
in July 1912 the Bill had been held up while the Commons dealt with
other legislation, and it was not until 23 January 1913 that it went
into Committee and final eclipse.   In this period the Government
had been proceeding on the assumption that the Commons would be
free to vote on the various amendments being prepared by Grey, Henderson, Dickinson and Lyttleton on the precedents of 1867 and 1884.
In view of the accusations of bad faith made subsequently by the
suffragettes it is valuable to have in the papers of Joseph Pease
some corroboration of the Government's intentions.   In the first
place the papers show that Pease sought reliable information about
how many women would be enfranchised by the various amendments;   it
was not apparently easy to discover, and Dickinson's, for example,
was expected to affect anything between five and nine million women;
he also enquired about the effect of raising the age limit for all
new voters to twenty-three or twenty-five in view of Hobhouse's complaint that the effect of enfranchising young female servants 'would
be to annihilate the Liberal Party'. (63)   In the second place
Pease was considering in November 1912 the procedure to be adopted
when the House came to consider the women's amendments; (64)   they
would be taken in the order - Grey, Henderson, Dickinson, Lyttleton;
moreover no guillotine resolution would be applied to any of them.
It was in December that a Cabinet Committee (65) decided to allow
the women's amendments precedence over all others and confirmed that
they would be kept separate from the days on which the guillotine
would be used.   It is therefore clear that the Cabinet were not
attempting to sabotage the women by means of technicalities but,
rather, smoothing the way for them.   It is inconceivable that
Asquith, who sat on the Committee responsible, would have gone into
the matter in such detail had he intended all along to abandon the
Bill.   As late as 22 January 1913 the Cabinet resolved that in the
event of a women's amendment being accepted by the Commons, 'the
members of the Government holding diverse views would not regard the
result of such decision this year as calling for their resignation
of office'. (66)   Instead the antis intended to rely upon ordinary
political pressure to secure the defeat of the amendments, and
Pease assured Curzon that he was doing everything he could privately
to this end. (67)

Thus until January 1913 there is no evidence to suggest that the
Bill's sponsors were aware of the procedural hazard which killed the
measure.   The possibility emerged apparently as a result of Pease's

own proposal to amend the Bill by deleting the occupation qualification which the Speaker considered would render the Bill out of
order.   The Unionist Leader then took his chance and, according to
James Lowther: (68)

> Mr. Bonar Law, on the evening of Wednesday 22nd of January, came
> to my Library and raised the point that the proposed amendment
> would completely alter the intention and character of the Bill.
> I asked him to postpone raising the question until I had had time
> to consider the matter fully, but I informed some Members of the
> Government of what had happened and of my difficulty.

In fact Bonar Law arose the next day in the Commons to demand a
ruling; (69) the issue he took up in the first instance was the
proposed withdrawal of the occupation qualification clause, and he
quoted a precedent - the 1889 Tithe Rent Bill - when a ruling by
Speaker Peel had forced the Government to abandon a measure in similar circumstances.   Lowther refused to give a definite ruling on
this point, but he made it clear that he inclined to the view that
the woman suffrage amendments would have the effect of creating a
new Bill.   With this threat hanging over the legislation the House
went on to discuss the Government's proposals for dealing with the
Bill in thirteen days.   Over the weekend the Speaker arrived at a
firm decision (70) which he communicated to the Commons on 27 January. (71)   He based his ruling in the first instance on a techni-
cality; the precedents of 1867 and 1884 were not binding because
the amendments then had been debated but not approved: therefore
the Speaker had not been called upon to give a ruling.   Second, the
1912 Bill, in Lowther's view, was not a Reform Bill of the previous
type; hitherto such Bills had been designed to enfranchise unrepresented *classes* of people, whereas this was basically a measure for
registration and plural voting.   The Government's Bill, therefore,
could not be amended with a woman suffrage clause.

This dubious and politically slanted ruling destroyed the Franchise and Registration Bill and the hopes of the women.   On 25 January, after receiving intimations of the Speaker's opinion, the
Cabinet was hastily summoned to consider his verdict which was 'in
flat contradiction of the assumption upon which all parties in the
House have hitherto treated the Bill', as Asquith told the King
later. (72)   A further session on 28 January confirmed the feeling
of the Cabinet in favour of withdrawing the Bill in its entirety,
and it was decided (73)

> that any legislation in regard to plural voting must be deferred
> till next session, and that facilities for the reasonable use of
> Government time should be offered to a private members' Woman
> Suffrage Bill next session, the members of the Government being
> free to vote as they pleased, and the Government assuming no res-
> ponsibility, then or thereafter, for the Bill, beyond the giving
> of the necessary time.

In this way perished the Liberals' only attempt at a comprehensive franchise measure before the war.   No doubt Asquith indulged
in a little *schadenfreude* over the defeat of the women, but the
fiasco had been no less a blow to him and his Government.   In the
constituencies the Liberals were obliged to carry on with the expen-
sive business of registration under the old system until the next
election.   There were only two further developments on the fran-

chise front before August 1914.   Willoughby Dickinson, a staunch
Liberal suffragist who was successful on the ballot, made use of the
Government's offer to introduce his Representation of the People
Bill, only to see it defeated by 48 votes in a House of almost 500
Members.   His Bill would have enfranchised five or six million
women, a step which only 28 Unionists were prepared to support.
The Nationalists, still with an eye on the Prime Minister, voted it
down by a margin of 40;   and the Liberals themselves were now only
two to one in favour of the Bill.   Their lack of enthusiasm was
understandable;   for through the pledge to the women they had lost
the reforms of the male suffrage and registration, as well as some
more useful parliamentary time, while the suffragettes carried their
civil disobedience to still further extremes.   After Dickinson no
backbencher was much inclined to waste another opportunity on a
woman's measure and so the exercise was not repeated in the remaining months of peace.

The second development was that on 13 March the Cabinet determined to go ahead with yet another Plural Voting Bill comprising a
single clause. (74)   They did not wish to find time for a reintroduced franchise Bill especially as that would have entailed including a women's clause on which they were still divided.   Another
factor was that in February 1913 the Labour Party Conference had
committed the Parliamentary Party to oppose any franchise legislation that left out the women, (75) and the Government appeared to
take this threat fairly seriously. (76)   Thus the abolition of
plural voting remained the only way of improving the party's chances
at the election.   Labour Members such as Snowden, (77) resentful at
the abandonment of the Franchise Bill, argued that plural voting was
by no means the aspect of the system most urgently in need of
reform.   However, despite a widespread feeling that the Liberals
were merely doctoring the Register to suit themselves there was only
a minor revolt by Snowden, Hardie and James O'Grady;   the Bill received approval in the Commons twice and awaited only its final passage when the First World War broke out.

The absence of any successful measure of electoral reform before
1914 may be ascribed to several general causes.   Of these the
underlying one was the inability of the unorganised non-voters to
exert pressure and the disinclination of the Labour Party to make a
major issue of the franchise at least until rather late in the day.
The attitude of the radical parties towards the franchise was tempered by perceived electoral interest;   for the Nationalists had
Ireland too neatly sewn up to desire any potentially disturbing ad-
ditions to the electorate;   Labour's democratic ideology was qualified by the realisation that they were at a stage of development at
which the Liberals were more likely to derive benefit from one-man-
one-vote.   On the part of the Liberals the complacency after the
victory of 1906 gave way to a mood of confidence about the working-
class voters;   but for their immediate purposes the advantage arising from a purge of plural voters on the existing register was considered sufficient.   The particular factors responsible for thwarting the Government were the crowded timetable, the state of which
was the result of the Peers' obstructionism and the reduction in the
life of Parliament to five years under the Act of 1911;   the Cabinet's differences over woman suffrage;   and finally the outbreak of
the Great War which ultimately put paid to the Plural Voting Bill.

These frustrating episodes set the scene for the wartime struggle over franchise reform.   Liberals, deeply dismayed at finding the Plural Voting Bill marooned in the shallows of the Party Truce after August 1914, tended to blame Asquith, and to accept with good grace what Lloyd George was able to offer in 1917.   The Unionists were well aware how narrow had been their escape from damaging reforms, and therefore found it worthwhile to split the difference with their opponents under the Coalition Ministry.   On the woman suffrage front Asquith had retreated stubbornly up to 1914 under pressure from his colleagues and the disaffection of women Liberals in the country, but had not yet capitulated.   His Government, like the Opposition, still found itself unable to produce a policy on the issue.   The central problem was the Liberals' insistence upon achieving adult male suffrage before any concession could be made to the women;   on the Unionist side their hesitation over male suffrage had not yet been overcome, but once it was, the road to a compromise that included women suffrage would become clear.

Part two

Chapter 4

WAR IS UNDECLARED

I loathe coalitions - the alternative is a General Election which
in war time would be very unpatriotic.   (Margot Asquith to
J.A. Pease, 11 June 1915)
You know what the Army out here think of Squiff and his ways.
(Sir Henry Wilson to Colonel Page-Croft, 30 August 1916)

Twentieth century experience has established the idea of coalition
as a natural response to periods of crisis; in 1914, however, there
was no automatic recourse to this expedient.   Unity among the politicians so recently and bitterly in conflict could only be skin
deep, and the precedent for their situation was the Boer War.   The
prospect in 1914, in other words, was of a period of more or less
muted controversy leading to a 'khaki' election if and when the admirals and generals crowned the efforts of the administration with a
few victories.   The difference between 1900 and 1914 was, of
course, that a Liberal Government now enjoyed office and lacked the
patriotic gloss with the Unionists defended themselves in the absence of military success.   Once Asquith had accomplished the mir-
acle of taking the country to war without disrupting the Liberal
Party the prospects were by no means unfavourable.   Professor
Wilson's lucid analysis (1) leaves one with a vivid impression that
the Liberals were doomed from the very start, the inevitable victims
of Tory ruthlessness.   But this is to anticipate; Asquith himself
thought otherwise, as his much-quoted but unexplained self-analysis
shows: (2)
    The same *Luck* helped you in external things - in unforeseen op-
    portunities, in the disappearance of possible competitors, in the
    special political conditions of your time: above all (at a most
    critical and fateful moment in your career) *in the sudden out-
    break of the Great War.*   (My italics)
On the basis of the prevailing interpretation of the politics of the
war Asquith would have been mad to have written this in March 1915.
He was not: but what did he mean?
    The early days of the war spawned a new spirit of unity and pat-
riotism, (3) yet of a spurious and hollow kind.   The Cabinet felt
very loathe to abandon measures for Home Rule and Disestablishment
of the Welsh Church, the first fruits of the Parliament Act, for

which their allies had been waiting so long.   These two measures,
which had thrice passed the Commons and only awaited Royal Assent,
were offered up by the Government as the first political casualties
of the war.   There was some communication between Asquith and Bonar
Law on the subject of the Government of Ireland (Amendment) Bill,
the Second Reading of which was postponed on 30 July 'without prejudice to its future - in the hope that by a postponement of the discussion the patriotism of all parties will contribute what lies in
our power, if not to avert, at least to circumscribe, the calamities
which threaten the world'. (4)   It was not until 15 September that
the Prime Minister appeared before the Commons with a long-winded
speech to request that in view of the changed circumstances since 30
July when war had only been a possibility it would be impossible to
proceed with debate on the controversial Amendment Bill; it was
therefore to be dropped, the Government of Ireland and Welsh Church
Bills sent for Royal Assent and a Bill passed to suspend their
operation. (5)   In a sharp reply Bonar Law accused the Prime Minister of breaking pledges and led his party in walking out of the
Chamber in a body.   This display of pre-war Unionist tactics went a
long way to undo the initial effect of John Redmond's famous speech
on 3 August in which he had heralded the unity of Irishmen in mutual
defence against Germany.   The Government's case rested on the argument that they were gaining nothing and losing nothing over legislation as a result of the war; the advantage they really won, of
course, was the lifting of the threatened civil war in Ulster which
removed at once the Unionists' only hope of destroying the Liberals.
Worse than that, there was no real role for the Opposition to play
beyond supporting the Government over the war; the walk-out of 15
September had to be their last fling lest they discredit themselves
in the eyes of a patriotic electorate.
    Asquith appreciated that if the first consequence of the war had
been to suspend Liberal legislation, the second was the other side
of the same coin: the Opposition became practically paralysed.   By
January 1915 Lord Curzon was fit to burst with frustration: (6)
    [The Government] tell us nothing or next to nothing of their
    plans, and yet they pretend our leaders both share their know-
    ledge and their responsibility....   The Secretary of State for
    War reads us exiguous memoranda of platitudes known to everybody,
    is acclaimed by the Liberal Press as having delivered an almost
    inspired oration and scored off his impertinent antagonists....
    I do not think this state of affairs can continue indefinitely
    ... the temper of our Party will not stand it.
His colleague Walter Long put the same view: (7)
    the Government has persistently pursued those Party aims which
    occupied them before the War.   Last Session it was Welsh Church
    and Home Rule: this Session it is to be the Plural Voting Bill,
    and nobody will pretend that the taxation proposals were con-
    ceived in a spirit that would recommend them to all Parties.
The trouble was that any Opposition criticism would 'be treated - as
indeed Liberals treat it now - as little less than High Treason'.
In fact many Unionists believed that the Government was taking advantage of their enforced good behaviour to give the impression that
a kind of *de facto* coalition actually existed; (8) however, for the
Liberals this could only be a temporary situation: for as a result

of the 1911 Parliament Act their term of office was due to run out
in December 1915.   Although the General Election did not take place
until the end of 1918 its shadow fell heavily across the three
intervening years and became the focal point around which the politics of the war revolved.

It is a basic and amply authenticated fact that after August 1914
each party continued to work on the assumption that a dissolution of
Parliament was more or less imminent, even though to say so openly
was bad form.   In February 1915 Joseph King blatantly informed the
House of Commons: (9)

In the whole of the West of England, in which my constituency is
situated, Liberal agents have been prevented from going to the
War, or offering their services, because they have been told that
they must stop until the General Election is over.   (Hon. Members: 'Oh!')

In the same month the National Union of Conservative and Unionist
Associations (10) instructed its agents in the constituencies to
carry on with registration work as usual except in places where an
arrangement could be made with the opposing party;   and they apparently did so even after the Coalition had been formed. (11)   Meanwhile the Labour Party was quietly preparing for an election;   in
January the National Executive (12) approved a meeting to select a
candidate at Accrington and appointed a sub-committee on registration.   The Committee reported in April that registration to meet
the circumstances of wartime service should not be undertaken if
possible lest the party 'be severely handicapped owing to the condition of our electoral organisation making it impossible to conduct
the enquiries necessary to compile our lists'. (13)

One backbencher put the problem in the Commons thus: (14)
either you will have the process of revision going on with all
its concomitants of party feeling, or else you will have the
agents entering into a more or less legal compact to make such a
new register as may seem to them most fit.   What would happen,
for instance, in the city of Glasgow if the registration is to go
forward this year as in former years?   It means that almost
immediately the party agents and a large staff of canvassers -
the largest that could be obtained - would be scouring the
streets, closes and tenements of Glasgow to find out old lodgers,
new lodgers and possible lodgers.

Many party agents did appear together on recruiting platforms, but
under the facade of unity often lay a more cynical attitude: 'We
ought to take advantage of the rather sloppy sentiment (which I
hate) about "no party feeling"', commented Lord Hugh Cecil. (15)
Also, one must remember that the agents had a vested interest in
maintaining a decent level of political activity - a financial one.
As early as October 1914 the 'Liberal agent' had complained: 'As we
go to press we learn that one brother had been "stood down" for a
month without salary.   We sincerely trust this is an isolated
case.' (16)   Like the Labour Party the Liberal organisers anticipated extra difficulty over a war Register, but the 'Liberal Agent'
was prompt with advice: (17)

Objections to voters absent on military service will be unpopular....   Agents should guard against allowing bogus claims to
pass in cases where rooms have actually been given up during the

present qualifying period; the best way of dealing with such
would be to produce strong evidence at the customary private
meeting with the opposition agent before the court, and induce
him to withdraw his support or pair.

One definite concession by the Unionists to the 'Party Truce' was
the agreement to avoid by-election contests, signed by the Whips on
24 August and periodically renewed, (18) though even here the spirit
in which the compact was interpreted proved rather restricting; for
example, Steel-Maitland tried to commit Asquith to the view that the
truce applied only to the replacement of Members already near re-
tirement by local candidates, not to attempts to fill vacancies with
'good men': this, he said, would be snatching an unfair advantage
especially where the seat was a shaky one. (19)   One such candidate
was Charles Masterman who vainly sought a seat at Swansea. (20)

Even the Coalition from May 1915 did not put an end to the manoeuvring for advantage: a dissolution still seemed probable.   John
Gulland, a Liberal Whip, was reported to have told the party agents
in July 1915 (21) that 'he could not foretell when the election
would come, it was possible it might be fought on the Register now
made up: therefore the only moral was to do Registration as carefully and particularly as in past years'.   Later, in the autumn he
and Geoffrey Howard wrote to every Liberal Association, 'may we urge
upon you as far as possible to keep the organisation alive by the
retention of your agent'. (22)

It was because a General Election continued to be a real possibility that the state of the parliamentary register became a subject
of absorbing and urgent interest to the Government.   In the first
instance the problem centered around the qualification for the
troops: the wider franchise question arose in consequence of this.
In fact had it proved possible to retain on the register all the
soldiers who possessed a vote already it seems unlikely that any
Government would have embarked upon what was thought to be the impossible task of electoral reform.   A 1915 election would have been
fought on the 1914 register - admittedly inaccurate because the outbreak of war had interrupted revision work.   However, the register
being prepared in 1915 would encounter even greater difficulties as
anticipated by Herbert Samuel, then President of the Local Government Board, and put before the Cabinet in March 1915; (23)   since
some 84 per cent of electors qualified by virtue of being householders of a separate dwelling place for a continuous period of twelve
months, the men who had volunteered to fight abroad or left home to
work in munitions factories had lost the right to be registered for
the period up to July 1915.   Thus the new register on which an
election would be fought would be shorter than usual and the competition in the Courts correspondingly keen.   The Government had
indeed passed an Electoral Disabilities Removal Act the previous
August to overcome this problem, but, apart from the fact that it
did not cover munitions workers, it did not adequately meet the
case, according to the 'Liberal Agent'. (24)

It is clear from the very short discussion on this Bill (25) that
the immediate impact of the war situation was upon Liberal and
Labour Members who anticipated that men who would shortly find themselves unemployed and in distress as a direct result of war would be
driven to accept Poor Relief and would consequently forfeit their

franchise.   To this fear there was no reply since the   Government
did not envisage altering the Poor Law.   The most that Pease would
offer in the Bill was the guarantee that men in the Forces would not
be disfranchised because their wives and families were receiving
Poor Relief, and a provision to allow claims for the franchise to be
made on behalf of lodger voters who were away in the Forces.   This
only partly mollified those afraid of a reduced working-class electorate.   As the war wore on the increase in employment put paid to
the expectation that millions would be on Poor Relief;   and the concern to maintain the soldiers' franchise gradually became a Unionist
concern even more than a radical one.

The war, however, killed off more than just the old registration
system: it undermined the Opposition's fear of male suffrage.   The
military vote had always been thought of as Tory in sentiment, and
now the working-class volunteers became transmogrified by the Army
such that the Unionists could not brook the idea of an election
without the 'best quarter' of the population, as Lord Salisbury
called them.   General Sir Henry Wilson wrote of the troops:
'True, if they get the vote they will send Squiff, and many of his
Government, packing, so Squiff will have 1,000 reasons ... to prove
it is impossible.' (26)   Even a Liberal soldier, Arthur Murray, MP,
believed in 1916 that 'the majority of the Trench vote would be cast
against the P.M.' (27)   However, these impressions of the troops'
voting intentions did nothing to deter the Liberal War Committee who
were equally vociferous in demanding a franchise for servicemen.
And Lloyd George, in a letter written but not, apparently, sent to
Asquith, referred to an 'insuperable' obstacle to his accepting the
War Office: (28)

> I have taken a strong line in Cabinet on the question of the en-
> franchisement of our soldiers.   I feel they have a right to a
> voice in choosing the Government that sends them to face peril
> and death.   Were I now to accept a new office in the Government
> it would fetter my action when the Cabinet come to decide that
> great issue as they must soon.

Lloyd George evidently considered the soldiers' vote a sufficiently
respectable reason to justify any action: 'It would be a proper
question on which to resign', he told Lord Riddell. (29)   As a
reason, however, it was spurious, since it was not so much the principle as the practical impossibility of enfranchising the troops
that troubled his colleagues.

Early in 1915 Samuel reported to the Cabinet (30) that consultations with the other parties revealed general agreement that it was
futile to pursue registration under ordinary methods and that many
voters would have to remain disfranchised until peacetime.   However, the Liberals' course of action was essentially dependent upon
whether the 1915 register was to be used as the basis for an election;   if not, then the inaccuracies might reasonably be overlooked.
Samuel accordingly proposed that after the Easter recess, Parliament
should be asked to pass a Bill extending its own life for an extra
two years or until six months after the declaration of peace.   All
work on registers could then simply be postponed.   This course, he
noted, had been adopted in France in 1914 where it had followed upon
the initial decision to form a National Government.   Two days after
Samuel's memorandum, Asquith informed the King, (31) the Cabinet had

a 'somewhat desultory discussion' on the subject, but without reaching a decision, a pattern that was to be repeated many times in the
months ahead.   On 7 April they agreed to consult the Opposition
leaders about postponing the elections, (32) without much hope of
success, one feels.   A solution acceptable to the Liberal
Party (33) involved allowing the normal Register to be produced
each year and supplemented at the end of the war by a Special Register to include all those excluded as a result of war work; for them
a shortened qualifying period would have been necessary.   Thus at
the cessation of hostilities a month would have been allowed in
which to terminate war contracts so that munitions workers could
return to their homes; then would have followed a one-month period
for qualification.   The essentials of this scheme were made known
to the Unionist organisation. (34)   However, the Cabinet had only
got as far as considering it in mid-May 1915 when they were overtaken by the formation of the Coalition.

As the prospect of a quick military victory began to fade in the
early months of 1915 the idea of a wartime election became less and
less attractive for the Prime Minister.   It would tend to divide
the nation and the Liberal Party at once especially if the pacifist
wing raised a debate over Britain's entry into the war, or conscription or the treatment of aliens; this would place Ministers like
Sir John Simon in a very difficult position.   The possibility of
a military victory might well have covered up the cracks, but while
the end of the war could not be seen all candidates in the election
would be obliged to prove their enthusiasm for the prosecution of
the war and their hostility to all things German; in a competition
of this sort it was a foregone conclusion that Toryism would triumph. (35)   As Bonar Law put it afterwards, 'We abandoned what we
believed to be the prospect of getting office ourselves and dispos-
sessing those who had so long occupied it'. (36)   Indeed, the
Unionists' impression was not only that they would win but that they
would shatter the Liberal organisation.   F.S. Oliver wrote: (37)

I can't think that a general election would be anything like so
discomposing as you imagine.   On one side there would be
practically the whole of the Unionist Party and a considerable
portion of the Liberal Party.   The watch-words would be - more
resolute prosecution of the War; more efficient management and
a firmer support of our allies.   *The Liberal Party would be
split and the Liberal machine would be pretty near a breakdown.*

To avoid an election at the appointed time would require the consent of Parliament to a Bill prolonging its own life: this could
scarcely be done without approval of the Peers who relished the idea
of a final veto over the Liberal Government.   Only by destroying
the case for a General Election by means of a Coalition Government
could Asquith obtain the prolongation of the 1910 Parliament.   The
problem, however, was that the Unionist leaders, far from wanting a
coalition, desired above everything to be dissociated from the Government and its mistakes.   This is true of Bonar Law, (38)
Long, (39) Chamberlain (40) and Curzon. (41)   'It should be stated
definitely that the Opposition does not desire - and ... is not prepared to assent to - a Coalition Government', said Long; Curzon
wrote:

A Coalition would tie our hands and close our lips even more

effectively than at present.   It would make us responsible for
many things which we ought to criticise....   If the country were
actually and seriously invaded a Coalition Government might
become expedient and even necessary.   But for the present it
does not seem needful to discuss it.

And Bonar Law concurred:

Much as I dislike the present position, there are I think only
two real alternatives open to us: one is to go on as we are
going, without responsibility and with a very limited amount of
criticism ... or to face a coalition.   The latter proposal I
should certainly be against, and on the whole, therefore, I am
reluctantly driven to the conclusion that the only proper course
for us in the meantime is to continue on the lines on which we
have acted since the war began.

In taking this line he had, not surprisingly, the full support of
Balfour. (42)   Only Lord Robert Cecil (43) liked the idea of joining the Government, though he too was in no doubt that it was something that would suit the Liberals better than the Unionists.   Even
after Law had committed himself to joining the Government, Long refused for a time to serve personally, (44) as did Lansdowne, (45)
Carson (46) and Cecil. (47)   Even the loyal Chamberlain found it
an unpalatable necessity: 'There are no two ways about it!   If our
help is asked by the Government we *must* give it.   God knows each
one of us would willingly avoid this fearful responsibility; but
the responsibility of refusing is even greater than that of accepting and in fact we have no choice.' (48)   In the event the doubters
were persuaded by appeals to their patriotism to join: Law could
hardly have risked leaving them out, for to do that would have been
to split the Unionist Party and threaten his leadership.

   This situation in mid-May 1915 serves as a corrective to the
long-standing assumption among historians that there was a sort of
inevitability about the divisive effect of war upon Liberalism.
All the indications were that the Conservative Party would be the
second to split (after Labour); that they did not do so is to be
ascribed to the fact that Bonar Law's very precariousness as Leader
led him to be ultra-sensitive to the mood of his supporters.   Different decisions by Law and his colleagues in May 1915 would have
shattered party unity just as in December 1916 different decisions
by the Liberal leaders would have averted the split in their party.

   However, reluctant as Bonar Law was to take any initiative in the
direction of a coalition, he could not resist indefinitely the criticism that his own restraint in allowing the Liberals 'an immunity
accorded to no other Government in the past' (49) had been overdone.
He was under pressure from the Unionist War Committee to take up
issues like the supply of munitions more vigorously, (50) yet to
have done so would have effectively started the General Election cam
campaign.   Now Bonar Law shrank from this prospect too: (51)

His only reason for joining [the Government] was that, in the
circumstances, the only alternative was a General Election; that
nothing could have prevented that General Election being held on
ordinary party lines; that he believed it would have resulted in
the return of a Tory majority and that after a little bit there
would have been an ordinary Party Opposition in the House of
Commons with effects most disastrous to the country.

Admiral Fisher's resignation in the middle of May 1915 proved to be
the last straw for Bonar Law; he did not wish to put down a censure
motion against the Government on behalf of a man who, in Asquith's
words, 'strictly speaking ... ought to be shot'. (52)   Hence his
hasty visit to Lloyd George on 17 May before news of the resignation
had got around.   It was by chance that Bonar Law found himself, at
this critical moment, without the advice of Max Aitken who was away
in France; (53) had he been at hand Law might well not have acted
as he did.
     Meanwhile Asquith had been weighing up the three options that
were open to him.   The most obvious and least troublesome was to
sack Churchill: this would have appeased the worst of the Opposition's anger and given more than a little satisfaction on the Liberal benches.   Fisher for one had the impression that this was what
the Prime Minister would do after his meeting with him on 15 May.
The next alternative, advocated by Churchill, was simply to defy the
Opposition and rely upon the radical majority in Parliament to see
them through; even in wartime departing admirals do not easily
bring down Governments especially when their manner of leaving is so
extraordinary and difficult to defend as that of Fisher.   Churchill
had moved fast to repair the damage caused by Fisher's resignation;
by Sunday 16 May he had established that Sir Arthur Wilson was willing to replace Fisher as First Sea Lord and that the Second, Third
and Fourth Sea Lords would continue in office.   He then visited
Asquith at his weekend retreat in Berkshire to inform him of these
arrangements to which he 'understood him to assent'. (55)   Asquith
had been sufficiently sympathetic to both Fisher and Churchill to
keep two courses open.
     Yet on Monday morning, Lloyd George tells us, (56) he agreed to
form a Coalition Ministry 'in less than a quarter of an hour'.
This was the third option, about which Asquith had been thinking,
for he already had a scheme for the distribution of offices drafted. (57)   Though the decision was a quick one Asquith had been
mentally prepared for it for some time; the drift towards an unhappy election in the winter of 1915 had almost begun, and if he
were to avoid it he had to lure Bonar Law into his Government before
the autumn when he would be too committed to the campaign and his
followers eager for office.   The snap decision in May enabled
Asquith to keep the maximum number of key posts in the hands of his
nominees.   The real obstacle for him, as for Bonar Law, was his own
party's reluctance to accept a coalition: that is why he gave them
no opportunity for consultations.   Even so, the Prime Minister had
to face a very rebellious backbench meeting as MacCallum Scott recorded: (58)
     [The rebels] took the Party line that the Prime Minister owed
     some explanation to his Party - ought to take his Party into his
     confidence - They wanted to have it out with him but they could
     not attack the coalition in the House - it had gone too far for
     that....   Asquith was fetched by Gulland who had heard how
     things were shaping.   Asquith spoke with deep feeling - his
     voice husky and his face twitching.   He looked old and worried.
     He flung himself on our mercy.   Within a week a wholly new sit-
     uation had been revealed to him.   There had been unexpected dis-
     closures which had taken them wholly by surprise.   He could not

reveal the truth to us yet without imperilling national safety.
But the situation was of the gravest kind.   Coalition became inevitable.   He had no desire to retain office - he could not do
it without our confidence.   He was ready to resign tonight....
He appealed to us not to have any discussion in the House at the
present stage.   It would be disastrous....   The meeting gave
him an overpowering ovation.   Pringle tried to raise his point
but the Chairman hurriedly closed the meeting and the P.M. hastened away.

Thus what had been achieved was in no real sense a Coalition Government, rather an uneasy blend of two separate elements brought
together by the collusion of Asquith and Bonar Law, aided by Lloyd
George, with the deliberate intention of keeping their followers in
the dark until it was too late to protest effectively.   The Unionists thought Asquith had hoodwinked Bonar Law and kept full control
of the personnel and policy of the Government;   both sides felt
freer to criticise in the House of Commons;   and, what was worse,
the Allied cause still did not prosper.   Asquith won a new lease of
life, but not a free run until peace: 'To tell the House that there
can be no General Election while war lasts and for six months is to
play the Liberal game.'   Steel-Maitland warned Bonar Law: 'If the
very possibility of a General Election is removed their position is
strengthened and the virtue goes out of any representations which we
make.   Not only are they strengthened, but they can sit and watch
philosophically the disintegration increasing among Unionists.' (59)
In short, the antagonism between the parties continued unabated;
beneath the formal Party Truce they manoeuvred for advantage.
Since the Unionists would not rule out a General Election the question of franchise reform stayed alive when it would otherwise have
died.

Chapter 5

VOTES FOR HEROES?

Will not this Coalition be weak and discredited from the start,
without any common purpose or object? Will not a general election be necessary after all? (Francis Hirst to C.P. Scott, 21
May 1915, Scott Add. MSS. III)

In view of its origins it is no surprise that the establishment of a
Coalition Government did not inaugurate a period of more efficient
and purposeful administration of the war; rather the opposite.
The formal machinery of Government, though much written about, was
probably of marginal importance; for even the small War Cabinet of
Lloyd George rapidly succumbed to the problem caused by extra members and lost its grip over the agenda. In the absence of military
genius and any technological breakthrough capable of winning the war
the only measurable criteria applicable to the new Government were
political and personal. In 1915 and 1916 Lloyd George as new Minister of Munitions was the one obvious gain; elsewhere the replacement of Harcourt by Bonar Law, Samuel by Long, or, worst of all,
Churchill by Balfour, represented no improvement at all. As for
the admittedly wobbly unity of the Government it plainly deteriora-
ted as a result of the Coalition. The Liberals remained utterly
unconvinced as to the need for Coalition, and feared a slide towards
conscription; the admission of men like Carson to office was quite
as offensive to them as to the Irish Members. As for the Conservatives, they resented the retention by Asquith of all the key jobs in
the hands of his supporters - Kitchener at the War Office, McKenna
at the Exchequer, Lloyd George at Munitions, Balfour at the Admiralty and Runciman at the Board of Trade. The Unionists were in
effect excluded from war work yet committed to the Asquithian methods of running it. Too many ambitious and energetic men now felt
frustrated in their desire to make a contribution among whom Curzon,
Carson and Churchill stand out; hence the tendency for the Dardan-
elles Committee to grow rapidly in size. All in all the Prime
Minister's critics considered he had them perpetually muzzled; Coalition was the first step; he kept Kitchener and Grey protectively
around him; he negotiated the rapids of McKenna's tariff budget and
conscription without going under. It is thus no surprise that
throughout 1916 Lloyd George felt depressed and out-manoeuvred.

Until towards the end of the year he was still a very isolated man
both in Cabinet and in Parliament.   Far from being a rival Prime
Minister Lloyd George was still a tool in Asquith's hands;   first he
attended to Munitions, then to Ireland, then to the War Office where
he was responsible for but not in control of the military effort.
However much he talked to Frances Stevenson of the joys of resignation the fact was that Lloyd George shrank from the prospect.   He
even missed Cabinet meetings which he could see no chance of influ-
encing, (1) while Asquith threatened to go on for ever doggedly
arbitrating between the Liberal and Unionist elements within the
Government.

It was a time of frustration all round.   Backbenchers were
largely deprived of their usual role;   a number of Liberal ex-Ministers lacked a job;   Unionists felt under-used;   even Ministers in
many cases had less to do now that war had swept away many of their
normal functions in terms of parliamentary duties and legislation.
Hence it was inevitable that minds should turn upon the circumstances in which the Coalition or the war might end.   Liberal minds
could turn towards salvaging something from the wreck of their
social reform programme when peace returned;   Asquith's decision in
March 1916 to establish what turned out to be the very significant
Reconstruction Committee (2) was the chief vehicle of this.   Yet it
must be emphasised that *political* reform could hardly be envisaged
as a part of 'reconstruction' at this stage.   If the Cabinet could
not work harmoniously on the war, there was little chance that Ministers so resentful of each other's presence and suspicious of partisan motives could tackle electoral reforms of the sort that had
divided them before 1914.

As a result of the manner in which the First Coalition had been
brought about the new Cabinet found itself unable to settle the
question that had brought it into existence: the life of the 1910
Parliament.   Conservative Ministers were no more ready than before
May 1915 to rule out a General Election in wartime.   In consequence
of this they had to deal with the vexed question of the Register to
which no solution was found during virtually the whole of the nineteen months of life enjoyed by Asquith's last Ministry.

At the Local Government Board the new Minister, Walter Long, and
his deputy, Hayes Fisher, were at once put under observation by the
National Union of Conservative and Unionist Associations. (3)   Long
lost no time in making recommendations to the Cabinet; (4) he proposed to postpone local government and parliamentary elections for
one year, halt registration work and conduct an *ad hoc* registration
at the end of the war without any change of franchise except a shor-
tening of the qualifying period from twelve months to perhaps two.
The scheme was not very different from Samuel's except, significantly, in the length of the extension being suggested for Parliament's
life.   The Cabinet ducked this issue and their Elections and Registration Bill, introduced in July, postponed only Municipal Elections
for a year, while suspending all work on the parliamentary registers
from 31 of that month;   the existing register was to remain in force
until Parliament provided for a new one, but in no case later than
31 December 1916.

On the Second Reading of the Bill, Long contended rather optimistically that his proposals met an almost unanimous demand. (5)

The money and manpower devoted to producing a new Register in 1915,
he said, would not be worthwhile because of the inevitable omission
of many soldiers and munitions workers.   However, the Overseers'
Lists, already prepared, would form the basis of the next register
and so would not be wasted.   What was important was to prevent the
Revision Courts getting to work on the lists because this would
generate the usual party conflict and disrupt the Truce.   This
point was well taken in the House for it meant that the Agents
could be spared the misery of uncertainty; McKinnon Wood offered
the support of the Scottish Agents, and Sir George Younger anticipated that more agents would now be able to undertake recruiting work
as an alternative to revision of the lists.

However, this debate showed the House of Commons starting to
seize the initiative and harry the Government from both Unionist
and Liberal benches.   The preservation of the 1914 register seemed
a dubious constitutional practice; it was also impractical to stop
the work on 31 July at a stage when two-thirds of the money
(£200,000) had already been spent; all that remained was the revision without which the lists were, by common agreement, useless.
Now the contracts made with the Revising Barristers had to be
broken.   Once the Register was left for a year it would become very
difficult to correct since thousands of removals took place each
year in every constituency, especially in the major cities.   Also
the 1914 register was a poor one to preserve since the outbreak of
war in August had led some agents to abandon the revision work then
underway.   In view of these considerations the Government's case
was not entirely convincing. (6)   None the less, despite a tendency
for Members to indulge in criticism, the Commons and Lords gave the
Bill a passage without a division.   Thus was preserved the register
that reflected the state of the electorate in the twelve months up
to July 1914: the more stale it became the less attractive was the
prospect of an election fought upon it.

During the autumn, however, the Cabinet had still to decide for
what period Parliament's life was to be extended and what ultimately
should be done with the register.   Long (7) insisted that a register compiled in 1916 to come into force in January 1917 would be
just as inaccurate as the existing one; therefore the work ought
not to be re-started at all.   This view the Cabinet accepted and
incorporated in the Parliament and Registration Bill, introduced on
9 December. (8)   Of course the Government had to give an assurance,
which it found difficult to fulfil, that all the men returning from
the war would be enrolled on a special register on the strength of a
reduced qualifying period; no other change in the franchise was
anticipated.

The second proposal in the Bill was to extend the life of the
1910 Parliament from five to six years.   Sir John Simon explained
that the 1916 Session would be treated for purposes of the Parliament Act as though it were immediately successive to that of 1914;
in other words any measure which had passed the Commons twice and
would have lapsed if not re-passed in 1915 could now be voted
through in 1916 instead.   The Bill in question, as Simon did not
attempt to conceal, was the Plural Voting Bill.

According to Harcourt (9) this 'unexpectedly good settlement'
over plural voting was reached through a committee appointed by

Asquith and comprising Bonar Law, Long, F.E. Smith, Simon, Harcourt
and Henderson: 'I was to do the fighting', said Harcourt, 'and I
did!'   In fact the arrangement over plural voting was a quid pro
quo for the refusal of the Unionists to keep the old House in being
until peacetime.   Bonar Law received plain warning from Steel-Maitland (10) on 25 November that the backbenchers would not accept an
extension of Parliament's life if it would have the effect of resus-
citating the Plural Voting Bill.   He made it known that he was
under pressure on this point, and on 29 November Simon pointed out
to him (11) that the Liberals would never consent to a mere one-year
extension of Parliament's life, and went on: 'W. Long and F.E.
Smith and I agree that it is only right to provide for passage of
the [Plural Voting] Bill in the first peace session of the next Parliament if the War drags on.'   This makes it look as though the
Unionist Leader had been too conciliatory and now wanted to draw
back under pressure from the backbenches: it was a danger he had to
live with all through the war.   Three days later an influential
group of Unionists signed a letter opposing the continuation of
Parliament beyond the end of 1916; (12) clearly the Liberals could
not have everything they wanted and compromised with a twelve-month
extension.

That Asquith should have insisted on preserving the Plural Voting
Bill at all under a Coalition Government is some measure of the continued strength of partisan feeling; according to the explanation
given in the House of Commons both by Sir John Simon (13) and Bonar
Law (14) the Coalition had been formed on the understanding that
neither party should suffer any loss as a result of joining; whatever had been achieved by one side in twice passing the Plural
Voting Bill was not to be forfeited but simply treated as a frozen
asset.   In any case while the Coalition lived the Bill could hardly
be passed again.

However, this line of argument was open to the objection that in
the period up to May 1915 the Bill had been becalmed in the sense
that there was no prospect of the Liberals taking it up a third time
in the middle of the war - thus the Coalition was being used to preserve a Bill which would otherwise have perished.   This added still
further to the heavy price the Unionists had paid for joining the
Government.   However, it was a right-wing Liberal Member, Mr
Cowan, (15) who led off the attack on the extension of Parliament's
life, claiming that MPs should not draw their salaries until they
had won a new mandate; electors serving in the Forces should be
allowed to exercise their votes by appointing their wives as proxies.   Coming from a Liberal this was an embarrassing line of
attack, for Cowan was making the Unionists' case for them.   Liberal
stalwarts rushed to defend the Bill, notably J.A. Pease who had returned 'hot foot from France' to rescue the Plural Voting Bill according to 'The Times'. (16)   Other Liberals cited the Septennial
Act as a precedent for parliament extending its own life, and, since
the existing House had been elected for seven years, its mandate
could hardly be deemed to have vanished after five.

There was in fact nearly as much support for the postponement of
elections on the Unionist benches as on the Liberal: what angered
them was the provision for plural voting.   So serious was the
unrest that Bonar Law had to intervene at some length to justify

himself to his party. (17)   Freely acknowledging their resentment
that a Ministry of which he was a member should preserve a partisan
Liberal measure, he urged his followers to see the other side's
point of view; basically the Bill could not be passed during the
life of the Coalition, and the chances of its being put through in
the period between the dismissal of the Unionist Ministers and a
dissolution was very slight.

Mr H.E. Duke, assuming the role of Leader of the Opposition, rose
to debate these points with his Leader, (18) and it began to seem as
though thé Liberals were eavesdropping at a private meeting of the
Unionist Party.   Duke was anxious to assure Bonar Law that the
party was really grateful to him for his services, 'even if he made
mistakes, and really, if a man made mistakes in a time like this -
and I am not suggesting that my Rt. Hon. Friend has made mistakes -
who could wonder?'   After handing out this menacing accolade Duke
turned reluctantly to the question of plural voting with the words,
'I am not going to discuss this miserable controversy'; he then
devoted nearly a column of Hansard to doing just that before concluding with the further assurance, 'Now, as I said, I do not intend to
discuss this matter.   I decline to discuss it.'

Ultimately the House granted a Second Reading without a division,
though most speakers had been unable to resist the temptation to re-
lapse into the indiscipline of pre-war partisan debate.   C.B. Stu-
art-Wortley, a supporter of the Bill, confessed that he spoke only
because 'I do not wish it to be thought that my silence is a mark of
absolute unbounded confidence in the Ministry'. (19)   By raising
this issue at all Asquith had certainly helped to undermine Bonar
Law's already precarious standing in his own party, and had subsequently to give him a firm promise that the Plural Voting Bill
would be abandoned. (20)   The face-saving expedient embodied in the
1915 Parliament and Registration Act can be seen as a sop to Liberals already irritated at the Government's failure to abolish
plural voting by this time.   It was the only consolation they could
offer in return for the failure of the Cabinet to save the party
from a dissolution until peacetime.   As Mr Duke truly said, 'I
could not help feeling that it did show that there is not yet a real
Coalition'.

In Committee on 20 December Asquith made a further concession to
Unionist opinion by reducing the extension from twelve months to
eight; this was approved by 158 votes to twenty-three.   When the
Peers dealt with the Bill in January (21) they fully enjoyed the
irony of a situation in which it lay in their power to spare the
Commons a General Election.   However, the debate was perfunctory
and the outcome not in doubt, though Earl St Aldwyn advanced the
theory of the irrevocable lapse of Parliament's mandate after five
years, and proposed to delete the subsection which kept alive the
Plural Voting Bill.   The Unionists were quite bemused at being
treated to a lucid exposition of the Liberal case by Lords Lansdowne
and Curzon, (22) and the hostile amendment was withdrawn.

Thus the intractable problem of the register was pushed from the
view of busy Ministers, only to reappear before them ten weeks
later. (23)   Parliament's life now ran until 30 December 1916, so
that the Government would have to go before the House with another
Bill sometime during the year.   Far from being solved the problem

was seen to have been exacerbated as the register grew less and less
representative.   Even MPs who disliked the idea of an election accepted that one might well become unavoidable, perhaps as a means of
settling an issue like conscription if the Cabinet were too badly
divided to do so.   In such circumstances Members did not wish to
prejudice their own chances in an election fought on the old register.   In short, the Commons grew increasingly reluctant to acquiesce in further extensions of Parliament's life unless the Government presented concurrently plans for preparing a new Register
during the war. (24)

On the Liberal side much resentment was now vented upon Asquith
whose stubbornness over woman suffrage was widely held to have frustrated Registration reform in 1913. (25)   But for that fiasco they
would not, in 1916, have been in such a muddle over the register.
In this situation the Liberals' concern to maintain 'workers' on the
register coincided with the Unionists' anxiety to put the 'soldiers'
there too.

As a result the Cabinet were inundated from March to August 1916
with a plethora of memoranda - eloquent testimony to the complexity
of the problem raised as a result of the suspension of registration
work.   The orthodox Liberal school of thought, represented by
Edwin Montagu, (26) Herbert Samuel (27) and Lewis Harcourt, (28)
held an election to be unthinkable until six months after the end of
the war.   Many cogent reasons were produced for not compiling a
wartime register, chief among them being that such a register would
still be so defective as to be unacceptable for use at a General
Election.   Also it would encourage attempts to place soldiers on
the register for votes which, for practical reasons, they would not
be able to exercise.   The money and manpower devoted to registration would therefore be a waste of scarce resources.   Moreover,
several other changes ought to be made before the next election, in
particular a general extension of the franchise and a redistribution
of seats;   such questions could best be resolved by a concordat between the parties.   Meanwhile if some action had to be taken to
appease the House of Lords, registration should involve no changes
other than a reduction of the qualifying period to three months.

As usual Bonar Law was left in no doubt as to his party's views
by a word from Steel-Maitland; (29) a sub-committee of agents meeting from 12 to 16 May had agreed on the need to prepare immediately
a civilian register based on a three- or four-month qualifying
period.   In addition they wanted a 'War Franchise Register': every
man who enlisted was *ipso facto* to qualify.   Steel-Maitland had
long since been urging the Government to enfranchise all the soldiers and let them sort themselves out into constituencies as best
they could. (30)   The Unionists went in dread of an election fought
on a register without the troops and filled instead with shirkers
and Conscientious Objectors;   and their wishes could not be ignored
because of their power to force a dissolution at the end of 1916:
'this policy of postponement may tend to defeat itself', warned
Steel-Maitland, 'the temper of the Unionist Party, at any rate, is
such that the very attempt to make a General Election impossible may
help to hasten a crisis.... I am not sure whether members of the
Cabinet realise how widespread is the feeling!' (31)

According to W. Jenkins of the National Union (32) the register

in June 1916 represented less than 60 per cent of those entitled to
vote; with Steel-Maitland and Sir John Boraston he advised Bonar
Law to have the register revised and supplemented by an *ad hoc* list
for servicemen; (33) but all other reforms including redistribution
they wanted left until peacetime: the Liberals stood to gain too
much from any concordat made during the war.   Bonar Law also heard
from John Gulland (34) of the conclusions of a private conference of
Principal Liberal Agents who also favoured the preparation of an
'Emergency'War Register' with a three-month qualification for occupiers and lodgers, but thought any other alteration in the franchise
would be too controversial; the registration of servicemen was not
a practical proposition and they would have to be placed on an *ad
hoc* post-war Register.   Thus both Parties, anxious to retain as
many 'workers' or 'soldiers' as possible on the Register, edged towards an election.

In Cabinet the question of a franchise for the troops divided the
parties: Lloyd George told Addison at the end of May that 'soldiers' registration was going well in Cabinet, except that there was
a more or less shamefaced movement against it as being impossible or
unnecessary'. (35)   And he instructed Addison to prepare a memorandum on the registration and voting of soldiers as the Cabinet had
accepted the idea in principle.   Long, on the other hand, as the
man who would have to translate it into practice, was highly dubious. (36)   For one thing, the troops could not simply be given a
vote in a wartime or post-war election - it would inevitably become
a permanent reform.   Second, the allocation of soldiers to constituencies would inevitably invite gerrymandering by the agents.   And
finally their votes would have to be cast either in the trenches, or
by post or by proxy - all very unsatisfactory methods.   It was
while struggling with these problems that Long began to come to the
conclusion that only a comprehensive measure for franchise and registration would do, (37) but in the summer of 1916 he still regarded
this as too controversial to be undertaken.   He was quite sure,
however, that it was impossible to prepare a satisfactory Register
for an election that autumn, and so, with only four months to go, he
appealed to the Cabinet for a quick decision. (38)   Beyond accepting Long's view about an election that year the Cabinet could agree
on nothing except that a committee should be set up to look at the
problem again. (39)

To this situation Arthur Henderson contributed the Labour point
of view.   Since April 1915 the Party Executive (40) had been at
one with the Liberals in wanting elections postponed, registration
suspended and avoidance of a list based simply on war service.   In
March 1916 the sub-committee on Electoral Reform advised: (41)

In view of the fact that the electoral machinery throughout the
country has broken down and the electors scattered, and that insuperable obstacles lie in the way of bringing them back to their
constituencies, no election should take place until a new scheme
of franchise reform (including Women's Enfranchisement, Registration and Redistribution) has been effected.

Henderson was instructed to bring this view to the Cabinet's attention which he did in a paper entitled 'Necessary Electoral
Changes' (42) in May 1916; he reminded his colleagues that Long had
already conceded the need to enfranchise munitions workers on the

same terms as the troops, and these men now formed a majority of the
eighteen- to forty-two-years age group.   Further, if the vote were
being given as a reward for patriotism it would hardly be fair to
exclude volunteers rejected on medical grounds or men in reserved
occupations withheld from military service on grounds of indispen-
sability.   In short Henderson arrived at a proposal for male suffrage based on a simple residential qualification.

Additionally he claimed that public opinion now favoured women's
suffrage as a result of their patriotism during the war; the
women's organisations would be satisfied with a franchise for women
over twenty-five, he suggested.   However, the women were only just
waking up to the fact that their cause was becoming serious politics
again (pp. 140-2).   The existence of a Coalition Ministry facilitated the raising of the issue in Cabinet, though from the evidence
available it seems that only two Ministers did so.   Lord Robert
Cecil (43) followed up Henderson's memorandum with a letter to
Asquith: 'it would be impossible to assent to any change in our
electoral laws which did not include some measure of woman suffrage.'   Subsequently Cecil and Henderson even sent the Prime Minister a joint letter in which they hinted at resignation if the
Commons were not allowed to discuss the women's case when a motion
for soldiers' franchise was raised. (44)   As Cabinet Ministers they
could not easily initiate such a debate in the House, but this function was performed by Simon - a free agent after his resignation in
January - who invariably followed Sir Edward Carson when he demanded
votes for the troops. (45)

Thus, by the summer of 1916 the Cabinet was in the position of
fearing to ask for a further extension of Parliament's life without
preparing for a new register, and yet appreciating that any registration proposals would open up a pandora's box of electoral reforms
and risk dissolving the Commons into pre-war parties, thus bringing
about the election they were trying to avoid.   Then on 2 June A.J.
Balfour threw his colleagues a lifeline. (46)   The Cabinet had
examined all the possibilities without reaching a conclusion; very
well, let the House of Commons be asked to lay down a policy itself
through a committee of backbenchers.   Austen Chamberlain (47)
agreed that the Government ought not to expose itself to attack by
producing a Bill: once a Select Committee had been appointed they
would soon realise the practical impossibility of dealing with registration at all.   He appeared to think that the Commons, thus
sobered, would then allow the Cabinet to proceed with the business
of the war.

In view of the appalling reception this plan received from MPs
Balfour and Chamberlain were being excessively sanguine - an indication of how easily Ministers became out of touch with backbench
opinion.   So specious a scheme did not commend itself to Long. (48)
He insisted that unless the Cabinet came out with a definite scheme
for registration the opposition would simply refuse to prolong Parliament's life.   Any new register would have to be based on a reduced qualifying period to be of any use, and this was tantamount to
a franchise reform: thus the question of franchise had to be faced.
Balfour's plan relied on sympathetic co-operation from MPs whose
patience was fast running out.   One feels that in pressing the Cabinet for a firm decision Long was struggling for the attention of
men whose thoughts were concentrated on the war.

By mid-1916 dissatisfaction with the war effort was reaching a
peak; the conscription debate had rent the Cabinet in two; Carson,
Churchill and Simon from their various viewpoints were assaulting
the Government in the House of Commons; and Lloyd George, faced
with the prospect of a futile tenure of the War Office, now that
Kitchener was dead, viewed a spell on the backbenches with interest.
The disintegration of the Ministers' will to work together manifested itself in their truculent and argumentative approach to the
parliamentary register.   Some of the Liberal Ministers were not
unwilling 'to use this as the means of breaking up the Coalition;
Lloyd George and some of the Unionists were keen to take their stand
on a soldiers' franchise if a split came.   And even Ministers like
Cecil felt the position over the register was becoming intolerable:
'If the Cabinet takes a strong line it will not lose, but if we have
lost the confidence of Parliament then let our opponents try to form
a Government.' (49)   Meanwhile many Unionist Peers were anxious to
settle the problem for the Cabinet by declining to renew Parliament's life, (50) a step which would have precipitated either an
election or a new Government or both.   This whole dispute had a
wider significance than the intrinsic importance of the parliamentary register, for it established, some six months before December
1916, that the will to maintain the Coalition had disappeared.
Those who were willing to keep it alive, Chamberlain, Balfour and
Cecil, looked for a solution for the register; their and Asquith's
ability to find one served to thwart the alternative Government but
only for a matter of months.
     Against Long's better advice the Cabinet decided to try Balfour's
plan.   Accordingly, on 19 July Herbert Samuel, now Home Secretary
in place of Simon, introduced a motion for a Select Committee to enquire whether it was practicable and desirable to prepare a new
electoral register and give representation to those engaged in war
work, and to conduct an election on such a register during the
war. (51)   So graphic was Samuel's exposition of the difficulties
involved in registration that J.M. Hogge interrupted to enquire
whether the Home Secretary was in order in opposing his own Motion!
Samuel confessed frankly that he was asking for a committee instead
of introducing a Bill because the problem had become so intractable,
and he relied upon the reasonableness of the House to solve it;
this was not forthcoming from any side.
     Carson charged the Government with failing to live up to the pro-
mises made earlier by Simon to create a special register to prevent
war workers losing their votes: nothing had been said then about
women's suffrage and the difficulties of elections in the
trenches; (52)   for a year the Cabinet had been humbugging the
House by keeping them in expectation of a Bill they had never drafted; it was clear they were too badly divided to agree on anything.
Thus the debate proceeded with hardly a word spoken in favour of the
Motion; one of the Members nominated to serve on the Committee, Mr
R. MacNeill declined the honour of covering the Government's retreat.   Members found it faintly quixotic that they should be asked
to decide whether an election should be held in wartime; a minority
including Carson plainly did desire a dissolution and were therefore
eager to exploit the Government's difficulties over the register.
However, it was appreciated by most politicians that if the Coali-

tion appealed as a body for a renewal of its mandate to get on with
the war, and the two party machines co-operated as they had at by-
elections, the result would have been the return of the same Government.   The exercise would thus have been a waste of time and a dangerous distraction from the war.   On the other hand, if no alternative Government would emerge from an election, it was feared even
by Unionists like Bonar Law that the party organisations would be
powerless to stop the electorate massacring many Members of the old
House of Commons;   there were ominous suggestions of this in the
by-election contests where pro-war independents challenged the established parties. (53)   Many Liberal and Labour Members would have
been defeated even if unopposed by the local Unionist Party with a
formal candidate;   and to attempt to prevent Unionists contesting
the constituencies of anti-war radicals would only have involved the
leadership in a disruptive and probably unsuccessful struggle with
local activists;   thus the prospect of an 'agreed' election was unattractive for Ministers in each Party.

Asquith had no alternative but to withdraw Samuel's Motion for a
Select Committee;   the attempt to put the registration and franchise
issue out of bounds for a few months had failed dismally, lowering
the Government's prestige in the process.   With only two months remaining of the life of Parliament, Long asked the Cabinet to introduce one Bill for a further extension, one for a new register, and a
third in the autumn to deal specifically with servicemen. (54)

The question then narrowed to a debate on whether a register
could be prepared in the usual way;   Long believed it could not because it would be fatal for the Government to propose, in effect, a
major reduction in the electorate, and therefore urged a three-month
qualifying period to counter this. (55)   However, according to Lord
Lansdowne (56) even this would not satisfy the 'Salisbury Peers' who
wanted nothing less than the total enfranchisement of the Armed
Forces, not merely the preservation of the votes of those men already on the pre-war register.   Lansdowne himself opposed this as
he believed it would be impossible to deny the vote to millions of
munitions workers and women.   In a note on Long's memorandum Henderson (57) asked that if the Cabinet reduced the qualifying period
the Bill should be so framed as to allow the introduction of amendments for woman suffrage.   He was backed up as usual by Cecil (58)
who insisted that a reduced qualifying period constituted a permanent franchise reform not just a temporary expedient.   He threatened to raise the women's case in Committee on any Government Bill
and to vote against the Third Reading if unsatisfied with it.
Cecil's own plan was to take the existing register, strike off the
dead and add those who had qualified since it had been compiled;
then anyone whose name was still on the register but who was no
longer living in the district for which he had qualified should be
allowed to vote by post for a period of up to twelve months after
the war. (59)   Since this involved no *franchise* change he believed
the Government could logically resist all amendments as being outside the scope of the Bill.   The real weakness of Cecil's plan was
that it left most of the troops without a vote and preserved only a
nominal vote for the rest: many Members were not content with this.

The main alternative to Cecil's approach seemed to be the Long-
Lansdowne scheme for a new register based on a three-month qualify-

ing period which was once more put forward on 8 August; (60) the
next day, however, the Cabinet met and rejected it in favour of a
simpler plan: (61) both the franchise and qualifying period were to
remain as before, but all 'war workers' were to be registered if
they would have qualified but for war service.   This was just a
glib formula, difficult to put into practice.   'What exactly is the
conclusion at which the Cabinet arrived yesterday is very obscure',
Long reminded the Prime Minister, (62) 'All I am clear about is that
they disapproved of a shortened period of qualification.'

This can be taken as an illustration of the disadvantage of a
Cabinet system in which decisions were not formally recorded; in
fact, Long was reluctant to have to come to grips with a proposition
which he felt to be impractical.   However, Long did have a note
made by Duke during the meeting - apparently the only account he had
salvaged from the discussion - which read: 'a) presence on the register prima facie proof of present qualification.   b) residence interrupted by military service or other war service to be declared
not to have been interrupted.' (63)

Long then interpreted this to mean that a new register should be
compiled on the basis of a twelve-month qualification, and that to
it should be added the names of all those on the 1915 register who
would have qualified for the new one but for their war service; the
Special Register Bill followed this plan.   However, its introduction was preceded on 14 August by another Parliament and Local Elections Bill which prolonged the old parliament for a further eight
months until 31 May 1917; such was the mood among Unionists that
'The Times' (64) found 'unanswerable reasons' against what it considered so long an extension, and suggested that three months would
be enough!   In his speech on 14 August Asquith (65) dwelt upon the
objections to any franchise changes and emphasised that the women's
organisations would accept the *status quo* only if the Government did
the same.   It was in this speech that Asquith implied for the first
time in the House his conversion to woman suffrage, but ruled out
the possibility of a Bill during the war.   His argument that a soldiers' franchise would provoke the women was refuted by Commander
Bellairs (66) who said he was authorised to state on behalf of the
WSPU that they would never oppose votes for the troops even if women
were not included in the Bill - a complete reversal of the Pankhursts' previous position.

The passage of the first Bill proved uneventful for Members realised they had little option but to pass it unless they were bent
upon an election.   In Committee the extension was reduced to seven
months and Sir Frederick Banbury received a promise that the Plural
Voting Bill would not be re-introduced during that period.   One
amendment to limit the life of any Parliament elected on the old
register to a maximum of two years was ruled out of order, but the
Peers dared to insert it, knowing that the Government would acquiesce in the change, which they did. (67)

It was the second Bill that foundered.   Asquith had already reviewed the proposals: (68) where people had kept their premises
they would not be disqualified for want of residence, but 'war workers' would be placed on the register even if they had lost their
premises or left their homes. (69)   So as to have as fresh a register as possible the end of the qualifying period would be postponed

from 15 July to 15 November.   All this involved no change in the
franchise, but if the House wished they would be able on the Second
Reading to turn the Register Bill into a franchise measure, a course
which, he warned, his colleagues all deprecated.   Carson amused the
House by promising to 'wait and see' this Bill before actually con-
demning it, but on 16 August he and Simon sought rulings from the
Speaker as to whether it would be possible to debate servicemen's
and women's franchise in Committee;   Lowther (70) replied that such
amendments would not be admissible: their sponsors would have to
move an instruction to introduce these classes onto the register,
and the machinery necessary to enable the troops to exercise the
vote would require a separate Bill to amend the Ballot Act.   Carson
responded by attacking the franchise being offered to war workers as
purely nominal and advocated Lord Salisbury's 'Trench Voting Bill'
instead. (71)

For the Liberal Party's registration experts the Government's
Bill provided a field day.   Simon characterised it as a 'bill which
is going to add a series of absentees to the register, and is going
to do nothing else'; (72)   taking the example of a lodger he said it
would have to be ascertained whether the man had, in the days before
the war, begun to lodge at a certain place in such circumstances as
would ultimately have entitled him to a vote;   meanwhile he might
have joined the army, returned home as an invalid and taken lodgings
elsewhere.   W.H. Dickinson (73) pointed out that anyone on the old
register not now to be found in his former constituency would automatically be dropped from the new lists unless he was a war worker;
one would have to trace several hundred thousand people who had gone
away up to two years before, and the result would be that most of
them would not get back onto the register.   Also those who had
never previously qualified would find it difficult to establish that
on 1 November 1915 they had been resident at a certain place, and in
practice their names would be omitted.   'These proposals are quite
unworkable', he concluded.

Thus the Government seemed to be heading for another humiliation:
it became vital to employ an alternative expedient if the Bill were
not to be withdrawn.   In reply to Simon's unequivocal demand for a
Franchise Bill (74) Asquith offered two contradictory views: 'to
bring about the great heroic measures which [Simon] has just adum-
brated ... you must devote weeks and months of parliamentary time to
a reconstruction of the constitution of this country.   Everybody
agrees that it is out of the question.' (75)   However, the Prime
Minister who was evidently feeling his way through the debate rather
than speaking from a firm position, then went on to concede that the
underlying need was to provide for the election of the post-war
reconstruction parliament, and, since this would necessitate an ex-
panded electorate, he went on to say:

let us by all means use the time - those of us who are not absolutely absorbed in the conduct of the War - in those months to
see if we cannot work out by general agreement some scheme under
which, both as regards the electorate and the distribution of
electoral power, a Parliament can be created at the end of the
War adequate for discharging these tasks, and commanding the
confidence of the country.

This mouthful of Asquithian prose contained only a vague indica-

tion that everyone might get what they wanted - a little later;   it
was a characteristic effort by a tired Prime Minister talking to
save his life;   and it was on the strength of these remarks that he
won a grudging acceptance of the Bill as a 'stop-gap to meet an
emergency'.   For, as the next speaker, Mr R. MacNeill admitted, (76) the Prime Minister's speech altered the whole nature of
the proposal, though this did not stem the flow of mockery and
abuse.   The idea of a general settlement had been hinted at from
time to time by Long, Balfour, Henderson and Montagu, but had foundered on the supposed Unionist refusal to start making the inevitable concessions to the radical programme. (77)   Now the Unionists'
zeal for a servicemen's franchise was about to bear fruit: too late
Lord Salisbury checked his demands: (78)

> I know that Bob [Lord Robert Cecil] is very nervous lest the
> result of the present agitation may not be universal adult suf-
> frage.   I have been so much impressed with these warnings ...
> that I did not put forward the general soldiers' franchise to
> which I had all but publicly adhered, but have fallen back upon
> the existing basis of qualification.

However, it was difficult to offer opposition to the Government's
new proposal: it was too vague a target.   The idea had been handed
across the floor of the House of Commons from Simon to Asquith, to
be picked up by Long who began to give it more definite shape;   but
there is no indication that Ministers knew what they were going to
do with the proposal in detail after the debate.   If they had some
idea, like Long, of the next step they wisely confined themselves to
generalities for the time being.   After his frustrating experiences
at the Local Government Board Long was evidently converted to the
reform of 'our absurd, cumbersome and ridiculous registration laws'
which he wanted replaced by a continuous Register on the Canadian
pattern; (79) the virtue of using a representative Conference to
deal with the whole question would be that it would free the Cabinet
from the need to intervene constantly in the matter.

   In fact they had not quite finished with registration: the
Special Register Bill had won a stay of sentence and had to be seen
through.   Now that the House was being offered a new register it
was disinclined to accept it unless an effective soldiers' franchise
was included.   As the parliamentary recess drew to a close
Long (80) optimistically advised the Cabinet that since the Conference would probably have some recommendations the Bill could be
abandoned;   however, he had to spend October devising expedients for
enabling the troops to vote in a wartime election;   these labours
led him to the conclusion that all absent voters would have to be
content with a proxy vote, (81) in which he was supported by Montagu, now Minister for Munitions, who flatly opposed any attempt to
allow munitions workers to return to their homes in order to
vote. (82)   Thus on 1 November the Government faced the Commons in
Committee with no new proposals;   Carson was still prevented by the
Speaker's ruling from introducing his amendment to the Bill.   As a
result the Government had 'one of their periodical bad days' as 'The
Times' put it, and, in the absence of any support the measure was
withdrawn: everything then waited upon the Conference which by this
time was at work.

   The evidence points clearly to the birth of what became the en-

during practice of Speaker's Conferences, less as a bold act of
constructive statesmanship than as a desperate expedient, the last
of a series in fact.   Its immediate object was to relieve the Cabinet of the tedium of registration debates and exposure to attack in
the Commons on a subject which they still believed to be basically
insoluble under a Coalition Ministry.   The Speaker himself accepted
the Chairmanship of the Conference without enthusiasm, believing it
would prove 'impossible to achieve unanimity on the main
issues'. (83)   Was the Conference merely a means of shelving the
problem?   Certainly it would have suited the Cabinet to have had
the Conference endlessly debating intractable franchise issues, thus
leaving them free to concentrate on the war and always able to
advise the Commons to wait for the report.   The conference would
have become a first line of defence against the backbenchers.   However, at least one Unionist backbencher regarded the new move as a
genuine one;   J.R.P. Newman wrote: (84)

> It is now certain that both Parties are pledged to an extensive
> and thorough measure of electoral and franchise reform before a
> normal Parliament of normal term of life is elected.   We shall I
> imagine have what will be a simple adult franchise for men and
> women and of necessity a complete redistribution of seats.

No doubt this exaggerated the chances of success;   for the Cabinet
did not anticipate that the Conference would be so quick in generat-
ing what proved to be the most sweeping measure of electoral reform
ever introduced in Britain.

What the Conference achieved was no less than the preservation of
the Coalition Government at a time when it would otherwise have
fallen or split for want of will to face a critical House of
Commons.   In this light the kind of status conventionally accorded
to the First Speaker's Conference is exaggerated.   Indeed no one in
August 1916 envisaged the Speaker as Chairman in view of the possibility of less politically compromised persons than Lowther being
available.

Chapter 6

MR LOWTHER'S TRIUMPH

You tell me not to be afraid of a drastic Reform Bill.   Well I
am not afraid - in the sense that I have great confidence in the
ultimate good sense of my countrymen, rich and poor, male and
female.   But ... we should do better to go slow.   Why not say
so?   Why not perform the essential function of a Conservative
Party?   (Lord Salisbury to Lord Selborne, 4 September 1916,
Selborne Papers, vol. 6)

The work of the First Speaker's Conference spanned a crucial period
in the First World War.   It began in October 1916 at a time when
continued lack of success in battle threatened to dissolve the
feeble bonds of Coalition; within two months Lloyd George had resigned office and replaced Asquith with a new Coalition based on
Conservative support with some Labour and Liberal backing.   This
development in no way affected the Liberal and Labour Members of the
Speaker's Conference, for a settlement of electoral reform was quite
as desirable under either Prime Minister; moreover, the majority of
Liberal Members, at least in the early months of 1917, were in no
sense divided into two parties, and could pursue the interests of
Liberalism through the Conference without disloyalty or doubt.   Although three Conservatives left the Conference when Lloyd George
became Prime Minister, their colleagues stayed on - a significant
indication of their faith in the new administration.   With Bonar
Law properly elevated as Chancellor of the Exchequer and flanked by
Milner and Curzon on the War Cabinet there was no longer any doubt
that the country had at last a Government dedicated to winning the
war; this, paradoxically, is what rendered the task of working on
domestic reform unconnected with the war more palatable for Conservatives.
    Between the parliamentary debate on 16 August and the first sit-
ting of the Speaker's Conference on 12 October the guiding hand in
the preparations was that of Walter Long.   In his determination to
promote a general measure of electoral reform Long epitomised the
pragmatic Conservative statesman; to act quickly meant a moderate
Bill; delay brought the danger of a really radical one. (1)
Long's role in this cannot be overestimated, for alone among Ministers he devoted himself to pushing ahead with reform from August

1916 onwards.   His usual tactic was to act before his opponents had
time to object;   for example, on 23 August 1916 Salisbury reassured
Selborne: 'Lansdowne thought that Walter's idea of a Conference was
not very substantial';   (2)   but a week later he was dismayed to find
that Long had been concealing his intentions: 'It has a most unpleasant appearance of the same old stunt as on the Irish Question-
Crisis;   rash proposal;   settle the whole business straight off;
negotiations behind Lansdowne's back.' (3)

For a man who is known to history as an archetypal Tory back-
woodsman Walter Long played a distinguished role as reformer during
the war;   it was he who pushed the scheme for a Speaker's Conference
ahead at every stage from August 1916 onwards despite the severe
loss of popularity which this caused him in the Conservative Party.
Long, and his subsequent collaborator on the Reform Bill, Sir George
Cave, were typical of politicians at the dangerous stage of life.
They nourished no further ambitions and therefore had nothing to
lose by taking up an unpopular cause in the comparatively short time
remaining to them in active politics.   Their support proved of crucial importance in helping Bonar Law to stand out against the Cur-
zons and Carsons who threatened to make him surrender either the
Reform Bill or the leadership of a united party.

Long in fact did his best to secure a Conference that would sal-
vage as much as possible of his party's position from the all-party
compromise that must emerge.   The membership, the Chairman, the
terms of reference and the general nature and status of the proposed
conference had all to be determined;   in August none were at all
clear.   The scope of the Conference occasioned little difficulty;
virtually everything relating to elections was to be thrown in.
Only two days after the debate in the Commons, Long proposed to
Asquith four main fields: franchise, redistribution, registration
and methods of election. (4)   Subsequently the Conference decided
that the local government franchise was within its terms of reference and resolved to avoid Irish redistribution, but otherwise followed this comprehensive programme.   It was also understood before
the Conference was set up that 'methods of election' included Proportional Representation,   a Unionist backbencher, H.J. Mackinder,
had been entrusted by the Proportional Representation Society with
the task of pressing upon Long the necessity of having their views
represented at the Conference. (5)   Though the Proportional Representation Society had run down its activities during the war its
leading personnel, Courtney, Humphreys and Aneurin Williams watched
the situation closely, so as to be ready to act when a favourable
opportunity presented itself. (6)   Asquith had for some time been
toying with the idea of an experiment with Proportional Representation, and Long, though he disliked it, acceded to the Society's
request. (7)

From the start the Conference was not envisaged as a Select Committee, but was to have wider representation and a frankly ambiguous
status;   it was, as the 'Manchester Guardian' later observed, 'not
even a formally constituted Committee of the House of Commons or a
joint Committee of the two Houses;   it was, so to speak, a private,
even a personal, Committee'. (8)   An innovation of this sort naturally allowed the Government room for manoeuvre when deciding what
to do with any proposals produced by the Conference;   no precedent

limited their options.   According to 'The Times' (9) it was intended to include in the Conference all the political parties, though
not the Government itself, and representatives of the women's movement, organised labour, trade and the Universities under the chairmanship of an impartial ex-judge.   This was a fairly accurate summary of Long's intentions; (10) he also thought of including a town
clerk and a rural district representative.   As for the political
elements, he proposed to Asquith (11) six Unionists, six Liberals,
two Irish, two Scots, two Labour and four Peers.   The party representatives, he thought, need be 'not necessarily M.P.'s', but in
other words additional Peers.

These suggestions were strongly contested by Edwin Montagu who
feared that Long had obtained Asquith's acquiescence without the
Prime Minister having given the matter serious consideration. (12)
Montagu objected to the Unionists having two more members than the
Liberals and to the inclusion of Peers who had nothing to do with
franchise; it would be 'monstrous' to have a Peer in the
chair. (13)   Long's answer to this was that he would have to raise
the matter in Cabinet, but that Asquith had already agreed that a
Peer could be the chairman. (14)   John Gulland, the Liberal Whip,
joined in with a direct protest to Asquith, (15) and was answered
by Long apparently for the Prime Minister: (16) some Peers would
have to participate, according to Long, since it was 'necessary to
ensure the passage of a drastic reform bill'; as for the chairman,
he ought to be an impartial figure like a judge, but whether a Peer
or a Commoner hardly mattered.   Even with ten Unionist representatives to eight Liberals they would still be in a minority since the
three other parties shared the same view on electoral issues.   Long
closed with the warning that if they could not agree on these points
they were unlikely to be able to produce a Bill and would then be
forced back to the Special Register Bill with the amendments of
Carson and Simon.

Doubtless the prospect of further confrontation with the Commons
helped to clarify the situation.   On 18 September Asquith received
a note from the Lord Chancellor who called to say that 'a Judge
could not be spared from [the] judicial Committee for Conference on
Franchise and would not be suitable anyway.' (17)   This left the
field clear for the candidate who possessed a politician's insight
while retaining some claim to impartiality: James William Lowther,
the Speaker.   His formal acceptance was conveyed to Asquith on 1
October just before Parliament reassembled. (18)

It was with some hesitation that I accepted the task; feeling
upon these topics had run very high before the war, the members
of the Conference were not to be officially appointed by the several parties, and there seemed to be no security that even if we
could agree, Parliament would ratify our decisions.   On the
other hand, however, the war was acting as a strong cementing
force, a Coalition was in power, and the time was perhaps oppor-
tune for an agreement if such a thing were possible. (19)

For the other members Gulland (20) advised following the practice
for Select Committees: 6 Unionists, 6 Liberals, 2 Nationalists, 1
Labour.   In the event they compromised between this and Long's
scheme.   A total of 32 were selected comprising 13 Unionists, 12
Liberals, 4 Nationalists and 3 Labour representatives.   Of these 3

Liberals and 2 Unionists were Peers.   Exclusion of the pressure
groups was probably wise; the NUWSS had been considering whom to
send, and the Proportional Representation Society intended to
appoint John Humphreys as a delegate.   Humphreys, with his broad
knowledge and detailed practical grasp of the working of electoral
systems, would have been a valuable member, but the admission of too
many groups could easily have led to deadlock between rival advocates whose interest was restricted to single causes.   In the event
Long was shown a list of MPs known to be favourable to Proportional
Representation, through the offices of Major Newman, (21) and he
intimated to Lord Courtney (22) that he would recommend as members
Earl Grey and Aneurin Williams MP, the president and chairman respectively of the Proportional Representation Society.

The balance of opinion on woman suffrage was a delicate question.
Long believed that there should be a 'preponderance' of anti-suffragists, (23) and the women's organisations took alarm at the news
that the Conference would actually meet at the local government
board with one of its Secretaries, Walter Jerred.   'The concatena-
tion of Mr. Long and Mr. Lowther is of evil augury for women', as
the WFL put it. (24)   However, events were to show these fears to
be misplaced.   The Speaker's brief was to select equal numbers of
suffragists and anti-suffragists, which he endeavoured to do. (25)
In fact, as Lowther himself admitted, one could no longer be entirely sure of Members' views on the women's question.   He enjoyed the
final choice, but within certain limits: (26)

A list of proposed members of the Conference was prepared by the
Whips and submitted to me, and while staying at Nuneham for some
shooting in September, I invoked the assistance of my host, Mr.
L. Harcourt, in making a selection designed to represent and
balance as fairly as possible the several interests concerned.
One should observe in passing that the original list included three
members, Viscount Bryce (Liberal), Laurence Hardy (Unionist) and Mr
Mooney (Nationalist), who withdrew before the Conference met, and
whose places were filled by Lord Southwark, Sir Robert Williams and
P.J. Brady respectively.

None of the members were politicians of the first rank with the
exceptions of Sir John Simon and Lord Salisbury, neither of whom
were likely to join a Government in the near future.   Sir Robert
Finlay had emerged as Unionist front-runner for the Lord Chancellor-
ship, the post to which he succeeded in December 1916 at which point
he retired from the Conference.   For the rest the MPs were mostly
backbenchers of some years' standing without prospect of office,
though Colonel James Craig later became first Prime Minister of Northern Ireland.   Some like Earl Grey and Herbert Gladstone had been
prominent in public life earlier in their careers or, like George
Lambert and Lord Southwark, had held minor office.

Certain positive reasons may be adduced for the selection.
Among Liberals Willoughby Dickinson stood out as an acknowledged
expert on electoral affairs, as did Simon; these two were also the
closest Liberal associates of Mrs Fawcett's National Union.   The
others included radicals like William Pringle and Aneurin Williams,
both inclined to the Asquithian side; Ellis Davies was a Welsh
Lloyd Georgeite, and MacCallum Scott a radical opponent of women's
suffrage.   Sir John Bethell and Sir Ryland Adkins represented res-

pectable Liberal orthodoxy, and George Lambert the rural right.
Earl Grey, though ranked as a Liberal, and justifiably in view of
his pronounced if eccentric democratic opinions, occupied a somewhat
ambiguous position between the two parties; illness kept him away
from most of the meetings. The three Labour members were all co-
operative, pro-Government men, and Walsh and Wardle actually served
in Lloyd George's administration.

Among the Unionists Sir William Bull, a former party agent and
currently secretary to Long, occupied a position similar to Dickinson's; Colonel Craig represented Ulster, and Sir Joseph Larmor sat
for Cambridge University.   Sir Henry Page-Croft was a notable
tariff reformer and right-wing rebel, balanced here by Sir Harry
Samuel, Chairman of the Council of the National Union of Conservative and Unionist Associations.   Apart from Salisbury the only
Unionist Peer was Lord Burnham, more familiar as Harry Lawson, the
Member for Mile End until January 1916, and also proprietor of the
'Daily Telegraph'.   An examination of the voting record of the
Unionist members is enough to dispel the notion that they were un-
typical or constituted an amenable liberal wing of the party.   In
fact the most uncompromising champion of the electoral *status quo*,
Sir Frederick Banbury, was included, 'a gentleman whose reputation
rose chiefly on his strange pleasure in obstruction'. (27)   This
redoubtable Member for the City of London had rarely been silent in
a debate on the franchise, and his selection was hardly a good omen
for the success of the Conference; nor was Lord Salisbury who had
earlier told Selborne: 'I do not say I would not take part in a
Conference if I were asked, but I don't want to take part - except
with a view to disintegrating it.' (28)

The actual division of opinion on woman suffrage was rather
blurred; a tentative estimate suggests 17 supporters to 10 opponents, (29) but these figures are not firm, and still leave 5 members whose attitude is in great doubt. (30)   Two who are not known
as suffragists had staunchly backed the women in the Commons even in
1912 and 1913 - Sir John Bethell and Lord Burnham.   The 4 Irish
members who had voted against the women in 1912 and 1913, could now
be ranked as suffragists, if unreliable ones.   Of the Unionist
'antis' only 4, Banbury, Peto, Williams and Finlay, were absolutely
irreconcilable, while Page-Croft, MacMaster, Samuel and Salisbury
accepted woman suffrage in 1917 and may, therefore, not have opposed
it very strongly at the Conference.   Pringle, Adkins and Turton
were all claimed by the NUWSS as recent converts, but even here one
cannot be sure what is meant.   Adkins, for instance, was on record
as having abandoned his opposition because 'their war work establi-
shes their claim for any of the electoral privileges which they
demand'. (31)   Yet a few months later he declared at a meeting at
the National Liberal Club that he was still 'in theory opposed' to
woman suffrage, but had accepted the majority view in the Conference
as being representative of a majority in Parliament and in the
country. (32)   This makes it difficult to generalise about the size
of the 'suffragist' majority at the Conference.

One person whose influence also seems difficult to estimate is
the Secretary, Walter Jerred, with whom the Speaker had 'long and
anxious discussions' and who was, 'although in many respects an advanced reformer, a disbeliever in Proportional Representation'. (33)

As to the most influential members one may only surmise, but in a committee in which expertise was at a premium Dickinson and Bull must have played a major role.   Dickinson was suited to this kind of work;   a sober, persistent speaker in debates, he tended naturally to eschew general principles and concentrate upon details. There is some indication of which members Lowther found most congenial in the short list of those he chose to thank in retrospect for their work: Burnham, Bull, Adkins, Dickinson, Healy, Samuel, Simon and Aneurin Williams. (34)

The authority of the chairman himself did not become established until the Conference was underway.   Long delivered an opening speech on 12 October 1916, and then departed: 'the Speaker - august personage - has replaced Mr. Walter Long as the presiding genius of the Electoral Reform Conference', commented 'Vote', (35) 'that is, he first nominates his conference and then dominates it.'   A truer prophecy than the ladies realised;   for despite his reputation for anti-suffragism Lowther did not play the evil genius that was expected of him.   After his initial despondency about his task the Speaker rapidly developed a determination to succeed: (36)

I felt very strongly that to renew these party and domestic polemics at the end of the war would bring discredit upon Great Britain in the face of her Dominions and Colonies, at the very moment when the nation should be occupied in the consideration of large and novel problems of every kind arising out of the war and the peace which must eventually follow.   As time went on I became more and more impressed with the soundness of this view, and frequently pressed it upon my colleagues when there seemed to be any danger of a breakdown.

He refused the offer of the post of Food Controller from Lloyd George because 'my heart was by this time set upon carrying the Electoral Reform Conference through to a satisfactory termination'. (37)

It is customary to regard the First Speaker's Conference as the epitomy of the spirit of patriotic conciliation which prevailed at this time;   G.J. Wardle declared that he had 'never sat in any conference where there was a more evident desire shown to reach a practical agreement', (38) and the Speaker expressed the members' attitude thus in his letter to the Prime Minister: (39)

They were desirous of rendering, at a time when the national energies were almost wholly centred upon the successful prosecution of the war, a service which might prove of the highest value to the State, and result in equipping the nation with a truly representative House of Commons, capable of dealing, and dealing effectively, with the many and gigantic problems which it will have to face and solve as soon as the restoration of peace permits of their calm and dispassionate consideration.

Such sentiments, even though retrospectively expressed, do throw some light on the success of the Conference.   There can be no doubt of their determination to reach an agreement;   between 12 October 1916 and 26 January 1917 twenty-six meetings took place;   they neither stopped for the parliamentary recess, nor were halted by three Unionist resignations and the change of Government in December.   In the third bitter winter of trench warfare this group of thirty-two middle-aged and elderly politicians found in the Confer-

ence one of the few ways that was open to them of making a personal
contribution to the cause of national unity; at the least they were
sparing the Lloyd George Government from a disruptive distraction
from the war, and at best they might conjure all-party unity out of
a dismal and perennial controversy.

However, the triumphant conclusion of the Conference has obscured
the discouraging start; indeed Grey, after the initial meeting felt
there was 'not the slightest chance of our being able to make a unanimous recommendation on any subject'. (40)   The mood of conciliation was as much the *product* of the Conference as a cause of its
success.   MacCallum Scott described it thus: (41)

> The Speaker's first suggestion that we should begin with the
> small things and proceed gradually to the bigger things was re-
> jected.   We were anxious to go to the root of the matter - the
> franchise - at once.   We tackled it forthwith and came to a com-
> plete deadlock.

This was precisely what had been expected in view of the formal positions adopted by the radical parties.   The three Labour members,
for example, stood for the programme laid down quite recently by
the national agent (42) which included adult suffrage, a simple
residential qualification, quarterly registration, the Alternative
Vote, simultaneous elections, extension of polling hours, restric-
tion of maximum expenses and redistribution of seats.   Similarly
Dickinson, (43) writing on the eve of the Conference, had urged the
sweeping away of all existing franchises in favour of a new personal
franchise in which every citizen would automatically be listed on a
continuously made up register.

Lowther knew that the Unionists could not be expected to capitu-
late in the face of such demands: 'Do not let us take a vote at
this stage', said the Speaker, in MacCallum Scott's account, 'Let us
go back to the smaller things and work up to this again gradually.'
Scott goes on to say:

> He told the Conference plainly that it was not a Parliamentary
> Debating Society ... the Government had asked us to find a way,
> and we had got to find a way....   From that moment he took the
> Conference in hand.   When the two sides sat and stared blankly
> at each other he took the initiative and put proposals for their
> discussions.   Over and over again he withdrew the proposals
> which discussion had convinced him were impracticable; but he
> had watched the discussion narrowly, and he was ready with other
> proposals which represented the largest measure of common agree-
> ment of the Conference.   He had no political axe of his own to
> grind, but he was determined to find a way, and he succeeded in
> dominating the Conference.   He created the atmosphere of concili-
> ation.   We were, first of all, pleased to find how reasonable
> we ourselves could be on the smaller points, and then as we
> approached the bigger points surprised to find that there was a
> prospect of our opponents being reasonable.

Dickinson perceived two main reasons for their success, the first
being that the members felt obliged to produce a scheme of some kind
before the end of the war; the second reason was that: (44)

> the deliberations of the Conference were so guided by their
> Chairman in the early meetings that no decisions were arrived at
> until the main questions at issue had been fully talked out and

understood by every member.   By this means those who wished for
one thing were able to appreciate what was in the minds of those
who desired something else and then it became possible to envisage the whole problem before either side had committed itself to
a definite proposition.

In other words the ground was cleared for a grand bargain in which
everyone might obtain some desired object: 'I consented at the
Speaker's Conference', explained Aneurin Williams, (45) 'to a large
number of things which I did not like, in order that I should get
certain things that I did like.'   Clearly it would have served no
useful purpose for the radical majority to have dictated a Report
which the Unionists in Parliament would have rejected;   Lloyd George
could never have accepted it.   The Unionists had to be conciliated
and compensated for certain inevitable losses, but most of them were
evidently willing to be conciliated with good grace.

Even so, the Conference required tactful handling;   as Lowther
pointed out later, there was no agenda, all proposals being sent to
him so that he could decide which to raise at the next meeting. (46)
Nor were there any minutes taken, though he took some rough notes:
'Our discussions were conducted on much the same lines as a discussion in Committee of the Whole House of Commons but with rather more
licence to irrelevancy.'   As a rule he avoided divisions, and where
they were inevitable he never took the names on each side;   whenever
the possibility of agreement arose he postponed the issue and talked
about something else.

The Conference's work fell into two periods, the first of two
months running up to the departure of four members in mid-December,
and the second ending effectively on 18 January during which woman
suffrage and some lesser matters were settled.   On 14 December the
Speaker reported to Lloyd George who had just displaced Asquith as
Prime Minister: (47)

the Conference has passed 24 resolutions: all but four of these
were unanimous: of the four, three were passed with one dissen-
tient and the other, in which the figures were 11 to 8, related
to the method of election known as the Alternative Vote which is
in no sense a party question....   We have in fact reviewed the
whole of the present system of Registration of Voters and propose
to remodel it entirely.   On the Franchise question we are very
nearly in agreement....   As regards Redistribution we have
agreed on a complete scheme, with the system of Proportional Representation in the larger boroughs.

How had agreement been achieved on such a wide range of issues in
so short a time?   In part the explanation lay in the fact that certain changes already commanded wide support, or at least did not
divide the politicians on party lines: redistribution (see Appendix
9) is a case in point.   The only general division here was between
those who accepted something like equal constituencies and those who
wanted the principle modified lest the rural areas lost representation and suffered huge, unwieldy constituencies.   This latter view
was urged at the Conference by George Lambert, the Liberal Member
for South Molton, to whom they 'paid no attention'. (48)   The
basic provisions agreed to were to deprive of representation all
existing seats with under 50,000 population, and to grant new seats
for every surplus of 70,000 and remainders of 50,000 in counties,

boroughs and urban districts.   The draft resolution for the scheme
that was actually adopted is to be found in Asquith's Papers; (49)
this made certain assumptions: 1, that the total number of Members
should remain unchanged; 2, that the basis of redistribution should
be a standard unit of population, 'say 70,000'; 3, existing constituencies below 70,000 but above 50,000 should retain their MP;
4, extra representation should be granted for every multiple of the
standard unit including remainders of 50,000; 5, three-Member seats
formed by boroughs or thickly populated county areas should use the
Single Transferable Vote; 6, London should be treated as a single
borough and divided into three- or five-Member seats; 7, the City
of London should retain its two Members; 8, parliamentary boundaries should, as far as possible, coincide with administrative ones.
All this formed part of the Report, yet it differs seriously from
Gerald Balfour's 1905 Memorandum on Redistribution (50) only in that
it sacrificed the small boroughs which Balfour had wished to save if
their population reached 18,500.

The Unionists had in fact been keen on redistribution since well
before the war, (51) but considerations of geography and chronology
posed problems for both parties.   Taking England, Wales and Scotland the Unionists estimated a net loss to themselves of nineteen
seats through redistribution (see Appendix 6), their losses in England being offset to some extent by the abolition of small Liberal
boroughs and counties in the Celtic Countries.   However, Ireland
drastically altered the picture; the iniquity of a situation in
which the average electorate of an Irish constituency was 6,700 compared to the English average of 13,000 had provided the Unionists'
standard argument against Liberal franchise reforms: 'every Irish
elector is, in effect, a plural voter and has two votes to the
Englishman's one.' (52)   Enthusiasts of the British Constitution
Association like Major Clive Morrison-Bell had produced vivid pic-
torial material, models and exhibitions to demonstrate this point to
the people at large, and used it to underline the Unionist case in
pamphlets like 'Votes Not Words OR Home Rule And The Welsh Church In
Mr. Redmond's Nutshell'.   By 1916 it was calculated that the advantage to the Party from a redistribution in Ireland would be twenty-
nine seats, (53) enough to give them a balance of ten for Great Britain as a whole.

Now the Speaker's Conference did not touch the existing 103 Irish
constituencies, but only because this had already been provided for
in the Home Rule Act; it was understood that in the event of this
Act being abandoned the question of redistribution would be settled
by the Irish Convention.   Conference saw no reason to duplicate the
work of this body.   It was not until towards the end of 1917, when
it was becoming apparent that the Convention was unlikely to succeed, that Lloyd George's Government gave way to Unionist demands to
make up for this omission in the Conference's Report.   However, in
the winter of 1916-17 the Unionist members did not feel that they
were giving away their position by accepting a redistribution that
left out Ireland.

On the central issue of franchise-registration there could be no
genuine agreement between the radical doctrine of one-man-one-vote
and the Unionist desire to preserve various forms of plural voting;
and so, as Dickinson put it, 'the solution of the problem was found

in the acceptance of both'. (54)   The foundation of the new electorate was to be a simple residential qualification for men and the
abolition of all other existing franchises except two;   instead of a
three-month qualifying period with four registrations per year they
compromised on a six-month period and two registers;   still splitting the difference on successive registration the Conference
allowed an elector to carry his vote with him if he moved to premises within the same constituency, or within the same parliamentary
borough or county, or to a 'contiguous' borough or county.   The
geographical anomalies entailed in this provision show the lengths
to which the Conference was prepared to go in order to avoid making
one side surrender all of its position on any issue.   A simple
decision to sweep away the 1885 system of registration which deprived about two and a half million men of the franchise for which they
had a legal qualification was more than the Unionists could swallow,
which is a measure of how little their views had changed on the
franchise under peacetime conditions.

None the less, the Report took a long step towards adult male
suffrage with the basic residential franchise;   why had the Unionists acquiesced in this?   It was often said subsequently that the
Unionist Members had allowed themselves to be taken in by the superior technical knowledge and dialectical skill of Liberals such as
Simon.   However, the Unionists had access to plenty of expert
advice from their own Central Office under the party chairman,
Arthur Steel-Maitland.   The first comprehensive set of proposals
the Conference considered were largely based on the 1912 Franchise
Bill and put forward by Walter Jerred who was naturally familiar
with them.   Confronted with this Sir Robert Finlay sought specific
information on behalf of his Unionist colleagues, and received some
very plain advice from Steel-Maitland.   He pointed out that it was
an illusion to think that the party's losses from the abolition of
plural voting would be balanced by their gains from redistribution; (55)   the latter, as we have seen, would have yielded only ten
seats net.   Against this Steel-Maitland claimed that the Ownership
Vote gave the Unionists fifty to seventy seats in England and Wales;
the loss of the £10 Occupiers would cost them a dozen existing boroughs plus a prospective gain of eight more at the next election.
He advised against surrendering the Ownership Vote since 'there is
no public demand for its abolition': (56) but they could afford to
give up multiple votes above four, three or even two since these
did cause some offence as a result of 'the silly letters of those
who write to "The Times" to say that they have voted in eleven constituencies'.   One qualification that seemed to be of little value
was the Freeman's franchise;   its loss 'would mean very little
except in boroughs like Exeter, Gloucester or Chester where the majority is very small':   his conclusion, therefore, was to 'abolish
if desired'. (57

A better alternative which Steel-Maitland did urge was one-day
polling: 'All concessions, of course, on this point mean votes to
the radicals, but if any are to be made, this would give them least
votes, meet such popular feeling as exists, and be otherwise desirable.'   As for the Liberal proposal for a new residential franchise
for men, this would 'amount practically to adult suffrage minus
tramps and nomads';   in numerical terms he reckoned that only 20 per

cent to 25 per cent of the new voters would be Unionist, thus giving
the Liberals a 50 per cent to 60 per cent net gain.   The result
would be to inflict upon the Unionists damage from which 'except for
some unusual wave of opinion - they may not recover for years'.

Thus fortified the Unionists managed to retain the principle of
the plural vote by persuading the radicals to allow one extra vote,
other than the one for residence, which might be claimed either in
respect of business premises of £10 annual value or as a University
graduate.   Understandably the party agents tended to panic at the
thought of what the Unionists might be giving away behind the doors
of the Conference, and the memoranda supplied by Central Office
showed wide variations in the number of constituencies expected to
be adversely affected by the loss of certain franchises; their figures could not be taken literally.   It was appreciated that Steel-
Maitland drew his illustrations in rather harrowing terms in order
to stiffen the resistence of the Unionists to the blandishments of
Sir John Simon.   When they presented their own terms early in
December (58) they included a six-month qualifying period and two
registers a year, successive voting within counties, divided boroughs or boroughs within counties, equal constituencies, polling
within two days and payment of registration costs by the exchequer
and local authorities equally.   With the Unionists going this far
one can see that similar concessions from the other side would lead
to a bargain.   These proposals were not, of course, the starting
point: they came in December after the whole range of franchise and
registration had been discussed, so that they were now aware that in
offering such terms they were bound to draw a conciliatory response
rather than making a fruitless concession.

Nor were registration reforms to be seen simply as a concession
on the Unionist side.   For before the war, as Lord Selborne pointed
out, (59) the Unionists had been 'prepared to agree to put all the
cost of registration on public funds and the work of it on public
officials, and to reduce the term of residential qualification to
six months'.   What is misleading is that the vociferousness of the
Liberals' demands for reform of registration rather pushed the
Unionist organisers into automatic opposition.

Yet there remains the possibility that after two years of war the
Unionists, or some of them, had changed their minds on the merits of
adult male suffrage.   We have already noted Lord Salisbury's enthusiasm for enfranchising the volunteers quite early on in the war:
'No doubt there is no logic in this', wrote Selborne, (60) 'but the
feeling appears to me to be very general, and so far from the bulk
of the Conservative Party not sharing this view they appear to me to
hold this view in a larger proportion than the Liberals.'   And no
wonder, for he accounted for the attitude of his colleagues as a
desire to

secure the votes of the men who have fought as a deliverance from
the domination of the Trades Union influence.   They will have
seen that only two days ago the Trades Union Congress passed an
apparently unanimous resolution against compulsory service after
the war, and they will be confirmed in the opinion ... that the
only men to save them from such folly will be the men who have
fought, and I think their instinct is sound.   I think these men
will be an immense support to us for many years to come against

radical and Liberal insanity in the matter of foreign policy, navy, etc.

These observations should be read very carefully in the light of the assumption that there exists a direct relationship between the level of mass participation in the war effort and the extension of political and social privileges. (61)   Lord Salisbury had done his best to force the Asquith Government to ensure the franchise for active soldiers - and then drawn back in alarm upon realising that he was pushing them towards adult male suffrage which was not his object at all. (62)   Unionists of Salisbury's type were essentially concerned to maintain the effective franchise of soldiers under the existing rules; they were not interested in a man's contribution to the war unless it took the form of *active service in the forces*. This view manifests itself again in the willingness to make an exceptional franchise available to boys of nineteen if they had fought, and their refusal to make exceptions for those Conscientious Objectors who worked for the war effort *at home*.   The essential virtue was that one fought, served in the Army, and experienced the moral and physical advantages that this entailed.   Unionists had long believed in conscription as a panacea for national degeneration but feared to apply it; now it seemed, as Selborne's remarks show, that the men themselves had seen the light, and in consequence they were increasingly to be viewed as a reservoir of Conservative votes waiting to be tapped.   One can observe the application of this theory in the activities of Lord Milner who in June 1915 accepted the chairmanship of the British Workers' League. (63)   The war had demonstrated what Milner had always believed, namely that working men were patriots if given an alternative leadership to that of the TUC; and at the Merthyr Tydfil by-election they had proved it conclusively.   Thus the work of the British Workers' League developed beyond the role of propagandist against the Union of Democratic Control and the ILP, until, by 1917, they began to construct an alliance between the Unionists and what Bonar Law called the 'Imperialist Section of the Labour Party'.   In the event Milner's quirky brand of socialism did not prove an adequate basis for a Conservative version of Lib-Labbery.   For the Conservative confidence in the working-man-as-soldier was at least in part misplaced.   Lord Selborne's belief that experience in the trenches actually created support for peacetime military service turned out to be a pitiful delusion; it sprang from a confusion in his mind between the regular soldier, as known to the officer class, and the volunteer whose reactions were far more critical.   Yet this belief, however unreal, helps to explain politicians' attitudes to working men as voters. The masses had not become citizens; but they had shown that as voters they were no more to be feared than the enfranchised classes.

At the level of the Speaker's Conference, however, it was not possible to obtain a vote for soldiers and no one else; indeed the recommendations for dealing with the troops were unsatisfactory from the Unionist point of view, which helps to explain Salisbury's resignation in December.   The position of the remaining Unionists depended upon the willingness of Liberals to make concessions; in return for adult suffrage Long had argued that they must seek a six-month qualifying period and the 'representation of interests rather than mere numbers'. (64)   This they won by the retention of the business and University qualifications.   But in practice the exercise of the second vote was to be limited, partly by holding all elections on the same day, and partly by grouping the large boroughs and thickly populated districts into three, four or five-member constituencies using the Single Transferable Vote.   The practical effect of this arrangement was that since many electors' business premises would be within the same multi-Member constituencies as their residences they would be unable to use their second vote.

The inclusion of a unanimous recommendation for Proportional Representation in a limited number of seats was the most striking and novel feature of the Report.   Though Grey and Williams showered Proportional Representation memoranda upon the Conference the only other members known to be sympathetic were Simon, Burnham and Lord Stuart of Wortley.   Their best ally was Lowther who was a convert to Proportional Representation, in his own words, and included it in his own plan for redistribution. (65)   He willingly took up the proposals of Grey, who had to drop out because of illness, which involved adopting Proportional Representation only in three-member boroughs and thickly populated areas. (66)   Burnham attempted to persuade Lowther to include County Divisions too, 'but the practical arguments as to distance told upon his mind, and it was everything to have his sanction and support'. (67)

The question that is difficult to answer from the available evidence is whether the arrangement over plural voting had been explicitly linked to Proportional Representation so that the two had to stand or fall together.   This became of material importance later on when Proportional Representation had been dropped from the Bill and all the boroughs reverted to single-member seats, thereby widening the scope for plural voting.   Naturally this gave rise to some angry debates between the Liberals and Unionists in which the latter asserted that the Proportional Representation proposals had been approved quite separately from the business and University franchises.   In the absence of any authoritative record of the meetings, and the silence of the Speaker on the subject, Members relied on their own memories and notes, and the truth never emerged. For the Unionists the business qualification represented a valuable concession since the great majority of the 600,000 ownership voters, freemen and liverymen were expected to qualify for it.   The preservation of the University franchise was an equally remarkable achievement;   Oxford and Cambridge were to be confirmed in their status as two-Member constituencies, London was to be merged with eight English and Welsh Universities to form a three-Member seat, and the four Scottish Universities were to form a separate three-Member seat.   This amounted to an increase of three in University representation.   However, the existence of this electorate was rendered somewhat less obnoxious to the radicals by widening it to include everyone who had obtained a degree.   Moreover some guarantee was given that the Liberal minority would be represented;   in the case of the three-Member seats the Single Transferable Vote was to be the method of election, while at Oxford and Cambridge each elector would be limited to one vote.

This made University representation rather less of an anachronism and therefore more likely to survive.   It was designed to allow the radical minority some possibility of representation in the Universi-

ties just as the Single Transferable Vote was envisaged as a safeguard for the Unionists in the large boroughs.   Aneurin Williams,
in an article which explained the Report in terms of a conservative-
radical balance, (68) argued, in terms reminiscent of Mill, that
Proportional Representation would serve to protect the minority
against the weight of radical numbers.   This was designed to relieve the Conservatives' very natural fear of being swept out of
existence by violent swings of the pendulum as in 1906;   with male
suffrage in the boroughs this was felt to be inevitable.   This was
the logic behind the Conference's decision to experiment with Proportional Representation only in three-member boroughs or groups of
boroughs;   the existing representation of such areas was split
approximately three ways - though this is to ignore the chronic mal-
representation of Birmingham, Manchester and Liverpool - while the
regions most obviously in need of Proportional Representation were
omitted.   The experimental scheme would not touch the heartlands
of the main parties except marginally, but would protect the Conservatives, and perhaps the Liberals too, against a violent turn to
Labour among the new voters.   Though initially Proportional Representation would have opened out opportunities for Labour gains in
such cities as Glasgow and London, in the long run it would have
had the effect of keeping the Party within bounds in some of its
strongest areas.

How important was Proportional Representation at the Conference?
Lord Parmoor (69) considered that some members had 'agreed to the
alterations in the franchise only on the condition that they were
accompanied by a system of P.R.';   Lord Courtney, who was not a
member, claimed that it 'led to a consent on the part of Conservative minds which would otherwise have been witheld'; (70)   and Grey
maintained that without it he and others would have withdrawn from
the Conference thereby precipitating its break-up. (71)   These com-
ments are a little suspect in that they were made at a time when
Proportional Representation partisans were attempting to dissuade
the Government from dropping the Proportional Representation part of
the Report.

Unfortunately the Conference did not recommend wholesale application of Proportional Representation, for it could not be said that
the reform had achieved sufficient public approval to be acceptable;
an experiment was therefore the most that could be hoped for.   What
has to be explained is the refusal subsequently of a majority of
Unionists to support what had originally been conceived as a concession to them (pp. 160-1).   Undoubtedly some Unionists like the
Cecils regarded the Report as less obnoxious with Proportional Representation than without, and the House of Lords welcomed the experiment.   Yet to present Proportional Representation as a concession
to the Unionists only served to emphasise the Alternative Vote,
which was to be applied to all the remaining single-Member seats, as
a benefit for the Liberal and Labour Parties.   In fact the Alternative Vote was approved by only eleven to eight, according to Lowther, and in Parliament virtually the entire Unionist Party opposed
it subsequently which in turn helped to reduce Liberal support for
Proportional Representation.

While the majority of the thirty-two Conference members acquiesced in these proposals, three Unionists found the sacrifice too

great; on 13 December Lord Salisbury, Sir Frederick Banbury and
Colonel James Craig wrote a letter of resignation in which they gave
three reasons for their decision: (72) 'In our view these conclusions should be come to by general consent and not as an expression
of the wishes of a majority.'   Lowther's answer to this was simply
that nearly all points had so far won general consent.   Their
second reason was that they had lost the assistance of Finlay, now
Lord Chancellor, who had been acting as leader of the Unionist members; they went on: 'But there is another circumstance of even
greater importance ... the Government at whose instance this Conference was appointed no longer exists and it would be impossible
therefore to render to it any report.'   In forwarding this letter
on to Lloyd George Lowther emphasised that the remaining members
were 'unanimously of opinion that it would be a serious misfortune
to allow the Conference to break up in view of the progress made
and an evident desire to arrive at an agreement'. (73)   The new
Prime Minister was in fact anxious to receive their Report at an
early date, (74) and Lowther accordingly promised to continue sittings through the parliamentary recess. (75)   In seizing this particular moment to resign the Unionists had made a final bid to em-
barrass their colleagues who remained and to undermine the authority
of the proposals ultimately put forward: 'however, with their departure a more conciliatory disposition manifested itself, and in
the new year good progress was made.' (76)

Sir Robert Finlay was not replaced, but Edward Archdale MP joined
in place of Craig, while the substitutes for Salisbury and Banbury
were Lord Stuart of Wortley and George Touche, MP, respectively:
'This of course is a blessed change from our point of view', commented Mrs Fawcett, (77) correctly sensing a decisive shift in the
balance of opinion in favour of woman suffrage.   Indeed the replacement of two diehards with two staunch friends of the women's
cause at this stage can only have been a deliberate move by Lowther
to ensure that all the agreements achieved so far would not be
spoiled by deadlock over women's suffrage: (78)

I endeavoured to push off the burning question of women's suffrage as long as I could, and succeeded, for I felt that if we
could agree upon other matters ... there might be a greater disposition to come to some satisfactory solution of the women's
question.

In the second phase of its work the Conference dealt with Absent
Voters, One Day Polling and Returning Officers' Expenses as well as
woman suffrage.   Members were aware that they were expected to come
up with a solution for disfranchised soldiers, but were quite realistic enough to decide at the outset not to attempt the creation of
a special register for wartime purposes only. (79)   Instead they
resolved by a majority decision to establish on a permanent basis a
list of all absent voters which would include fishermen and merchant
seamen as well as soldiers and sailors.   Any person who could satisfy the Returning Officer that he was unlikely to be present on
Polling Day on account of his occupation would be placed on the list
and vote only on a ballot paper sent to him at his registered
address.   This arrangement seemed quite inadequate to many MPs and
was subsequently modified in Parliament.

Meanwhile the ladies of the WFL had been picketing the Confer-

ence's meetings in case their claim should be overlooked; it was
not until 10 January, according to Dickinson's account, that the
vexed question was reached.   The Speaker departed from his usual
practice by suggesting that opinion should be tested by a series of
informal divisions; thereupon the members voted by fifteen to six
in favour of conferring a parliamentary vote upon women, but rejected by twelve to ten a proposal for equal suffrage with men. (80)
Dickinson recorded the next step:

> I was then allowed to put forward my proposition, which was that
> the vote should be accorded to all women who were either 'occu-
> piers' themselves or wives of occupiers.   The division showed
> nine 'for' and eight 'against'.   Thus by one vote we secured for
> women's suffrage a place in the report that Mr. Speaker brought
> up to Parliament.   Had it not been for this I doubt if there
> would have been any positive recommendation on Women's Suffrage
> and the House of Commons would have found itself once again
> powerless to reconcile the conflicting views of its members, for
> the difference in effect of the various schemes was too great.
> The bill favoured by the Conservatives would have admitted about
> one million women voters.   Equal franchise about twenty million;
> whilst my scheme would give the vote to some seven millions.

It is clear from the figures quoted by Dickinson that the Conference felt bound to make a solid gesture to the women but not a capitulation.   Dickinson's proposal affected about the maximum number
that the members were willing to accept; for, as Sir William Bull
frankly explained, (81) they were anxious to avoid women becoming a
majority among the electorate, and therefore reduced the numbers to
tolerable proportions by combining an age limit with Dickinson's
scheme.   Their information, according to Dickinson, was that there
were ten million women over thirty years, which was too many, and
the Conference therefore decided to recommend the vote for those who
were local government voters or wives of such voters, leaving it to
parliament to impose an age limit of thirty or thirty-five.   It
seems that members thought they were enfranchising at most six million women instead of the 8,400,000 who were actually on the 1918
register.   This was only a majority proposal, but it meant that by
18 January 1916 Lowther was able to report to Lloyd George that the
basic work had been concluded and would be ratified at a final session on 26 January.

As the subsequent debates were to show, this rather involved
series of compromises had resulted in some rather illogical reforms.
The Report by no means reflected a coherent philosophy of political
citizenship, but instead, in the long tradition of English parliamentary reform, derived its strength from a certain political co-
herence.   The balance of party advantage was not so fine that
nothing in the Report could be altered without reducing the whole to
chaos; indeed, several minor and major alterations were made both
of addition and of subtraction.   Yet this was always at the risk of
dissolving the ill-assorted majority who supported it.   It could
hardly have been otherwise with a Report devoid of theme or principle patched together by compromise and skilful horse-trading.

'It is entirely thanks to you that the Conference has come
through so triumphantly', Walter Long congratulated the
Speaker. (82)   This was a widely shared view, though Speaker

Lowther has, none the less, slipped into obscurity; he observed,
somewhat wryly, himself: 'Mr. [Maurice] Healy had thrown out the
suggestion that the Act should be called "The Lowther Act", but this
proposal never caught on, and its formal official description remains rather a mouthful.' (83)

Chapter 7

LLOYD GEORGE'S DILEMMA

What was once the great Conservative Party has committed itself
to the wildest revolutionary change by this Representation Act
that England has seen since 1660.   And it has done this under
no compulsion.   It has nobody fit to lead it in the Lower
House.   (James Bryce to A.V. Dicey, 21 November 1917, Bryce
Papers, English Part I, vol. 4)

By the end of January 1917 the Speaker's Report lay in the hands of
the new Prime Minister, David Lloyd George.   What was he to do with
it?   Not until two months later could his Cabinet bring itself to a
decision to legislate on electoral reform.   For no irresistible
tide of reform swept it on, and in view of the natural public preoccupation with the war the Report might well have been shelved
until peacetime as were so many other measures of reconstruction,
had not certain leading politicians had good reason for taking it
up.
    Among the lower ranks of the political world the Speaker's Report
caused a ripple rather than a splash of excitement, for during the
winter of 1916-17 MPs had begun to lose interest in electoral reform
once again: (1)

Particularly is this the case with the keen supporters of the new
Government, who ... are more anxious that they shall have a fair
chance than that there should be an appeal to the country....
Indeed electoral reform and the Register have faded into the
background, where they will remain, probably, until the next
political crisis.

The new Government were certainly not anxious to create a major
issue out of the Report which, in the 'New Statesman''s words, had
'given rise to widespread satisfaction, but to little enthusiasm', (2) and the real danger was not so much that it would be
strongly opposed as that it would be 'pigeon-holed and forgotten'
amid the more pressing business of government.   The press, with a
few exceptions like the 'Morning Post' and the 'Yorkshire Post',
generally applauded the fact that so comprehensive an agreement had
been reached by the politicians themselves.   Even 'The Times' (3)
gave an unqualified welcome to the Report, professing to see nothing
in the least revolutionary in any of the proposals.   All this was

an expression of that vague belief in national progress through
goodwill that gripped many people in 1917;   Lowther was doing in
political affairs what his deputy was doing for industrial peace by
means of the Whitley Councils;   for men of liberal inclinations
Whitley and Lowther pointed to the end of the tunnel where the
light of reconstruction shone bright and clear.

On the other hand since the proposed changes could not be represented as an unqualified advantage or victory for any party the reception of the Report among the partisans was less than euphoric.
The National Liberal Federation welcomed the Report even though it
fell short of the reforms advocated by the Party, (4) while the
Agents offered only 'qualified support'. (5)   However, Liberal
backbenchers meeting on 6 March urged the Government to proceed with
a Bill (6) as did a variety of bodies in the Labour Movement.   The
party's National Executive (7) resolved to summon a National Conference to demand early legislation;   even at this stage when Arthur
Henderson was still a loyal member of the War Cabinet the adoption
of Labour candidates in Liberal seats was going ahead and the party
naturally anticipated making gains if the Report could be passed
into law before the next election.   Accordingly, some 436 delegates
representing the Labour Party, the TUC and women's industrial organisations met on 20 March and called upon the parliamentary party to
secure the franchise for the bulk of wage-earning women, but otherwise accepted the Speaker's Report 'as a minimum'. (8)   A deputation, including the three Labour members of the Conference, was dis-
patched to communicate these feelings to the Prime Minister.

Unionist reaction, as expressed by the agents, was understandably
cooler: (9)

Although sorely tempted we do not intend to indulge in useless
criticism of the capacity of the Unionist representatives on the
Speaker's Conference for the task allotted them, but the feeling
is justifiably strong among agents that the representatives in
question have let their party down very badly.

They ascribed this to the fact that the 'knowledge of the subject
and the power of plausibility possessed by [Sir John Simon] and his
political friends completely hoodwinked the unfortunate representatives of the Unionist Party'.   Constituency reaction, as reflected
in letters sent in to the National Union, (10) was also rather unfavourable in that 81 local associations were against adoption of
the Report compared to only 4 in favour, while as many as 169 agents
were hostile and 23 friendly. (11)   A typical letter from Bridgewater threatened the loss of the party's local majority if the
leadership 'betrayed' them by accepting the Report. (12)

However, despite these discouraging developments, Lowther's
Report survived because its timing proved to be highly fortuitous.
Under Asquith's Government it was highly unlikely that a sweeping
measure of reform could have emerged, basically because Asquith did
not enjoy the loyalty and confidence of Bonar Law upon whom would
inevitably rest the responsibility for holding the Unionists in
line.   Instead Lloyd George, never a man to pass up his opportunities, reigned over a two-month-old Government;   later on in his Premiership as his dependence on the Unionists increased even Lloyd
George would have found it all but impossible to force this measure
on his colleagues and supporters, as his record from 1918 to 1922

shows.   Early in 1917, however, he was the leader who had freed the
Unionists from Asquith's grip, and his Government was recognised, as
Asquith's had not been, as primarily a war administration; it was
this, paradoxically, that made it easier to tackle measures of domestic reform.   Under Asquith the Unionists would instinctively
have rebelled against another of his partisan schemes to ensnare the
gullible Bonar Law; under Lloyd George the Unionists were sensible
of their greater power and of Bonar Law's restoration to a position
of proper authority at the Exchequer and in the War Cabinet; they
were less resentful and thus more amenable to Law's influence.
    The loyalty of Bonar Law gave Lloyd George his vital lifeline to
the Unionist backbenchers without which his chances of enacting a
Reform Bill were negligible; indeed for Lloyd George, who never
dominated his Government in domestic affairs any more than in military, the Conservative Leader provided a substitute for the political base he lacked, just as his personal Secretariat made up for his
deficiencies as an administrator.   It is difficult to follow the
Prime Minister's connection with the Reform Bill during 1917 not
simply because his papers give such a sketchy idea of his role but
because he deliberately avoided detailed day-to-day discussions on
the handling of the Bill in Parliament.   From the outset it had
been recognised that the Cabinet could not possibly keep meeting to
settle each difficult point that arose, (13) which for Lloyd George
was politically wise since it would not have done for a radical with
his record to have inaugurated his Premiership with a time-consuming
Reform Bill; constant attendances in the Commons for this as for
most other business were therefore out of the question for Lloyd
George who left the invidious task of foisting the Bill onto the
backbench rebels to his Tory minions.   Thus the credit due to him
is that for taking the initiative and pushing out the venture;
after that he left the work to others in the belief that the details were less important than the fact of a Bill itself.
    Nor should one forget the most obvious reason for Lloyd George's
apparently tenuous association with the Reform Bill: he had bigger
battles to fight elsewhere.   It was but natural that electoral
reform should have failed to dominate politics in 1917 in the way
that it had done in 1832, 1867 and 1884.   No doubt it aroused a
certain amount of debate and even emotion in the House of Commons,
though there was more controversy over Proportional Representation
and the Alternative Vote than over the rest of the Bill put together.   Perhaps, too, it penetrated to the general public; reform
was mentioned in the press, though one had to search for it amongst
all the war news.
    No one could catch Lloyd George neglecting the war for electoral
reform.   In the early months of 1917 one finds him very much absorbed in attempting to convince his generals of the wisdom of an
attack on Austria, and he is soon steeped in intrigue against Sir
Douglas Haig; in April British shipping losses from unrestricted
submarine warfare reached a peak; Woodrow Wilson brought the United
States into the war while Russia's effort was disintegrating.
These were some of the momentous events of the spring which distrac-
ted a Cabinet as yet undecided what to do with the Speaker's Report.
After April's attack on the Vimy Ridge the summer of 1917 was
marked by a series of Allied offensives as Haig used his free rein

to pursue fantasies of victory through the mud of Passchendaele
from August to November.   October brought the Italian disaster at
Caporetto, November the Bolshevik Revolution and Lord Lansdowne's
appeal for a negotiated peace.   Such was the background against
which MPs debated the Reform Bill during the summer and autumn of
1917.   It is, perhaps, surprising that the divisions on the Bill in
the House of Commons were as large as they were and debate so prolonged.   Yet the number of Members serving with the Army was only
approximately 150, many of whom enjoyed desk jobs in Britain.   Further, the Bill was received gratefully by many Members since it
helped to relieve their role as impotent spectators and restored
some of the normal functions of the House.

   Now there existed an intimate relationship between the Reform
Bill and the timing of the General Election.   For the 1918 Act,
destined to be Lloyd George's one *Liberal* achievement, was the product of the Parliament of 1910, the last fruit of the long and constructive partnership between Asquith and Lloyd George, as well as
of the new one with Bonar Law.   Without the Reform Bill it was unlikely that the Prime Minister would have tolerated until the end of
1918 a Parliament he so much disliked;   yet once committed to the
Bill he felt compelled to await not only its passage through Parliament but the preparation of a new register.   It was his choice from
these alternatives that determined the political timetable for 1917
and 1918.

   Consequently when Lloyd George hesitated over Lowther's Report he
was thinking only in part about the expected Unionist opposition:
he had his own reasons for holding back.   Not that he disliked the
proposals;   on the contrary he was tempted to enact them at once.
Bold radical Lloyd George, speaking to C.P. Scott in January wished
to embody the recommendations of the Report in a Bill and ask the
House to make up its mind. (14)   Yet his careful, calculating self
had had in his mind from the start an alternative strategy which
left no room for the reform project;   within days of assuming the
Premiership he was 'inclined to think that, if things went moder-
ately well, it might be as well anyhow to have an election in
March'. (15)   His administration had been formed on the specific
understanding, in which the King had acceded, that Lloyd George was
free to dissolve Parliament whenever he deemed it necessary. (16)
Now the Speaker's Report forced him to think hard about this possibility: 'As to passing a Reform Bill now his difficulty was that if
the Bill were carried he would be morally estopped from dissolving
until it could come into operation which would take some time.' (17)
Lloyd George returned repeatedly to the idea of an election as a way
through his difficulties.   In April he spoke to Lord Riddell (18)
about the terms to be offered to the Liberals and Labour for an
election, and to Addison (19) about a dissolution if the Irish obstructed the Bill to prolong the life of Parliament.   In a House so
full of hostile elements Lloyd George never felt very secure and was
a prey to fears, especially early in 1917, of some attempt by Asquithians and the Irish to defeat him on an Irish issue and replace
his Government without an election.   This possibility inclined him
to delay any franchise measure until an Irish settlement had been
reached. (20)   When considering prolonging Parliament's life in
April 1917 he demanded in exasperation: 'Why not just let it lapse

and get rid of Snowden, MacDonald and the other extremists.... He
should not hesitate to hold an election on the existing register,
however imperfect; at least a House elected on it would be more
representative than the existing one.' (21)   Again in October Lloyd
George informed C.P. Scott (22)

> with some irritation that he was getting rather tired of the
> Party truce and was not sure it would not have to be broken soon
> ... a new Franchise might compel a new Parliament.   Asken when,
> he said about November of next year.

Of course some suspicion attaches to these oft repeated threats
about a General Election designed for consumption by the Opposition.
Lloyd George was not likely to share with C.P. Scott, with whom his
relations were periodically strained, a definite intention to go to
the country; but Scott was precisely the sort of person to whom one
would reveal these thoughts if one wanted them spread among the Asquithian faithful, there to exercise a wholesome restraining effect
upon rebellious spirits.   None the less Lloyd George plainly had a
special interest, in view of his weakness under conditions of normal
party warfare, in an election fought around war issues, especially
the basic one, who should fight the war.   Milner shared this pre-
dilection for a dissolution, but Bonar Law continued to resist the
idea as he had all through the war because of his concern to stave
off the disruption of the Tory Party on which his rivals, Carson and
Curzon, and the unattached politicians, Lloyd George and Milner,
thrived.

This problem raised the whole question of Lloyd George's future.
If he saw himself as a war Premier, and could be content with that,
there was much sense in the strategy of a dissolution leading to a
markedly more Conservative Parliament, even though its life if
elected on the old Register was limited to two years. (23)   The
consequences of this for electoral reform are apparent; a Conservative Parliament would have argued that the Speaker's Conference had
represented the 1910 Parliament which, as the election had shown,
was out of touch with opinion in the country; as a result any Bill
could not have amounted to more than an emasculated version of the
Report dealing only with a scheme for voters absent in the Forces
for which a general desire could be said to exist.   Thus the spring
of 1917 was a critical time for the cause of reform; since there
existed no widespread popular desire for such a measure Lloyd George
stood in danger of succumbing to the temptation to put his Government on a sounder footing by bringing forward a khaki election at
the first opportunity.

However, after a matter of weeks as Prime Minister was Lloyd
George prepared to commit his future to the Conservative Party?   It
was doubtful: longer term considerations still pointed to a future
on the left of politics.   He was sensitive at this time to charges
of betraying his supporters and his principles, and he owed it to
them to demonstrate that he had not been shackled by his new associates.   What better way than by snatching a Reform Bill from the
jaws of the Tory tiger, thereby succeeding as a Liberal where
Asquith had for years failed?   On this basis the Bill had to come
first and the election later.

At the end of January, however, the Prime Minister could not be
entirely sure that a decision to go ahead with a Bill would not be

sufficient to dissolve his Government.   Immediately on the publication of the Report, Walter Long (24) pressed the Cabinet to adopt a Bill, which created 'great consternation in Unionist Central Office', (25) as well it might, for the Cabinet meeting was fixed for 5 February.   Steel-Maitland obtained a copy of Long's memorandum with the intention of circulating it among the National Union, whereupon Long threatened to expose him before the Cabinet.   (26) Steel-Maitland, as former party chairman, remonstrated with Long: 'Since your control over the Unionist Members of the Conference has been released through your leaving the L.G.B.   I think that they have really gone mad'; (27)   and he requested a personal interview so that he might demonstrate with the aid of statistics the disastrous nature of the proposals from the Unionist point of view. Long, however, had already been treated to one stern lecture by Sir George Younger, who had replaced Steel-Maitland as party chairman, without being dissuaded from his belief that a Bill should be prepared. (28)

   Yet Long's attempt to rush the Cabinet did not quite come off; they decided, 'Henderson dissenting, to "wait and see" re electoral reform'. (29)   Then the opposition had time to mobilise.   On 8 March Carson sent Lloyd George a resolution (30) signed by over 100 Unionist MPs denouncing the whole project on the grounds that the time was inopportune to indulge in such contentious proposals, that parliament had been prolonged beyond its legal term for the sole purpose of winning the war, and that no reforms ought to be submitted which omitted Ireland, as was the case with redistribution of seats.

   During February such fears had been stoked up by the experts of Conservative Central Office (31) who dismissed most of the registration reforms as 'all in favour of the Liberal-Labour Party';   the effect of losing the Ownership Vote they now put at thirty seats, plus twenty-seven prospective gains, much less than their estimates of October 1916;   as for the new franchise it would add two million men, 30 per cent to the urban and 20 per cent to the rural electorate;   of these three-quarters would be aged twenty-one to twenty-six years, 'young men of no fixed political opinion and over one million of these would belong to the Labouring classes'; (32)   the other half million were reckoned to be older men presently disfranchised by the registration system.   No calculation was now made as to the supposed voting intentions of these people, but the Unionist organisers noted the ominous rise of over two million in Trade Union membership since 1913 (33) as sufficient evidence of the danger. At the same time, however, they obviously expected the soldiers to help their cause in the boroughs (34) and believed that the Conference ought to have enfranchised all men of *military* age who had taken the Oath of Allegiance to the King.   It seemed unlikely that many men would take advantage of the Conference's proposals for absent voters since 'it will be difficult for anyone to say for certain where he will be six or seven months hence'. (35)

   Among a host of objections the main lines of the Central Office position were becoming clear: the troops' franchise had to be a real and effective one, the women voters were not a threat, the Alternative Vote must be scrapped, and Irish Redistribution included. Similar conclusions were being arrived at by a special sub-committee of the National Union which reported on 13 March; (36) but its detailed suggestions were designed for use only in the event of a Bill being presented; as yet it was not certain that matters would go that far.

In Cabinet the Central Office view found support from Carson (37) and Curzon, (38) the latter being particularly opposed to woman suffrage; Milner would also have preferred a General Election to a Reform Bill (39) and, as he frequently met Steel-Maitland, judging by his diary, he was doubtless urged to use his influence with Lloyd George to kill off the project. However, Milner twice missed Cabinet discussions on the question on 5 and 15 February when he was away on a mission to Russia, and he does not seem to have taken an active part in the later talks, leaving the matter to the regular politicians instead.

It was the backing of the Bonar Law-Long-Chamberlain-Balfour group that enabled the Prime Minister to get his way over the Bill and stood between him and the Unionist organisation, though Long alone represented the hard core of resistance. Law's initial verdict on the Report had been that while he had no objections to a Bill on the same lines he did fear excessive controversy (40) particularly over the great stumbling blocks of woman suffrage and Irish Redistribution. Like Lloyd George he had to weigh up the alternatives of dissolution or a Reform Bill. Long pointed out the dangers: on the one hand if they sought a further extension of Parliament's life without presenting a Bill to deal with the register they would provoke a dangerous situation in the House: (41) 'Asquith would be a fool not to take advantage of it'; on the other hand he shrank from an election 'which will mean handing the party over to Sir F[rederick] Banbury and the Party Agents'. Meanwhile Dr Addison urged the same point upon Lloyd George: 'if we are not to have an Election we must have a Bill to embody [the Report].' (42)

Long had been promoted from the local government board to the Colonial Office in the new Government, but he enthusiastically undertook to combat all Curzon's objections to parliamentary reform; (43) the proposed Bill, he thought, should be in the charge of a Minister, though the Government need not take an official view of the various clauses; it was immaterial that Parliament had outlived its normal span of life - the need was to settle the whole question at once in a spirit of compromise so as to obtain a representative post-war Parliament, a task which might be facilitated by encouraging Asquith and Henderson to place their names on the back of the Bill; as for Ireland the omission of redistribution could be rectified later if necessary by means of an amending Bill. On the question of the women's vote Long could substantiate his claims about the possibility of reaching a compromise for he had spoken with Mrs Fawcett who had given an assurance on behalf of some twenty-two suffrage societies that they would accept the Speaker's proposals provided that the Government incorporated them into a Bill at the start. (44) This would enable the Cabinet to avoid any public agitation by the women in the middle of the war.

In urging acceptance of the women's claim Long was somewhat imprecise in his use of statistics; when he described the proposed franchise as 'really extremely limited' (45) Walter Jerred pointed

out that not less than five million women were involved; Long amended his remark to 'limited'!   Certainly the Cabinet were under a
misapprehension about the numbers involved; Long himself apparently
worked on the assumption that a six-month residence qualification
would add two million men to the 6,758,000 on the existing Register, (46) deductions being made for removals which would cut out
aliens, criminals, lunatics, the common lodging house population,
vagrants and navvies.   In fact the estimated total was five million
short of the electorate on the 1918 Register, while the women exceeded predictions by two and a half million (see Appendix 10).

While the argument developed in Cabinet some backbenchers began
to demand to know the Government's intentions; questioned by one of
the Conference members, Basil Peto, Bonar Law suggested that the
House might debate a resolution on the Report: would such a resolution be proposed by the *Government*?   'I think it is obvious that
there would be no object in having this resolution if we were to
decide in advance exactly what was to be done.' (47)   Law had to
prevaricate so long as the Cabinet were unable to reach a decision,
and Ministers were themselves anxious to know what attitude the
backbenchers would take before committing themselves to a Bill.   As
Lowther put it, the difficulty lay in deciding how to bring the
Report before the House 'in such a way as to avoid making the Bill,
to be founded upon it, a Government measure (which might provoke opposition) and yet procure the general assent of the House to its
contents.' (48)

The solution to this emerged from an unexpected quarter when a
motion to adopt the Speaker's Report was moved by the new Leader of
the Opposition, Asquith.   The actual timing of this arrangement is
difficult to pinpoint, but it seems to have originated with a suggestion by Sir John Simon at an informal gathering of Liberal backbenchers in February; (49) at the same time Harcourt also advised
Asquith to take the initiative in pushing the Government to bring in
a Bill. (50)   By 26 February Lloyd George had accepted the
idea. (51)

Asquith's decision here is an interesting one in that it was one
of the very few initiatives emanating from the ex-Prime Minister
after his fall from power.   Indeed Asquith's behaviour after December 1916 has been passed over in such haste by his biographers (52)
that one sees little more than an old man relaxing, reading books
and wondering how to replace his lost source of income, while being
determined chiefly to avoid becoming a centre of opposition to the
n w Government.   Undoubtedly he played a very limited role, conspicuously failing to give his followers a lead over such issues as
the Indian Cotton Duties, the banning of overseas editions of the
'Nation', and Irish Conscription on which he was expected to attack
the illiberality of Lloyd George. (53)   Even the Corn Production
Act provoked no more than a critical speech, while the Maurice
Debate saw Asquith attacking the Government with a feather duster
when more effective weapons were to hand.   In these circumstances
when one does find Asquith making a definite move one has to scruti-
nise it carefully.

At first sight the decision to propose a motion on the Report was
far from being a hostile move; the remarks of Scott and Lowther,
confirmed by Lloyd George, (54) indicate that it had been arranged

by mutual consent.   Assuming that the Prime Minister wished to
adopt a Reform Bill he required a convincing expression of support
from the House of Commons.   A Minister could hardly take the initiative in advance of a Cabinet policy;   a member of the Conference
might have been selected, but there was no one of real standing on
the Unionist side, and a lesser figure would have appeared a mere
nominee of Lloyd George.   Yet no one could say that Asquith was in
the Prime Minister's pocket;   he was both independent and authoritative enough for so important a task;   and what could be more natural than that the Prime Minister who had set up the Conference
should now inaugurate a discussion on its findings?

Thus Asquith's Motion was directly helpful to Lloyd George.   The
question is why he should have been willing to assist his supplan-
ter.   For this the explanation is two-fold.   First, by edging
Lloyd George towards a Reform Bill he might have been leading him to
his downfall as Prime Minister.   Faced with a wide range of sweeping reforms the Cabinet could well have been trapped in endless
debate as Asquith knew from experience.   Moreover, it was not yet
known what view the Commons would take;   during March the Unionist
rebels gathered strength under Carson and the Peers lurked in the
background.   Even if the Unionists agreed to embark upon the Bill
everyone realised that in the months ahead, as the strain of each
unwelcome clause told upon the party's loyalty, there would come a
point when the ever-fearful Bonar Law would have to insist on dropping a measure that threatened Party unity and his leadership.   In
parting company with his Bill Lloyd George would loosen the ties of
his Liberal followers too and the whole exercise would provide a
useful demonstration of the futility of trying to rule through a
Conservative majority.

The validity of this hypothesis is in no way reduced by the complete failure of Asquith subsequently to exploit the opportunities
open to him in the debates on the Representation of the People Bill.
After proposing his Motion on 28 March he never spoke except on Proportional Representation, and sedulously avoided criticism of the
illiberal parts of the Bill.   In fact the opportunity for defeating
the Government was reduced by the Cabinet's wise strategy of stick-
ing rigidly to the Report, and also by the unexpectedly large majority supporting it in the Commons;   when the House voted by six to
one in favour of Asquith's Motion the prospect of passing a Bill was
transformed.   More importantly, Asquith sought always to avoid
being seen to be contriving the Government's defeat especially on
purely domestic issues;   he could never have replaced Lloyd George
on any issue that did not vitally involve, as the Maurice Debate
did, the running of the war.   The virtue of Asquith's Motion was
that its hostile potential was only covert.

However, one should not overlook the essentially defensive nature
of his strategy.   Given the drift of the Prime Minister's mind towards an election Asquith had to avoid provoking him into the kind
of khaki poll that he had striven to forestall since August 1914.
For the Asquithians would hardly be able to make credible their
claim to be supporting the Government when their leaders refused to
serve in it.   Thus for the sake of his Party and his own hopes of
returning to the Premiership Asquith had to preserve the 1910 Parliament for as long as possible, and a major Reform Bill, undertaken

in the summer of 1917 and occupying the two Houses until well into
1918, would contribute much to this objective.   Whether Asquith
appreciated all the possibilities of his initiative one cannot say,
but its effect was to defend his own position while placing Lloyd
George in a potentially embarrassing one.

In the Cabinet's thinking the Reform Bill and a dissolution were
still rival plans until the 26 March when they decided to legislate
on the Report; the very next day they sought a first reading for a
Bill to prolong Parliament's life once more and on 28 March the
House debated Asquith's Motion.   It was touch and go on the Reform
Bill for Lloyd George became most irritated by the Irish Members who
obstructed the Bill to prolong parliament's life, and the Cabinet
reconsidered the measure on 16 April, the day before it was due for
a Second Reading debate. (55)   In the event they persisted and the
Bill was passed by 286 to 52, the main parties spurning the Nationalists' suicidal desire for an election.

After the large Cabinet meeting on 26 March Lloyd George had been
euphoric: (56)

> My attitude on the franchise has achieved great things.   I have
> forced the Cabinet to take a progressive turn.   I made it clear
> to them that I was not going to be dragged at the heel of the
> Tory reactionaries who support them.

Thus spoke the boy David; but in reality the Tory philistines had
done a lot to overcome their own Goliath as Dr Addison's notes indicate. (57)   For when the Prime Minister urged the adoption of the
Report he was swiftly rebuffed by Sir George Younger and Lord
Edmond Talbot, the Chief Whip, who had attended in order to explain
the views of the protesters.   It was Long and Lord Robert Cecil
who, according to Addison, poured scorn upon the prophecies of the
election experts and gave Lloyd George vigorous support, while Bonar
Law, though also supporting, was 'timid as usual'.   Lloyd George
had contrived to bring pressure on the anti-reformers from another
direction by inducing Henderson to play the 'heavy truculent wor-
kingman', which, if Frances Stevenson's account is to be believed,
he performed with *élan*: (58)

> While the meeting was going on, I was sitting in my room, when
> suddenly I heard someone shouting and banging their fist on the
> Cabinet table.   This went on for a long time and there was no
> doubt it was someone in a great rage.   I thought D. was having a
> bad time and that his Tory colleagues were going to resign in a
> body.   Not at all.   It was Henderson putting his case, as D.
> told me afterwards ... and the result was that the Cabinet agreed
> to accept the Speaker's Report....   This pleased the Liberals
> mightily.

Although the Cabinet Minutes do say that a decision was reached
to introduce a Bill embodying the Speaker's Report, Milner told his
private secretary that the discussion had 'veered towards introduction of legislation'; (59) since Milner was such a precise, meticu-
lous individual it is unlikely that he would have expressed it in
this way if a formal decision had been taken.   Certainly the Cabinet's agreement was subject to two major qualifications: the women
women's suffrage clause would be left entirely to a free vote of
the House - and its loss would not affect the Bill as a whole - as
were the other proposals that had not been unanimous; also the

Conference was to be invited to *reconsider* the question of Proportional Representation. (60)   There is no indication that the Speaker was willing to do this, and the Proportional Representation proposal which had been a unanimous recommendation went into the Bill though, again, without the Government's support.

It seems most likely that the Cabinet hesitated over legislation until they received a convincing display of support from Parliament; before the final version of the Minutes was produced the issue had effectively been settled by the debate two days later in the Commons.   In the intervening period, however, the Cabinet desired to withold the news of their 'decision' particularly from the Unionist Party representatives who had no doubt left the meeting after stating their case.   In fact, on 27 March some fifty-two Unionist backbenchers gathered under the leadership of Arthur Steel-Maitland, who was now an Under-Secretary at the Colonial Office, to declare their support for a hostile amendment to Asquith's Motion to be moved by Clavell Salter. (61)   On the previous day, when the Cabinet had been in session, Steel-Maitland had sent a note to Bonar Law to the effect that 'as it was an open question, I proposed to speak on behalf of Clavell Salter's amendment'. (62)   But the Cabinet no longer wished it to be treated as an open question, though they hesitated to say so;   thus, according to Steel-Maitland:

Later in the afternoon Mr. Bonar Law passed me in the lobby and said he had wished to speak to me himself, but not having time would I ask Lord Edmund Talbot as to what had happened at the Cabinet meeting that afternoon....   He [Talbot] told me that, as far as he could gather no decision whatever had been reached at that Cabinet Meeting.   Subsequently Sir George Younger told me the same.

Steel-Maitland thereupon allowed his name to go down in support of Salter's amendment, but on the afternoon of the Commons' debate, 'Mr. Walter Long leant across to me and asked me if I was going to speak....   He then spoke to Mr. Bonar Law and the Prime Minister who were beside him, and a discussion ensued, as a result of which I received a card forbidding me to speak.' (63)   Written by Bonar Law, this card read: (64)

The Government have definitely decided that they will recommend the House to adopt the proposals of the Speaker's Conference.   I do not think therefore that it is *possible* for a member of the Government to speak against this decision.

In this way Law and Long tried to crush opposition within the party, and with success, for the voice of Steel-Maitland, carrying all the authority of the ex-Chairman of the Party, was not heard in the Commons debate.

It was an unusually full House that awaited Asquith's opening speech on 28 March, a fact which the anti-reformers professed to see as an indication of the violent controversy about to be unleashed. Both Asquith and the Prime Minister chose to stress that the circumstances from which the Speaker's Conference had emerged virtually obliged them to adopt a more comprehensive approach to electoral reform than either had intended;   both were careful, also, to enthuse less over the actual proposals, though Asquith gracefully embraced the women's cause, than over the Speaker himself for his personal achievement in winning agreement.   This was shrewd tactics

for to present a compromise on electoral reform as a contribution to
national unity was to deprive the critics of the patriotic argument
from the start.   As the 'Yorkshire Post' somewhat sourly remarked,
it would be 'bad form' to oppose proposals emanating from the much
admired Speaker.

Hostile speeches were consequently confined to a few bolder
Unionists supporting Salter's amendment; their arguments may be
summarised briefly: a Reform Bill was calculated to arouse pre-war
party passions; public opinion demanded soldiers' registration not
wholesale reform; in its seventh year Parliament had no mandate but
to win the war.   However the critics won debating points rather
than votes.   For, with Bonar Law and Long as solid as the two Liberal leaders in support of the Motion the rebels entirely lacked
leaders of stature.   Despite being 'very nervous of the old fash-
ioned Tories', as Lloyd George (65) put it, Bonar Law delivered
another bold and candid defence of his colleagues, denying that the
policy had been foisted upon them by Lloyd George: 'This is not the
result of the contamination of the Friends with whom I know work;
it is original sin.'

In the event Asquith's Motion won approval by 343 votes to 64,
the minority being Unionist Members while the majority comprised 188
Liberals, 79 Unionists, 51 Irish Nationalists and 24 Labour Members,
plus Mr Pemberton Billing.   Unionist revolt at this stage might
have been expected to kill off the project, but Bonar Law remained
undeterred by this ominously even split in his party.   The vote
could not be represented as an overt attack on the Government since
the ostensible object of the debate had been to ascertain whether
they ought to introduce a Bill; if a Bill were now unavoidable at
least a show of strength would serve to demonstrate to Lloyd George
that he would have to conciliate Unionist opinion on certain points
unless he wished to face the collapse of Bonar Law's authority in
the party.   In view of the abstention of half the Unionist Members
it is difficult to estimate the full extent of their opposition, but
'The Times' (66) felt certain that after registering their protest
many Members 'will loyally abide by the decision of the Government'.

This view was partly borne out by the next division on the Second
Reading of the Bill on 23 May.   On that occasion the vote was 331
to 42.   Liberal and Labour voting hardly altered, though the Irish,
who recorded only 21 votes, had already lost interest.   However,
the Unionists shifted decisively in favour of the Bill by 110 to
42.   Of the original 64 opponents 11 had become supporters, 22 abstained, and 30 continued in their opposition, being joined by a
dozen extra rebels.   The months ahead were to show a hard core of
between 50 and 60 persistent anti-reformers whose numbers were liable to be swollen by more disgruntled Members on occasion.   Essentially, however, the leadership had won the battle for a Bill by
their resolution during March, and the National Union began to concentrate on skirmishing in Committee to retrieve lost ground without
challenging the whole Bill. (67)   The party chairman, Sir George
Younger, assured Long that serious opposition from the original
rebels would now cease - an optimistic prediction - and that the
machinery of Central Office 'will certainly not be used in any an-
tagonistic form to the main principles of the measure'; (68)   in
return for this Younger wanted an assurance that the Upper House

would be reformed;   for although the adult male franchise was acceptable 'I did not regard it as consistent either with wise statesmanship or with National safety that we should combine manhood suffrage
with Single Chamber Government'. (69)   Long hastened to assure
Younger that he was indeed pressing upon the Prime Minister the idea
of another Conference on reform of the Second Chamber; (70)   it
would have 'a very excellent and moderating effect upon those who
voted against us', he told Lloyd George. (71)

For the Prime Minister the debate on 28 March gave a clear invitation to proceed with a Bill;   the problem lay in the fact that
half of his Unionists might oppose him while possibly a half of the
'reformers' could be reckoned his political opponents.   He had
therefore to avoid provoking a union of these two, admittedly ill-
assorted, groups which could defeat him.   Since the Liberals and
Labour basically wanted the Bill it would be foolish to antagonise
them by trying to conciliate the Unionists at the outset;   nor did
he have either time or inclination for endless horse-trading over
each clause of the Bill.   The safest possible course lay in par-
tially dissociating the Government from the Bill, and instead,
appealing constantly to the authority of the compromise already
worked out by the Speaker.   Thus when taxed by a deputation of
women suffragists on the relationship between the Government and the
Bill Lloyd George trod warily;   declining Mrs Pankhurst's request
that he should take personal charge of the Bill he explained: (72)

> I am not sure what the arrangement will be about Government whips
> for any part of the Bill, because our view is that this ought to
> be a House of Commons measure - that is the principle upon which
> we have proceeded with this - and not a Government Bill....   We
> take the responsibility of conducting this Bill through the House
> of Commons, but the measure itself is a House of Commons measure
> which every section of the Commons is equally responsible for ...
> the strength of our position is that we are acting upon an agreed
> Report.   The moment you depart from that I think it will mean
> disaster to the whole of the proposals.

Government Whips were, in fact, put on, though with variable effect.
Lloyd George himself never uttered another word on any stage of the
Bill in Parliament after his speech on 28 March, and voted only
twice;   Bonar Law, too, kept out of the way except for one or two
critical occasions when he came down to rally the Unionist loyalists.   The Reform Bill was, in short, an illegitimate War Baby of
mixed parentage to which Lloyd George played uncle rather than
father.

Part three

Chapter 8

THE UNIONIST REVOLT

It seems to be thought that the mother of Parliaments has become
a toothless old crone, who cannot chew her own dinner, but re-
quires to have it prepared in a suitable manner by skilled persons in order that it may be sufficiently digestible for her.
She is to be given what I believe is called Benger's Food, and
this Bill is Benger's Food, and you, Sir, and your Committee are
Bengers.   (Lord Hugh Cecil, H.C. Deb., 22 May 1917)

By the summer of 1917 Lloyd George's new system of war administration had reached maturity; the hasty improvisations that became the
hallmark of his Premiership, though still in evidence, paled into
obscurity beside the apparently dominant figure of the Prime Minister.   He presided over the five-man War Cabinet, reinforced by his
own personal Secretariat at 10 Downing Street and serviced by the
Cabinet Secretariat under the indefatiguable Colonel Hankey.   Beneath this apex committees rose and fell in waves, and the new
Ministries and Controllerships sprang up to handle labour, pensions,
shipping, food, blockade, air, reconstruction and National Service.
Into them marched Lloyd George's battalions of non-political experts
and businessmen, Geddes, Maclay, Fisher and Devonport, as well as
the tribe of newspaper proprietors, Rothermere, Beaverbrook and
Northcliffe.   Since the new men possessed few party ties and little
following they were less of a threat to Lloyd George and served only
to elevate further the role of the Prime Minister in this period.
    Appearances, however, were deceptive, for within weeks Lloyd
George had reduced the new Cabinet system to a shambles and Hankey
to despair by his unbusinesslike methods of Government. (1)   The
vast apparatus of Government, designed to enable the Prime Minister
to maintain personal control, proved to be a power in its own right
rather than a prop to Lloyd George's.   Sometimes the new appoint-
ments were failures like Devonport; more often the politicians such
as Derby and Carson at the War Office and Admiralty respectively
proved to be the pliable tools of their departments not the agents
of Lloyd George.   Thus, for all his intrigues the Prime Minister
never got his way over the central questions of military strategy.
Apart from Munitions the major posts were in the hands of Conservatives whose followers provided most of the Government's majority in

Parliament.   Lloyd George's contacts with them, apart from his political breakfasts, were slight, and his appearances in the House
became comparatively infrequent lest he provoke where his Conservative allies had to be conciliated.

This problem became acute after the resounding vote in the Commons on 28 March in support of the Speaker's Report which obliged
the Cabinet Reformers to follow up their initiative with a Bill.
To escort the measure through the Commons Sir George Cave, the Home
Secretary, was selected.   This was a prudent choice; now sixty
years old, Cave had vacated the Solicitor Generalship in December
1916 on the understanding that he would be given the next important
judicial vacancy, for the only ambition remaining to him was to
become Lord Chancellor before retiring. (2)   Such a man would not
find his work on the Reform Bill too much of an embarrassment in
what remained of his career.   Moreover, Cave proved useful to Lloyd
George in handling awkward legislation; widely liked and trusted in
the House, his courtesy made him difficult to attack especially on
the Unionist side.   Neither Cave nor his assistant, Hayes Fisher
who was now President of the Local Government Board, were more than
mediocre politicians, but in view of the preoccupations of the leading figures with the war and the natural unwillingness of leading
Unionists to prejudice their future careers, it was the best that
could be done.

However, Cave had barely embarked upon the task of drafting the
Bill when he fell ill with pneumonia at the beginning of April. (3)
According to Bonar Law, he had set his heart on the Bill, (4) but
was adamant that no time should be lost; as a result Walter Long
stepped in on the understanding that Cave would take over the Bill
when well enough, (5) and little time was lost.   Long began work
half way through April and by early May had produced a draft Bill
for the Cabinet's approval. (6)

This original Bill was designed to reflect the wishes of the
Speaker's Conference, even though it was later modified on the
grounds that the draftsmen had not interpreted the Report correctly.
First, the franchise itself represented a considerable simplification of the seven-franchise system of the post-1884 era.   An adult
man would enjoy a six-month residence qualification which he could
carry with him if he moved within the same constituency or within
the same, or a contiguous, county or borough.   Nor would he forfeit
that franchise for receipt of Poor Relief of less than thirty days
during the qualifying period.   For men in the Armed Forces one
month's residence would serve as qualification in the present war,
while all those whose normal occupation kept them away from home
could apply to vote by post as absent voters.   Women, subject to
the age limit to be determined by Parliament, were to be granted a
parliamentary franchise as local government electors or as wives of
such.   Only one additional vote was to be permitted for which one
might qualify either as a University elector, or by possession of a
£10 business qualification.

Second, the simplified registration system was to be operated by
Clerks to the County Councils and by Town Clerks in boroughs.
Appeals against their decisions were to go before the County Courts,
and half the cost of registration would be paid by the Treasury.
Third, the conduct of elections was to be modified.   The work of

Returning Officers was to be performed by Town Clerks and Clerks to
the County Councils whose expenses were to be fixed by the Treasury;
each candidate would place a £150 deposit with them to be forfeited
if his poll amounted to less than one eighth of the total.   The
scale for expenses was to be fixed at 7d. per elector in counties
and 5d. in boroughs, while any meetings, publications or advertisements in support of a candidate but omitted from his list of expenses would constitute a corrupt practice.   Finally, all constituencies were to poll on the same day.   Fourth, the new system of constituencies, yet to be worked out in detail by the Boundary Commissioners, would be based upon units of 50,000 population for existing
seats and 70,000 for new ones.   The Alternative Vote was to prevail
everywhere except in three, four and five-Member boroughs which
would use the Single Transferable Vote as would contiguous boroughs
which could be grouped to form three, four or five-Member seats.
Cities such as London would be treated as single units for parliamentary purposes and divided into seats of not more than five and
not less than three Members.   Existing two-Member boroughs and
counties would be divided unless the Single Transferable Vote were
not adopted in which case the boroughs only might remain undivided.

    The general rule was that proposals which had been unanimously
agreed by the Conference were to be insisted upon by the Government,
while 'majority' proposals were to go to a free vote, for example,
woman suffrage and the Alternative Vote.   However, the Government
made two important exceptions to this; first the proposal for
Absent Voters, a majority proposal only, was to be treated as an in-
tegral part of the Bill, and second, the Proportional Representation
scheme, a unanimous recommendation, was to be put to a free vote.

    Only ten days after the Cabinet had inspected Long's draft the
Bill came up for its First Reading, a perfunctory affair without a
division.   A week later Cave returned to the scene to initiate the
Second Reading Debate on 23 May, and on 6 June the Reform Bill went
into Committee.   The object of such rapid advance was to obviate
the activity within the Unionist Party designed to amend the measure.   The Cabinet endeavoured to keep one step ahead of the party
all the way, and successfully, as is apparent from the correspondence between Lord Derby and the Lancashire Conservatives whose
criticisms he duly reported to Bonar Law but to which he declined to
give any support. (7)

    Meanwhile the Executive of the National Union had met on 22 May
to give urgent consideration to ways of improving the Bill;   the
meeting expressed particular dissatisfaction about the provisions
for the troops and decided to set up a sub-committee to prepare
amendments. (8)   Most Unionists had ceased to take the apocalyptic
view of reform expressed earlier by Central Office and concentrated
on the details.   Basically the National Union took their stand on
the terms laid down by their sub-committee in March, which allowed a
great deal: male suffrage if it included the troops, simplified
Registration, Redistribution provided Ireland was included, and a
concurrent scheme for reconstituting the House of Lords.   Beyond
this general position it was assumed that there existed much scope
for regaining ground by intelligent committee work which was undertaken by the National Union without either help or support from the
party leaders;   virtually all the amendments tabled by Unionists

during the summer can be traced directly to the sub-committee's
report in March.

Within two weeks of their meeting on 22 May the Executive had
amassed 150 amendments of which fifty had been circulated to Members
of Parliament. (9)   On 7 June, at the suggestion of Archibald Salvidge, the Liverpool Unionist boss, the National Union decided to
issue their own whips through the agency of Colonel Gretton MP.
Assistance had been received from the Lancashire Unionists who sent
a deputation to London to explain the faults of the Bill to
MPs, (10) leaving several experienced agents behind in order to
help draft amendments and coach the Members who were to move them;
a special committee of agents sat giving day by day advice while the
Bill was under discussion.   'I should like you to know', Salvidge
(11) piously informed Lord Derby, 'that all the amendments are
reasonable, not designed for any party advantage but to improve the
Bill.'   That Salvidge should have written in this way to his political chief is some indication of the handicap under which the
Unionists were operating.   They knew they had to reckon with the
active opposition, or at best, indifference, of Bonar Law, Long,
Cave, Chamberlain and Derby to any efforts at deradicalising the
Bill, not to mention the Government Whips issued against their
amendments. (12)

Long anticipated no real difficult at first, unless the Unionist
rebels managed to combine with the 'independent obstructing radicals' at some stage;   'Asquith is all right', he said, 'but the bulk
of the men who sit on that bench are all wrong, and would take advantage of any opportunity to cause trouble.' (13)   What really
rattled him were the preparations made by the National Union which
he urged Bonar Law to take in hand: (14)

> The Reform Bill is a Bill of the Government - you are a member of
> the Government, and the Central Office officials are your ser-
> vants, paid and appointed by you to carry out your policy - not
> to dictate to you and your colleagues what your policy should be
> ... there is nothing between this Bill and another shipwreck of
> the same kind as that which overtook the late Administration.

Some distinction should have been made here between the Central
Office and the National Union representing the constituency parties
and consequently less amenable to the Leader's control.   The unfortunate Bonar Law, who could please nobody, was apt to be written off
by his colleagues as a Leader 'especially as he was in Aitken's
pocket, and absolutely lacked courage'. (15)   So frequent are the
disparaging remarks that one easily forgets that he both kept the
Party together and survived to become Prime Minister.   His apparent
weakness no doubt led his potential supplanters to tolerate him as a
caretaker, but it also meant that he would not attempt to prevent
the party improving a Bill which they had accepted with reluctance;
a strong Leader would have been in danger of provoking a serious
split of the sort that the Liberals suffered.   Bonar Law retained
the personal loyalty of Sir George Younger, the Party Chairman, Lord
Edmund Talbot, the Chief Whip, and Sir Harry Samuel, Chairman of the
Council of the National Union, but never expected them to keep their
followers on too tight a rein;   by allowing them to work away for a
few concessions which he could expect to obtain from Lloyd George
anyway, he provided a safety valve for the pent-up emotions of backbenchers and agents already frustrated for lack of useful activity.

Meanwhile the other parties presented a similar spectacle of dis-
array.   The Labour Party proved to be a negligible factor in the
passage of the Reform Bill, both before and after Arthur Henderson's
departure from the Government; in fact there seems to have been
only one initiative from the party on the lodger vote; though
Ramsay MacDonald spoke from time to time there was no real leadership of the party with Henderson and Thomas preoccupied with organisation in the country.   No doubt the concentration of Labour on
the War Emergency National Workers Committee and, subsequently, on
the constituencies and the new Party programme reduced the damage
done by splits at the parliamentary level in the party.   But the
growth of the Labour Movement was by no means unrelated to parliamentary events; the neglect of Parliament had the unfortunate
effect of leaving approximately a third of the Labour Members to
vote with the Government against radical amendments pressed by the
Opposition thereby reducing to a handful the party's impact in each
division.   Now it is easy to see why this did not disturb Labour
politicians who felt convinced that any Reform Bill would help them;
but the changes in detail often hurt Labour's prospects and produced
an electoral system in which, notwithstanding the democratic franchise, Conservative Government became the order of the day for a
quarter of a century.

Until towards the end of 1917 the Irish Nationalists played a
minimal role in the passage of the Bill; their seventy-odd votes
properly disciplined as in the past would have turned the scale in a
number of the often rather small divisions particularly with regard
to Conscientious Objectors, Proportional Representation and the
Alternative Vote.   Later in the year they mustered some forty votes
for divisions on Irish aspects of the Bill, but during the summer it
was rare for as many as twenty Members to participate.

If Labour and the Nationalists neglected the Bill much of the explanation lay in the dissolution of the bonds that had bound them to
the Liberal leadership.   Just as the Asquithian Liberals were un-
clear about their general attitude towards the Government so they
found no very definite strategy with regard to a Bill which seemed
to represent the maximum they could expect under the circumstances
of a Coalition.   As a result Liberals comprised the majority of the
Bill's supporters, thereby creating the illusion of a Liberal measure
risen through the ruins of the party.   Not until the autumn and
winter of 1917 did the adherents of Asquith and Lloyd George begin
to be increasingly separated from each other by their voting on the
Reform Bill; at that stage the possibility emerged of reviving the
three-party alliance under pressure of the concessions being made by
the Government to the Unionist side.   In fact a radical alliance
never materialised, though the Reform Bill did breathe a little life
into the comatose Liberal leadership.   However, when the ex-Ministers did get around to arranging a meeting to discuss strategy on
the Bill - pathetically late on 5 June the day before the Bill went
into Committee - neither Asquith nor Harcourt attached much importance to the meeting. (16)   They saw no prospect of liberalising
the Bill beyond the compromise reached by the Conference and confined themselves largely to defending and accurately interpreting
the Report, a task for which Simon, one of the members, was obviously qualified; Simon, in fact, was absent on military service for

much of the time and Herbert Samuel became the closest approximation
to an Opposition spokesman that the Asquithian frontbench could provide.

In fact when the Commons plunged into Committee on 6 June the
Liberal ex-Ministers were ready only in the sense that Simon and
Dickinson were in attendance to ensure that the Home Secretary was
never edged away from the terms of the Report by his fellow Unionists.   The strength of the Unionist pressure was quickly put to the
test.   In ,the absence of a leader of real weight the most effective
backbench champions were Sir Frederick Banbury, whose efforts earned
him the wry compliment of being the only Tory left in the House, and
Lord Hugh Cecil to whom belonged the distinction of making the best
speeches both for and against the Bill; but Cecil was alone in
debating reform in terms of the theory of representation instead of
the compromises and expedients which had become the order of the
day.

In his initial foray Banbury rallied more Unionists than Bonar
Law could muster, a feat achieved by proposing at the commencement
of business that there should be an entirely separate Bill for redistribution of seats. (17)   Here Banbury capitalised on the feeling in the House that the Home Secretary was rushing the matter
along too fast; though the House had not been consulted yet about
the principles of redistribution, the Boundary Commissioners had
been put to work so that when their schedules were available in a
month or two's time it would be too late to challenge them.   The
opposition to redistribution especially from rural areas obviously
weighed with Long who had already entertained the idea of a separate
Bill; (18) but in rejecting this suggestion Cave carried the House
by 217 to 65 on a division.   Only a quarter of his majority were
Unionist Members who were actually outnumbered (62-54) by those
supporting Banbury.   This demonstration of strength prompted Cave
to conciliate the rebels by offering a special debate on the Instructions to the Boundary Commissioners on 11 June.   Long sought
out one of the leading rebels, Colonel R.A. Sanders after the debate
to suggest that he should arrange with Cave the wording of an amendment limiting the area of constituencies, so that the Government
might accept it. (19)

When the promised debate took place it proved advantageous to the
Unionists in two ways.   Members indulged in pleas on behalf of the
agricultural areas which were alleged to be in danger of losing
thirty seats through redistribution.   In view of the food shortages
in 1917 the cause of agriculture was much in vogue among MPs, but
Cave stood firmly on the principle of one-vote-one-value, with two
qualifications.   The first of these was Mr Salter's amendment to
take into account the size of electorate where the ratio of population to electors was abnormal, as for example in a barrack town such
as his own seat at Aldershott.   The second and more important
change emanated from the Unionist Member for Windsor, Mr Mason, who
desired to instruct the Commissioners to avoid producing constituencies of an inconvenient size or character.   Accepting this involved
Cave in throwing over Sanders' more precise and controversial amendment.   However, Long again tried to reassure Sanders afterwards by
promising that the Commissioners would be told to stretch a point in
favour of agriculture. (20)   'I don't trust him much', Sanders

noted; but conceded later that the redistribution proposals 'have
more than fulfilled my expectations as regards agriculture'. (21)
The effect of the two amendments in the final scheme was to allow
some fifteen to seventeen seats to agricultural counties which, on
a strict interpretation of their population, they could not have
had. (22)   Long did not worry about this increase in the total
number of Members because 'some form of Home Rule must be adopted
without much delay' (23) thereby substantially reducing the size of
the House.   The Unionists, content with these concessions, did not
challenge the radical redistribution proposals being incorporated
into the Instructions to the Boundary Commissioners.

During the same debate another Unionist moved that the Commissioners 'shall act on the assumption that Proportional Representation is not adopted'. (24)   On a division this was carried by 150
votes to 143, a narrow defeat for Proportional Representation which
may be ascribed partly to the fact that its supporters had not expected it to be debated so soon, and particularly to the heavy
Unionist vote (86 to 39) against it.   However this hostility had
been building up for some time as is evident from the March report
of the National Union's sub-committee (25) which had drawn especial
attention in its remarks on Clause 1 to the likely effect of Proportional Representation on the business franchise in boroughs.   The
problem arose because the scheme for multi-member constituencies in
the large boroughs obviously reduced the number of separate voting
districts;   and since Hayes Fisher had already confirmed that no
more than one vote might be cast in any one constituency (26) it
followed that many of the business votes would not materialise.
Parliament had only to omit Proportional Representation, and revert
to single-Member seats to open up a whole *new* field for dual voting
in large boroughs.   In this way the Unionists could win back a
number of plural votes without actually stating this objective and
with the tacit support of their leaders in view of the free vote
allowed on Proportional Representation.

To set against this, however, the Unionists had not made much
progress in debates on the central question of the male franchise in
Clause 1 of the Bill.   A series of questions and time-wasting
amendments by Hugh Cecil, Colonel Sanders, Colonel Gretton and Major
Newman paved the way for a serious amendment moved by Banbury to add
an extra franchise for owners of land or premises of £5 annual
value;   this amounted to a restoration of the ownership vote with a
minimum value on the property to limit the creation of faggot
votes. (27)   Cave flatly rejected this on the grounds that it would
entirely upset the compromise on which the Bill rested, in which he
was backed up by two of the Unionist Members of the Conference,
Donald MacMaster and Sir Robert Williams.   Faced with an impasse
the rebels - Major Hunt, Mr Burdett Coutts, Mr Rawlinson, Mr Nield
and Mr MacNeill - indulged in some rather bitter remarks at the expense of the Home Secretary.   'The Unionist leaders', Major Hunt
summed up, 'as they always do, have given the rank and file of the
party away.'   However, with Long, Cave, and F.E. Smith present
there was a modest rallying of sixty-eight Unionists to the Government against the thirty-seven mustered by the rebels (see Appendix
8).   Something more subtle than simple confrontations with Cave
were obviously necessary.

Ronald MacNeill then attempted this, at first with some success, when he tried to alter the provisions relating to successive voting. The Bill, in accordance with the Report, allowed an elector to retain his vote on moving if his new residence was within the same constituency, the same parliamentary borough or county or a contiguous one.   Now MacNeill proposed to require that such persons should be resident at their new addresses for at least thirty days prior to the date of registration, the justification being that the clause would otherwise facilitate 'swallow voting', or the transfer of voters into marginal constituencies by the party agents for a single night's residence and a bogus vote.   The Liberals prized the proposals in the Bill, even though somewhat anomalous, as a big step towards continuous registration, for most people were now expected to be able to carry their votes with them especially in London where the losses had been heavy.   Moreover with the increase in the size of the electorate to some 20,000 to 25,000 per constituency the impact of swallow voters was rendered less serious and the practice less attractive.   None the less it is clear that Long took the view that the new residence qualification would serve to encourage bogus votes of this sort: (28)   'If the Bill is passed without amendment, there are very few Unionist seats in Ulster which will be safe.' The Government therefore agreed to the thirty days requirement for residence which would have had the effect of reducing the number of electors considerably.

Luckily for the Liberals the debate on this amendment had to be terminated for lack of time which gave the registration experts the opportunity to devise a solution to meet both Unionist and Liberal fears.   Their suggestion, proposed next day by Aneurin Williams, (29) was neat and fair.   The problem lay essentially in establishing whether a removal was a *bona fide* one or not;   if a man moved a month before the end of the qualifying period it was a fair indication that he intended to stay;   similarly, if he moved on the last day of the qualifying period but remained at his new address for a month afterwards he had made a genuine change of residence; such persons ought not to be deprived of their votes.   Therefore Williams proposed that a man should lose his place on the Register if he moved within the last month of the qualifying period and stayed less than a month at his new residence;   assuming he did stay for a month he kept his vote.   In the face of this Cave abandoned the Unionist amendment to the irritation of Banbury.   Wiliams's expedient had narrowly foiled the rebels' best attempt to ease a plank out of the compromise.

Although the Unionists saw the futility of pushing their amendment to a division they could hardly stifle their resentment at Cave's decision.   Hugh Cecil took the opportunity to lecture the Government on the lack of theory or principle behind the Bill; (30) as he saw it they were abandoning the concept of the representation of *interests*, or at any rate severely modifying it by abandoning plural voting, while still refusing to accept the theory of the vote as an attribute of citizenship which plainly required that a man might take his vote with him wherever he went.   Sir John Simon and G.J. Wardle solemnly pronounced themselves convinced by Cecil's lucid exposition, but no one wished to act upon his suggestions.

Still undaunted, Banbury next proposed to leave out the provision

that London should be treated as a single parliamentary
borough; (31) this of course, would have had the same sort of
effect as the previous amendment in disfranchising voters who moved,
and it was therefore unacceptable.   Again Banbury, who did not find
it worthwhile to go to a division, seemed only to be filling up the
cup of Unionist anger, perhaps in the hope of squeezing concessions
from the Government later.   When Colonel Sanders proposed that the
new franchise for 'business premises' should be taken to include
land, both Cave and Simon agreed. (32)   Major Newman then attempted
to preserve the business vote for people who by taking a partner
might reduce the *per capita* value of their enterprise below the
level of £10 and consequently forfeit the vote; (33) but the Home
Secretary rejected this, and with Long and F.E. Smith rallied forty-
nine Unionists in the lobby against thirty-two rebels.

Banbury made one last effort to dislodge the compromise on Clause
1 with an amendment to omit the provision that in the counties only
two joint occupiers could be registered in respect of the same premises unless they were *bona fide* partners.   Back came the by now
familiar reply from Hayes Fisher: ordinarily he would have agreed
with Banbury, but the Conference had worked on the understanding
that the law relating to joint occupation should remain unchanged,
and so it must.   This time only twenty-two Unionists rebelled
against forty-three who backed the Government.

For the Liberals Willoughby Dickinson (34) raised one point of
concern; the Bill did not specify that a man with two qualifications in the same constituency could vote only once, a practice
which had been disallowed since 1878.   Since the present Bill re-
pealed the Act of 1878 Dickinson wanted some safeguard against dual
voting in the same constituency which the Conference had obviously
not intended to arise.   Hayes Fisher undertook to amend the rules
in the schedule to remedy this defect.   Thus the House disposed of
all amendments and passed Clause 1 after what was a rather inadequate debate (35) considering the radical nature of its contents.
While a handful of Unionists voiced their dismay, most Members
found it hardly worthwhile to join the discussion.   Unionists who
were accepting the clause without particularly liking it, found it
best to keep silence; while for the Liberals there was little
point either in rubbing in their victory or complaining that the
clause did not go far enough.   The outcome was therefore never in
doubt.   In the five divisions on 6 and 7 June the rebel vote had
fluctuated between sixteen and sixty-two; in each case some 70 per
cent to 75 per cent of the Government's vote had been provided by
non-Unionists.   All the efforts of Banbury and Cecil had foundered
on rigid adherence to the hallowed compromise.   Indeed the Government had hardly entered into debate at all except in so far as it
became necessary to establish what the intentions of the Conference
had been; nothing of significance had been added to or subtracted
from it.   The chief role of the radical parties had been to emphasise how much they were swallowing in the cause of compromise,
thereby to bolster the Home Secretary in his resistance to Unionist
amendments.

Clause 2 dealing with the University Franchise passed Committee
with little discussion and no divisions, but Clause 3, on the local
government Franchise inspired the first Liberal-Labour initiative.

Their objection to the clause stemmed from the fact that the Bill
incorporated two different franchise qualifications: residence for
parliamentary elections and occupation as owner or tenant for municipal elections.   Now since Clause 3 specifically ruled out votes
for lodgers, it would have disfranchised many people particularly in
London and in Scotland who had enjoyed a municipal franchise.   Mac-
Callum Scott (36) therefore proposed to rectify the Scottish case by
moving that those presently qualified as i) lodgers, ii) holders of
a service qualification, iii) non-resident owners who paid rates,
should be kept on the register.   He had the support of G.J. Wardle
for Labour and Sir George Younger for the Scottish Unionists, and
thus encountered no difficulty in obtaining an assurance from Robert
Munro, the Secretary of State for Scotland, that the Scottish Clause
would be amended so as to maintain the existing franchise in that
country.

The question of lodgers elsewhere was more tricky.   According to
H.G. Chancellor the words 'but not as a lodger' in the clause meant
the disfranchisement of 300,000 people, and, in accordance with the
instructions of the Labour Party National Executive, (37) William
Adamson moved their deletion. (38)   To equate the parliamentary and
local government franchises would have been a departure from the
Report, as Banbury was quick to point out; on the other hand the
Report had not used the offending words 'but not as a lodger' which
were in the Bill.   What had Conference intended?   According to
four Liberals - Dickinson, Simon, Williams and Adkins - they had not
envisaged the exclusion of all lodgers but simply the extension of
the vote to all who were tenants of rooms; and since this interpretation was not disputed by any Unionist Member it is a reasonable
deduction that that was the case.   Thus in place of Adamson's
amendment Dickinson put forward an alternative that would enfranchise lodgers who rented *unfurnished* rooms; this still left considerable numbers of lodgers off the Municipal Register, as in the
case of London where only 65,000 out of 108,000 lodgers were said to
be in unfurnished accommodation.   The Bill now would enfranchise
occupiers and tenants; Cave accepted the normal definition of
'tenants' as persons renting unfurnished rooms, justifying himself
on the grounds that they must reach a correct interpretation of the
Conference's intentions.   Thus the Liberals managed to achieve an
improvement in the Bill, but only by bringing it closer into line
with the Report; the original version had yet to be breached in a
Liberal direction.   This was attempted on Clause 4 when the radicals tried to extend the municipal franchise to several million
women whom the Conference had left out, but the matter was postponed by agreement until Report Stage in the autumn.   In general,
despite the pressures from right and left the compromise continued
to hold.

On 25 June the House came to Clause 5 which dealt with the Armed
Forces' franshie; it was proposed to allow all members of the
Forces and organisations like the Red Cross to be registered in respect of one month's residence for whichever constituency they would
have resided in but for the war.   This of course was not a franchise for soldiers as such, merely a means of retaining the vote for
them despite war service, a privilege which was to last for the dur-
ation of the present war and for twelve months thereafter; Cave extended this to cover 'any war in which His Majesty is engaged'. (39)

As has been shown, the Unionists' faith in the politics of the
troops led them to regard the clauses dealing with soldiers and
absent voters as the redeeming parts of the Bill.   However, they
demanded both a widening in the scope of the soldiers' franchise,
and some reassurance that the procedure for registering and casting
the votes had been made as perfect as possible.   Some Unionists
professed to see the Bill as a fraud on account of the practical
problems involved in this; but on Clause 5 their chief object was
to extend the application of the franchise to nineteen-year-old
soldiers.   In putting the case for this Colonel Leslie Wilson (40)
raised no fine debating points: if you could fight at nineteen you
could vote at nineteen - let anyone who was bold enough try to con-
tradict that.   Although this idea had been a long time coming some
Unionist statesmen like Selborne had already dismissed it as 'mischievous sentimentalism of the worst sort'. (41)   Yet this was
easier to write in a private letter than to advocate in the Commons.
Crude emotionalism spurted forth in the speech of Major Rowland
Hunt (42) who was so disgusted at the prospect of non-soldiers
voting while the troops could not that he went so far as to threaten
a military takeover unless the amendment was accepted.   However,
Banbury, Cecil and Sir William Bull all opposed him from the Unionist side, as did Herbert Samuel in a bold contribution from the
Opposition frontbench. (43)

Now the Home Secretary had stepped into the debate at an early
stage to warn that the franchise could not be treated as a reward
for service: (44) such an assumption, though he did not say so,
would have carried obvious implications for the women's franchise
too.   However, as the debate wore on with speaker after speaker
taking a contrary view, Cave's resistance evidently crumbled, and at
length Hayes Fisher rose to offer a compromise to be worked out in
Report Stage.   Indeed before the debate was over Cave had announced
his willingness to accept the enfranchisement of nineteen-year-olds
who had seen *active* service during the war.   Once the Home Secretary had taken up this position the onus fell upon the Opposition to
force a division against him which they understandably declined to
do.   However, Cave was apparently speaking on his own responsibility in the debate, and the question was not finally settled until
November when he eventually obtained approval from the Cabinet for
the nineteen-year-olds' franchise on condition that women were to
be excluded unless there appeared to be widespread support for them
in the Commons. (45)

In the same vein Ronald MacNeill proposed the disfranchisement of
all Conscientious Objectors exempted from military service on Clause
8 of the Bill. (46)   To purge the register of unpatriotic elements
in this way while adding infusions of young soldiers was envisaged
by Unionists as the best way of creating a suitable electoral body,
though hostility towards the Conscientious Objectors was not by any
means confined to their party.   The problem was that provision for
these men, some 16,000 altogether, had been made under the Military
Service Act of January 1916 which adopted the tribunals, set up by
the Derby Scheme to vet applications for exemption, to sit in judgment on appeals based upon 'a conscientious objection to the undertaking of combatant service'.   Now as Lord Hugh Cecil argued in an
eloquent speech, (47) there was no justification for placing a

retrospective penalty upon men who had merely availed themselves of
the exemption from military service specifically granted to them by
Act of Parliament.   It was basically wrong to penalise liberty of
opinion, and the requirements of the State must, in any case, be
subordinate to the laws of religion and morality; those who believed it wrong to kill would be committing the worst crime by joining
the Army.

In his speech Cave gave his position away with a personal confession of support for the amendment; but - it was the now familiar
'but' - it was so controversial as to imperil the Bill itself.
Thus the Home Secretary embarked upon a somewhat dutiful reiteration
of the case so skilfully made by Cecil, emphasising particularly
that Conscientious Objectors had already paid the penalty for their
views and could not be required to do so a second time.   Yet the
patent ambivalence of his speech served only to encourage the rebels
who raised 71 votes, in addition to 2 Liberal ones, in support of
MacNeill's amendment despite the imposition of the Government Whips.
Of the 143 in the Government lobby only 26 were Unionists, of whom
only 2 stuck to their view in subsequent divisions when the Whips
had been taken off. (48)   All the rest either frankly showed their
disapproval of Conscientious Objectors or abstained, which is some
indication of how precarious was the ground upon which Cave had
attempted to take his stand.   In short the apparently decisive two-
to-one vote against MacNeill's amendment could not be said to have
represented the true opinion of the House; the Unionist War Committee were well aware of this fact and intended to raise the matter
again. (49)

It was not until 15 August that the House began to deal with the
practicalities of soldiers' voting under Clause 18 on absent voters.
The new scheme provided for the absentee to receive a declaration of
identity and a ballot paper from the Returning Officet at an address
given against his name on the list; these two were to be sent back
to the Returning Officer before the Poll had closed.   The hazard
here, as Cave admitted, was that the transfer of ballot papers back
and forth from Returning Officers to men within the prescribed
eight-day period between nominations and Polling Day would be virtually impossible for about 80 per cent of the men.   Moreover, even
the relaxation of the residence requirement designed to cope with a
post-hostilities election seemed quite inadequate.   The Returning
Officer would have to attempt to ascertain who normally resided in
his area and to allow such persons to register after one month's
residence; yet as Long complained: (50)

> Supposing the war came to an end tomorrow, it must be months
> before thousands of our soldiers can be brought back from the
> scene of war, the Fleet will certainly have to be kept mobilised,
> and I do not think it is an exaggeration to say that a period of
> not less than twelve months after the termination of war and dec-
> laration of peace will elapse before a very large number of these
> men could qualify.

This of course represented an immense electoral risk in view of the
millions of votes at stake.   The Unionists therefore, could not
afford to let the clause go without some effective method of polling
the troops.   What could it be?   Cave tentatively offered three
alternatives: a poll in the trenches, an extension of the period

between nominations and the Poll or the Count, and a proxy system.
Led by Colonel Sanders many Unionists began to fasten upon the third
solution, not merely as a temporary expedient for a 'khaki' election, but as a permanent device for the Army in India and elsewhere.
Here they felt sure of their ground because Cave and Hayes Fisher
had advised Sanders well in advance that they meant to work for
proxies. (51)

However, Herbert Samuel took it upon himself, at the risk of
being labelled anti-Army, to criticise the proxy system in considerable detail; (52) essentially a proxy was not a real vote; how
were people to be prevented from acting as proxies more than once?
Would the soldier really go through the procedure for claiming a
proxy every six months in order to keep himself on the register?
No, in practice the soldier would not know where he would be six
months hence, with the result that he would not bother applying;
Instead the party agents would endeavour to contact him, fill up his
forms and provide him with a suitable proxy; the vote would not be
his at all.   Dickinson virtually lectured the Home Secretary:
surely he could now understand why the Conference had expressly not
proposed the proxy system?   In the debate Cave and Hayes Fisher
were so overcome by the arguments of the Asquithian bench that the
Home Secretary was reduced to the plea that the House should accept
the proxy in principle and settle the details later.   He gratefully embraced Simon's suggestion that Clause 18 be postponed until
the end, and meanwhile the amendment was withdrawn.   In the end the
Government was to accept Samuel's compromise which involved postal
voting combined with an extension of the period between the Poll and
the Count for electors in Belgium and France, and proxies for the
rest.

The gradual disintegration of the spirit of conciliation which
had manifested itself in the discussions on Conscientious Objectors
and proxies had been clearly heralded in the debate on Clause 7
which dealt with the right of a person registered to vote.   Reacting to the earlier setback to Proportional Representation, a Liberal
backbencher, Percy Harris (53) brought in an amendment designed to
prevent anyone voting in more than one division of a borough, and
thus maintain the *status quo*.   Harris enjoyed the support of the
Asquithian frontbenchers, Samuel and Simon, in the ensuing debate
which developed into a wrangle between members of the Conference as
to what they had decided.   In Sir William Bull's version they had
settled the dual voting plan long before taking up the question of
Proportional Representation which meant that the one could hardly
depend upon the other; Simon, on the other hand, insisted that this
very point of the mutual dependence of the two had been clarified at
the end of the Conference's discussions.   As the Speaker kept silence no conclusive answer emerged.   Although the Unionists were
anxious to have the matter settled at once, the Chairman ruled that
Harris's amendment could be withdrawn and raised again after a final
decision had been taken on Proportional Representation.   In view of
this it was not surprising that when the House voted a second time
on Proportional Representation on 4 July only eight days after the
debate on Harris's amendment there was a majority of 32 against the
scheme.   This time 137 Unionists turned out against Proportional
Representation and only 42 in favour, thereby overwhelming the small

Proportional Representation majorities given by the other parties.
Now that the threat to the business franchise was so widely appre-
ciated no fewer than sixty Unionists who had not previously voted on
Proportional Representation entered the lobby against it.

However, the remainder of the work done on the Bill during the
summer proved comparatively successful for the Liberals in terms of
defending the compromise.   They even managed to achieve one further
liberalisation over the disqualification from voting set out in
Clause 8. , The Speaker's Conference had only gone as far as to lift
the disqualification for receipt of Poor Relief for less than thirty
days for fear that they would not carry the House of Commons any
further than that.   Now J.H. Whitehouse proposed to abandon this
disqualification altogether on the grounds that it was anomalous to
discriminate against this one form of State subsidy at a time when
voters received aid in the field of pensions, health, education and
unemployment. (54)   Since members of all parties now came forth in
support of this view Hayes Fisher felt able to accept a revised version of the amendment without any serious controversy.

This sort of all-party consent was conspicuously absent when the
Alternative Vote came on for debate on 9 August.   The probability
that the experiment with Proportional Representation would be abandoned now meant that the Alternative Vote would apply to practically
the whole country.   As a majority recommendation it was denied the
support of the Government Whip with the result that the House split
sharply into its pre-war camps.   The 124 opponents of the Alternative Vote were all Unionists but for a dozen Liberals, while the 125
Members comprising the majority included only two Unionists.   The
very narrowness of the vote naturally served to aggravate the party
conflict in later divisions on the question.

How precarious was the Home Secretary's control of the House even
with the Whips became clear in another partisan division on 9 August
when Banbury attempted to delete the provision in the Bill which
prevented an elector in a two-Member University seat from voting
more than once; (55) this would have affected only the four Ox-
bridge Members, two of whom would have been displaced by a Liberal
poll of 34 per cent.   Though this was still perhaps unlikely the
very possibility of losing the Unionist monopoly infuriated Banbury
who urged that to divide the representation of the Univerisities
equally between the parties would simply render it null and void.
The furore on the Unionist benches seemed disproportionate to the
two seats at stake, but a certain emotional force attached to certain constituencies among which were numbered the Universities and
the City of London.

However, not only was the proposal in the Bill a unanimous one on
the part of the Conference, it represented also the absolute limit
to which the radicals were prepared to go with regard to University
representation.   They were in fact increasing it when they would
have preferred to abolish it altogether.   There was thus very
little room for manoeuvre on the part of the Home Secretary who
pledged the Government to accept the clause as it stood; to do
otherwise would have jeopardised Liberal and Labour goodwill.   Consequently the amendment fell by a two-to-one margin despite a truly
dramatic revolt of Unionists of whom sixty-eight resisted the Whips
while Bonar Law, appearing in person at this critical stage, took
only seventeen other Unionists with him into the lobby.

This division highlighted the precariousness of the Government's
position.   In such small divisions they were entirely in the hands
of the Asquithians to keep them from defeat.   Yet for Liberals who
wanted the Reform Bill it was worthwhile to co-operate with Cave so
long as he stuck to the compromise.   It was not until much later
in the year that there was any indication that the compromise would
be seriously breached under pressure of Unionist dissatisfaction.

Meanwhile the Unionists had been working away for another concession related to the Bill, though outside its scope: reform of the
House of Lords.   Ever since their defeat over the 1911 Parliament
Act with its notorious preamble promising reform of the Upper House
the Unionists had professed to consider the Constitution as in sus-
pense.   Now the National Union urged a scheme for a reconstituted
chamber to be enacted concurrently with the Reform Bill, (56) and
threatened to summon a Party Conference unless this demand were
acceded to. (57)   By the time the special Unionist Conference did
take place in November 1917 Bonar Law was able to dodge discussion
of the issue on the grounds that the Bryce Committee had begun work
on the question.

To have promised a *concurrent* measure for the Second Chamber
might well have encouraged the Peers to delay or tamper with the
Reform Bill, but it was worth making the gesture to mollify the
National Union as Lloyd George had readily conceded back in
March. (58)   However Long kept Salisbury and Selborne waiting for
some months for the plan to be launched.   It was not until July
that Bonar Law sought Asquith's approval for a Conference on the
same lines as Lowther's, (59) except that instead of Lowther, now
much out of favour among Unionists, Lansdowne was to preside.   In
fact Lansdowne was a reluctant and not generally acceptable figure,
and so James Bryce became Chairman; work did not begin until
October 1917 (pp. 156-7).

From time to time the National Union paused to assess what progress had been made in improving the Bill.   At their meeting in
July the Executive reported a substantial list of successes, though
mostly minor ones. (60)   They congratulated themselves particularly
on obtaining the special debate on the Instructions to the Boundary
Commissioners which, apart from the concessions directly won, had
led to the abandonment of Proportional Representation with the con-
sequent widening of the Business Vote.   The male franchise had been
leavened by the addition of the nineteen-year-olds, though the real
value of this franchise remained in doubt pending a decision about
postal and proxy voting.   Though this was not a great deal the
gains were felt to justify the effort.   Against this however, had
to be set the series of rebuffs suffered on Clause 1 over the Ownership Vote, successive voting, the Business Vote and Joint Occupation.   Nor were the National Union happy about the franchise for
lodgers since those in furnished accommodation were more likely to
be of substantial means than those in unfurnished rooms.   In addition the House had struck out the disqualification for Poor Relief,
a setback admitted by the National Union; the University Members
were threatened; Conscientious Objectors remained on the register;
and the Alternative Vote had been narrowly retained.

That the Bill remained a practical proposition despite all these
objections was a good measure of the loyalty to Bonar Law's leader-

ship at this stage in the war.   The Reform Bill revealed both the opposition and the relatively small number of loyalists who were otherwise, through their silence, difficult to count.   By examining the eleven critical divisions which strained Unionist loyalty during the summer of 1917 one can gauge the strength of the Government supporters and rebels within the party.   On this basis some 69 Unionists emerge as largely unqualified supporters of the leadership, while a group of 58 Members behaved in a consistently hostile manner.   There are exceptions among these lists, for example Sir Henry Page-Croft who recorded three votes for the Government and none against although, as a founder of the National Party, he was one of Bonar Law's strongest critics.   No doubt his complicity in the Bill, as a member of the Speaker's Conference, explains his behaviour.   Indeed all the mebers stayed loyal except two of the late-comers, Touche and Archdale, who doubtless felt unpledged on decisions taken before their arrival, and Basil Peto who voted three times against and eight times for the Government.   Leading figures such as Bonar Law, Long, Cecil, Cave, F.E. Smith, Duke and Talbot turned out in support of the Whips though not with any regularity, but Carson and Chamberlain were conspicuous by their absence. Among the 69 loyalists 18 held posts in the Government and a further 7 were to do so during the lifetime of Lloyd George's Coalition down to 1922;   even a rebel like Colonel Sanders was under pressure to moderate his activity by being kept in hope of a post by the Chief Whip, as his diary shows.   Sixty-nine was a remarkably slender basis of support in a party of 270-odd Members, but they served to make the Reform Bill just feasible politically during the summer and thereby to stave off an early dissolution of Parliament.   The rebels, however, ran them sufficiently close to make further concessions inevitable.   It was these that threatened to disrupt the shaky reform majority in the autumn, in particular the questions of Irish redistribution, the dual vote in the large boroughs, and the Alternative Vote.   Here the pressure would be very much on the Liberal and Labour Coalitionists to prevent the radical majority in the House from outvoting the Unionists.   How many would decide to save the Bill and preserve the Lloyd George Coalition at the same time?

Chapter 9

WAITING FOR ASQUITH

I thought Asquith looked a wreck.　His face was aged and care-
worn.　His figure had lost its sturdy square built Yorkshire
set.　His hand trembled.　His voice sank almost to a whisper.
...　I felt pity.　The strain had almost broken him up.　Whatever he may have been before he was no longer, for the present,
fit to hold the helm of state.　(MacCallum Scott's Diary, 8
December 1916)

More than any other item of legislation the Representation of the
People Bill helped to restore a sense of normality to the life of
the House of Commons;　yet no Member could easily mistake the divisions of the summer and winter of 1917 for the politics of peacetime.　Whereas before 1914 a Member was almost invariably drilled
by his Whips and his vote given automatically, the situation now had
become much less certain.　Turnout in divisions was regularly low
due to the absence of around 160 Members in the Forces, though many
of these enjoyed desk jobs in Britain and appeared not infrequently
in the House.　For the　Unionists Lord Edmund Talbot issued the
party Whips though they were treated with much less than usual respect;　while the Liberals were blessed with a Government Whip directed initially by Neil Primrose and subsequently by Freddie Guest, as
well as the Asquithian Whip from John Gulland.　To issue these
Whips to all Liberal Members served at first to maintain the fiction
of party unity, though as 1917 wore on the uncertain loyalty of
Members to one or other leader gradually emerged;　for most of them
two Whips reflected precisely the confusion in their own minds.
What is clear is that Gulland's whipping was comparatively slack and
ineffective, though not surprisingly in view of the failure of the
frontbenchers to support him.　The Chief Whip after all, merely
rallied the troops behind his leaders' policy, yet as is apparent
from the meeting of ex-Ministers just before the Committee State of
the Reform Bill, or more calamitously, in the Maurice Debate, the
frontbench could rarely find a real strategy to pursue.
　MPs on all sides were thus left much more to their own devices
than usual with the result that the luxury of voting against the
Government carried a greater risk of bringing the Government down,
which one would not do lightly at this critical time.　In this sit-

uation Lloyd George enjoyed not only the advantage of being virtually indispensable as Prime Minister, but also the comforting knowledge that, unlike his Liberal, Labour and Irish critics, he had no
cause to fear a General Election.   A defeat for him in the Commons
would not, therefore, carry the dire implications which it would for
a Prime Minister dependent on a normal party majority.   He would
dissolve and form a new administration even though the composition
of the House would have changed at the election.   Like a Prime
Minister from an earlier era Lloyd George rested upon no automatic
party majority in the House, but instead upon the support of groups
which, in the case of the main, Unionist, groups was somewhat erratic.   Yet he could invariably rely upon the old Asquithian alliance
to keep him afloat when the Unionists rebelled; this occurred most
obviously over the Reform Bill since Asquith could never bring himself to endanger the Bill, nor to allow the Prime Minister an excuse
for dissolving parliament.   Consequently the Government's majority,
as was clear by the summer of 1917, began to display the chameleon-
like qualities of its leader; by the autumn and winter the majority
for the various parts of the Reform Bill had been Conservative and
Liberal by turns (see Appendix 8).   Now that all four parties had
degenerated into groups relatively immune from whipping Lloyd George
had no alternative but to live off these alternating majorities;
more and more he assumed the role of an eighteenth-century chief
minister using a combination of patronage, personal charisma and an
astutely-blended Cabinet of group leaders to cobble together his
majority from one division to the next.
     The reassembly of Parliament in the autumn of 1917 brought the
Reform Bill to its climax in the Commons; during October and November adherence to the, by now well-worn, compromise of the Speaker's
Conference was so strained as to threaten a reversion to normal
party warfare.   What prevented this development going too far,
apart from the pusillanimity of the Asquithian leadership, was the
behaviour of those Liberal and Labour Members who chose to support
the Government when their colleagues were obstructing it.   The
force of habitual voting for or against the Coalition policy began
to conjure up a shadow of the three-party alliance on the backbenches and in the lobbies.   It was enough to irritate the Government, but, in the absence of any leadership from Asquith, the rebellion never gelled into a real Opposition; they were not looking
for power.
     Not least among the reasons for the failure to recreate an effec-
tive radical alliance was the deepening disenchantment of the Irish
Members with Asquith, (1) though their own disunity in this period
rendered them difficult to marshall in the lobby.   The suspension
of the Home Rule Act, the inclusion of Carson in the Government in
1915, the Easter Rebellion and the failure of Lloyd George's negotiations during 1916 had all conspired to sever the bonds between
Asquith and the Irish.   Yet he remained their only lifeline particularly after December 1916 when Lloyd George's alliance with the
Unionists presented the Liberal Leader with the opportunity of redeeming himself in their eyes.   They were not to be won round by
the soporific absentee leadership provided by Asquith, yet one can
understand from the parliamentary arithmetic why the Coalitionists
grew so nervous at every indication of Irish and Asquithian criti-

cism.   For of the 270 Unionist Members approximately 125 were
absent in the Armed Forces from time to time; while of some 260
Liberals only 32 were thus engaged, in addition to a small handful
of Irish and one or two Labour Members.   This should have left the
three radical parties even more dominant than usual but for the
difficulty in persuading them to turn out for divisions.   Of course
it was not so easy for Asquith to put together a majority now because of the adherence of a number of Liberal and Labour Members to
Lloyd George.   In fact the Lloyd George Liberal following remained
quite small, around 50 to 60 judging by the voting on the Reform
Bill, plus about 10 Labour Members; this still left around 200
Liberal and Labour votes to be mobilised by the Asquithians with a
reservoir of over 70 Nationalists - a total quite enough to dominate
the House of Commons in this period.   What made the position uncertain was the fluctuation in turnout, often extremely low among the
Nationalists, plus the conflicting loyalties among the Liberals.
Just how many Coalitionist Liberals there were was a question that
began to be answerable as a result of the forty-four divisions on
the Reform Bill which, by making Coalitionist voting a habit for
certain Members, became more important than occasional issues such
as the Maurice Debate in sifting the Lloyd Georgeites from the rest.
     The other element of uncertainty in the parliamentary equation
was the number of Unionists who might be prepared to free their
Party from Lloyd George's unwelcome grasp by co-operating with the
Asquithians to defeat the Government.   Unfortunately they were not
presented with suitable opportunities on the Reform Bill, a measure
which the radicals cherished too much to make co-operation with the
Carsonites possible.   Yet on war issues on which the Government
might properly have been overthrown the Carsonites shunned the embarrassing signs of support from the Asquithian benches.   For although the two groups were drawn together by a tendency to defend
the generals against Lloyd George, behind every vote stood the
prospect of Asquith's return to office; as Lord Salisbury wrote in
explanation for Unionist loyalty in the Maurice Debate, everyone
knew the Prime Minister was a liar but, 'whatever was felt about
Lloyd George no-one was prepared to put Asquith in his place'. (2)
     Essentially, then, Lloyd George survived because of the inability
of his enemies to combine against him.   Without a lead from Asquith
many Liberals felt reluctant to obstruct the Government (3) thus enabling Lloyd George to live with the 1910 Parliament for nearly two
years.   An Asquithian majority, though difficult to attain, was not
impossible if Asquith worked for it; his refusal to do this created
immense frustration among Liberals and Nationalists who, loathing
the Coalition, yearned for a lead.   These Members of course tended
to be those most hostile to the war itself with whom Asquith found
himself in basic disagreement; he therefore resisted for a long
time their desire for the more modest alternative of organising a
coherent minority Opposition which, though not an alternative Government in the immediate future, would at least have staked out a
longer term claim to the leadership of progressive opinion.   Instead Asquith's negative approach left Lloyd George's administration
looking like the only possible Government.   Meanwhile Liberal principles continued to be rapidly abandoned, without any improvement in
the war situation to show for it, thus leaving room for alternative

leadership; in short Asquith passed up the opportunity in 1917 of taking a stand to stem the drift of the radicals into socialism and of the ambitious into Coalitionism.

The summer of 1917 had demonstrated that the Reform Bill could survive substantial Unionist opposition and abstentions with Liberal and Labour support; now the Government put this, unavoidably, at risk by making certain concessions to their own right wing particularly over Conscientious Objectors and Irish Redistribution; the radicals themselves were determined to edge the Bill back in a liberal direction on several issues. In the event the consensus did not dissolve disastrously because the radicals, though invariably suffering defeat through defections from the Liberal ranks, still felt the Bill worth saving.

For the radicals two issues still remained to be tested in a division: dual voting and the problem of Scottish lodgers. Accordingly Mr G. Thorne (Liberal, Wolverhampton) brought forward in November an amendment to prevent a person voting in more than one division of a parliamentary borough. (4) Debate at this stage became rather pointless. Thorne's amendment would have deprived of their second vote a few people in towns with two or more multi-Member seats whom the Conference had intended to have it; (5) equally the Conference had not proposed that the second vote should be as widely available as it would be without the Proportional Representation multi-Member seats; this latter group included such cities as Bristol, Newcastle, Edinburgh and Leicester which would have become single multi-Member constituencies. All the familiar arguments about the deliberations of the Conference were reiterated without shedding any decisive new light upon the question. A division was again postponed until Report Stage on 20 November when Herbert Samuel both spoke and voted in support of Thorne. His amendment was, however, lost by 163 to 142 votes, with the Liberals dividing in his favour by 114 to 29. The minority, all blacklisted the next day by the 'Westminster Gazette', were solid Lloyd George men, 12 of them being members of the Government. Numerically this was the biggest triumph won by the Asquithian side in the battle for the Liberal Party, though it was still a poor showing for them in view of the fact that about 90 Liberals who were not in the Forces had not voted. Indeed only Samuel, Gulland and McKinnon Wood from among the ranks of the leadership participated in the lobby. In a similar manner the Labour Party split 11 to 5 in favour of Thorne; only Walter Hudson spoke in his support, while the 3 Labour members of the Conference, Goldstone, Walsh and Wardle, were conspicuously absent from the proceedings. Thus the adverse majority of 21 could be ascribed to the 34 Liberal and Labour Members whose votes had saved the Government from an embarrassing setback and helped shore up Bonar Law's position.

A virtual repetition of this occurred over the Scottish municipal franchise. Robert Munro, the Liberal Secretary of State for Scotland, came armed with the concessions he had promised in order to retain the local government franchise for lodgers, service voters and non-occupying owners of property of £10 value; the only category of former voters still disfranchised were the non-occupying tenants under long leases whose claim was not strong since they did not pay rates. The Liberals' main complaint about this was that

the lodgers would be put to the trouble of making a claim to go on
the register twice a year.   However, Munro resisted further amendments. (6)   On 28 November a Labour Member, William Adamson, moved
the deletion of the financial qualification for lodgers' premises
from the Bill (7) in which he was supported by Gulland, the Liberal
Whip.   Munro rejected this as tantamount to adult suffrage for
lodgers, and after a short debate Adamson's amendment was thrown out
by 151 to 114 votes.   Again the result rested upon 41 Liberal and
5 Labour Members who voted in the Government lobby;   also as before
the radicals received no frontbench support apart from that of
Gulland, McKinnon Wood and H.J. Tennant, hardly an impressive array.
    Of the two defeats inflicted upon the Unionists one was of com-
paratively little importance;   this was Sir George Touche's proposal
to retain the franchise for the Freemen of the City of London. (8)
Touche asked only that they be permitted to use the Freemen's qualification as an alternative to the business vote.   However, the
Government stuck rigidly to the Bill and defeated the amendment by
167 to forty-eight.
    An altogether more disruptive situation was building up as a
result of the protracted struggle over the Alternative Vote.   On
this point the Government, by taking the Whips off, stood aside from
the conflict, though in practice they could not but suffer from the
immediate division of the House into its pre-war groups which could
well have been the prelude to a general dissolution of the fragile
consensus on the Bill.   After their defeat by a single vote on this
issue in August the Unionists had to wait until 22 November for
another attempt.   This time the speakers were considerably less
guarded in their language;   Sir George Younger, (9) moving the deletion of the Alternative Vote, declared that he would prefer to have
the Liberal and Labour Parties settling their differences privately
and fielding a single candidate in each constituency to the prospect
of a 'corrupt' deal to combine the second preferences of their
voters for the purpose of defeating Unionists.   Younger's assumption and that of his colleagues, was that Liberal and Labour voters
would continue to regard the two radical parties as equally acceptable vehicles for resisting the Unionists.   The urgency of the
situation was much more apparent to the Liberals than it had been in
the earlier debates on this question.   For in August 1917, after
his return from Russia convinced of the need for British Labour to
be represented at the Peace Conference of socialists at Stockholm,
Arthur Henderson had been unceremoniously sacked from the War Cabinet.   As a result a free Henderson, now inspired by the dangers of
allowing working-class politics to develop outside the parliamentary
system, reversed his views on Labour Party organisation.   By September Henderson had persuaded the National Executive Committee both
to develop a new party programme and to extend membership, the constituency parties and the number of candidates.
    Edward Hemmerde, a backbench Liberal, frankly confessed that with
Labour threatening to field several hundred candidates after the war
the incidence of Unionist victories based on a minority vote would
greatly increase. (10)   Henderson freely confirmed this prognosti-
cation.   During the autumn of 1917 the Labour Party National Executive were working on the assumption that the new Register would be
prepared early in 1918, unless the House of Lords delayed the

Reform Bill, (11) and it is certain that anticipation of the enactment of the measure stimulated the adoption of candidates with NEC
approval more indiscriminately than hitherto.   Apart from the possibilities of the new franchise, which Henderson significantly did
not mention, there was the advantage of greatly reduced election
expenses in the Bill, which, taken with the payment of Members since
1911, facilitated the adoption of working men as candidates. (12)
But for the Alternative Vote, however, Henderson would hardly have
contemplated as many as 500 candidates in December 1917; (13)   he
apparently hoped to leave a mere handful of seats occupied by radical Liberals uncontested, relying in the majority of constituencies
upon 'the alternative vote and on a friendly understanding between
Liberalism and Labour to give each other their second choice'. (14)
Now it was not until February 1918 that the Alternative Vote was
ultimately dropped from the Bill;   thereupon the National Executive
Committee met to reconsider the number of candidates to be fielded
and to 'review the whole political situation'. (15)   By this time,
however, the constituencies had been given their heads and a mass
withdrawal of candidates would have been difficult, though the 388
who came forward ultimately fell well short of the 500 Henderson
had expected earlier.   On 27 February it was decided to fight
'wherever the local parties desire' despite the loss of the Alternative Vote (16) and vote splitting with the Liberals became unavoidable.

     The Commons' second division on the Alternative Vote only under-
lined the previous one for it was approved on 22 November by 151 to
123.   The three-party majority reasserted itself briefly in the
form of 109 Liberal, 22 Labour and 19 Irish Members, a total which
served to emphasise the opportunity open to the Asquithian leaders
to establish their dominance in the House.   The Unionists fell back
upon an attempt to sabotage the Alternative Vote, in which they were
assisted unintentionally by Major Chapple, (17) a Liberal Member who
wished to adopt a special method of counting the votes under the
Alternative Vote system known as the Nansen method (see Appendix 1).
The Unionists promptly espoused Chapple's amendment with unwonted
enthusiasm;   it was mathematically subtle - some Members boasted
that they could not understand it at all - and it robbed the single-
Member system of the virtue of simplicity;   moreover it had not been
tried anywhere.   In short it seemed an admirable means of turning a
dangerous proposal into an absurd one, ripe for excision by the
Peers.

     Hence, when Younger seconded Chapple most of the Unionists fol-
lowed suit with the result that leave was given to introduce a new
schedule into the Bill to provide rules for the conduct of elections
according to the Nansen method.   It was, as the 'Manchester Guardian' commented, a 'proof that party divisions have returned'. (18)
However, only two days later this mischievous attempt to take advantage of Chapple's interest in electoral reform was thwarted when
sufficient Liberal and Labour Members rallied to defeat the new
schedule;   as a result the Bill had to go to the House of Lords with
the Alternative Vote Clause but without the rules governing its
practical application.

     Fortunately for the Government there were only three areas for
this kind of brawling between the parties which would rapidly have

reduced the passage of the Bill to chaos.   The second of these opportunities was opened up over Conscientious Objectors by the Government's own decision;   for Cave had managed to stave off the
first Unionist attempt at disfranchisement back in June only by in-
voking the Government Whips.   In November a free vote was allowed
on Sir George Younger's amendment which the House accepted, thereby
disfranchising all the men who had been accepted by tribunals as
genuine Conscientious Objectors. (19)   One amendment was subsequently adopted which exempted those men who had done work of national importance in accordance with the decision of their tribunal.
  It is not certain at what point the Home Secretary changed his
mind over the vital use of the Whips.   Dr Rae (20) has pointed out
that at a meeting on 19 November between Curzon, Derby and Cave at
the War Office a major concession had been made in the form of an
agreement to authorise the release from prison of Conscientious Objectors reported to be unfit.   It seems possible that the withdrawal of the Whips on Younger's amendment two days later was a *quid
pro quo* for this;   but the Cabinet Minutes do not help us here, and
Sir George Cave's Papers, which might throw light on the question,
are not yet available.   It is more likely that the decision to
withdraw the Whips had come first, thereby facilitating the release
of the Conscientious Objectors rather than the other way around.
Certainly the pressures of the parliamentary situation on Cave were
great in view of the fact that in June seventy-one Unionists had
defied the Whip while a mere twenty-six reluctant Members had
obeyed.   Virtually the entire Party leadership wanted Conscientious
Objectors disfranchised, Cave being the only abstainer in November
on the grounds that he was committed by his earlier statement on the
subject;   perhaps he also wished to avoid offending the Liberals too
much.   Nor was there any prospect of Lloyd George and his fellow
Coalitionists resisting the strong emotions of their colleagues, for
with the exception of H.A.L. Fisher they seemed to share their sentiments.   As we know from C.P. Scott's (21) sad efforts to reclaim
the lost Liberalism in him, Lloyd George had no sympathy for Conscientious Objectors: 'I shall only consider the best means of
making the path of that class a very hard one', he had told the
House in 1916. (22)   He was, in deference to his well-advertised
Free Church connections, willing to except Quakers from disparaging
remarks of this sort.   Yet only a quarter of Conscientious Objectors took their stand on religious grounds, and the Free Churches
were little different from the rest of society in their enthusiasm
for fighting; (23)   indeed, their leading political spokesman, Sir
Joseph Compton-Rickett, spoke up strongly in the House for the disfranchising amendment. (24)
  Thus the temptation to abandon the issue to a free vote proved
too strong for Cave to resist;   his only fear was of the consequences later on of having unleashed a controversy on a matter that was
clearly beyond the scope of the Speaker's Conference.   However, by
November it was no longer the case that the Report had not been
altered by addition;   there was a precedent, as Bonar Law pointed
out, in the extension of the municipal franchise to six million
women, for adopting a change which had strong support in the House,
even though the Conference had not considered it.
  The intrinsic importance of the disfranchisement was dispropor-

tionate to the controversy surrounding it, partly because it was
limited to a period of five years after the war which meant in practice from August 1921 to August 1926.   Also a majority of the
16,000 Conscientious Objectors could gain exemption under Sir
Ryland Adkins' amendment which covered men who had worked as non-
combatants, serving as ambulance men or mine-sweepers, or had been
put to work under the Pelham Committee.   Finally, many Registration
Officers, in the absence of proper information, unknowingly left
Conscientious Objectors on the Registers. (25)
 However,. the issue helped to drive a deep wedge between Coalitionist and Asquithian Liberals in four emotional debates.   Some 10
Labour MPs gave votes for disfranchisement, (26) a high proportion
in a party of 38.   The Liberals had previously opposed the disfranchising amendment by 93 to 2; but in the absence of the Whips 12 of
these joined the other 2 and 34 abstainers to make a total of 48
Members who were willing to show their hostility to Conscientious
Objectors.   This group comprised the hard core of Lloyd George Liberals whose support remained firm in all the critical divisions
during the autumn.   Such was the process that drove the right wing
of the party towards Lloyd George, thus putting him in an increasingly false position, while the left wing looked for a new home.
On an issue which touched the Liberal conscience so painfully
Asquith might have been expected to give a lead, but instead, as
Richard Holt lamented, he 'failed to turn up and our front bench did
nothing, causing scandal and offence to many earnest Liberals'. (27)
It was left to Tim Healy (Irish Nationalist) to demand to know from
the silent Unionist benches why they did not include in their amendment the original Conscientious Objectors at the Curragh.
 The redistribution of seats, so troublesome an aspect of previous
Reform Bills, went through remarkably smoothly in 1917.   It is true
that the question of the constituencies caused controversy where it
touched upon Ireland and Proportional Representation, but the general principle of equal constituencies, with a few modifications,
met widespread approval; dissidents, whether Liberal or Unionist,
were few and concentrated upon local grievances rather than upon
basic principles.   Thus it was no surprise that the new Schedules
produced by the Boundary Commissioners were ratified by 225 to 72
votes on 5 November.   In the minority were to be found 31 Unionists
and 26 Liberals, the latter a mixed bag of radicals and Coalitionists without any coherent case against the new scheme.   The chief
complaint of the Unionists concerned the loss of agricultural representation and the intrusion of disfranchised boroughs into existing
county seats.
 A host of quite trivial changes were effected, for Cave gladly
took the opportunity to conciliate Members by allowing them to re-
name their constituencies.   Asquith, for example, was permitted to
retain the title''East Fife' for his constituency instead of adopting 'St Andrews' after the borough that was to be incorporated into
the division.   On any points of substance, however, the Home Secretary adopted an uncompromising attitude.   When General Hickman (28)
attempted to detach one of the three Wolverhampton seats and make it
a Staffordshire County division he received only thirty Unionist and
one Liberal vote in support.   J.G. Butcher's attempt to save York
as a two-Member seat was similarly doomed, (29) despite his eloquent

treatise on the singular historical importance of that city; he
succeeded in provoking spokesmen for the rival historic city of
Winchester, but silenced them with the aid of geography by pointing
out that Winchester had never been the capital of the North of England! Before the debate could turn into a convention of antiqua-
rians a vote was taken in which some seventy-four Members supported
Butcher's amendment in a futile gesture of protest. No better fate
awaited Colonel Gretton's bid to preserve Rutland as a separate constituency, (30) despite his claim that the county had been sending
Members to Westminster since 1265; support came from Sir Francis
Edwards a Liberal who was about to lose his seat at Radnorshire, a
county almost as small as Rutland in population and boasting a
parliamentary history stretching back to 1541. The Radnorshire
case explains why eleven Liberals joined with Gretton to raise
twenty-five votes for his proposal. The House treated these gal-
lant but forlorn efforts with indulgence, but firmly resisted them.
    One amendment alone met with wide approval on both sides: Sir
Philip Magnus's amendment to retain his London University seat
rather than have it merged into the new three-Member constituency
for the English and Welsh Universities. (31) Twenty-one Liberals
opposed this, doubtless out of a general dislike of University representation and the Unionist monopoly, but some sixty-two, including
Samuel, voted in support of Magnus. Cave acquiesced in this only
on the condition that the seat allowed for London would be deducted
from the total of three for the English Universities. His chief
concern throughout was to resist any increase in the total number of
Members, already too high at 705 (see Appendix 9), for fear of re-
leasing a flood of demands for clemency for disfranchised constituencies.
    The total of 705 included, of course, the existing 103 constit-
uencies in Ireland which had been left unchanged both in the Report
and in the Bill; the decision to redistribute these rather late in
the day reflected the development of the Government's general strategy on Ireland. From the start of his Premiership Lloyd George had
come under conflicting pressure to act; on the one hand John
Dillon, increasingly taking over from Redmond, stepped up the demand
to put the Home Rule Act into operation before the parliamentary
leaders of Nationalist opinion were irretrievably discredited, an
argument often communicated to Lloyd George by C.P. Scott; on the
other hand Carson represented, if he did not entirely accept, the
renewed resentment of the Ulstermen towards concessions in the face
of the violence that had been growing since the Easter Rebellion.
Lloyd George's own fading sympathy with the Nationalists stemmed in
part from his suspicions about co-operation between them and the Asquithians; he was also a prey to fears of German landings in Ireland; and, in deference to the pressure of President Woodrow
Wilson, his new war-winning weapon, he would dearly have loved to
find a settlement of the question. Given Lloyd George's insistence
on separate treatment for Ulster Carson was half-willing to accept
county option as a solution, though desperately afraid of losing
his supporters in consequence. (32) The appointment of the Irish
Convention in May 1917 was envisaged as a means of achieving such a
solution by agreement of all parties without embroiling the Cabinet
in the details, just as the Speaker's Conference had been.

In this way the Home Rule Act, which had included a new scheme
for the constituencies, in effect died, but had been replaced with a
new policy based on the Convention (33) which was also expected to
deal with the constituencies thereby relieving the drafters of the
Reform Bill of the task.   However, since the Convention did not sit
until 25 July any decision by the Government to pre-empt it by introducing their own scheme for the constituencies in the autumn carried the clear implication that they did not expect, or did not
want, the Convention to succeed.   In fact Carson had begun to push
the Cabinet towards remedying the 'gross injustice' of the maldis-
tribution of seats in June. (34)   This demand coincided with the
campaign being waged by Lloyd George to remove Carson from his post
at the Admiralty where the Ulster Leader was patently a failure. (35)   In July Carson was manoeuvred into the War Cabinet which
relieved him of departmental duties and enhanced his role as representative of hardline Unionist opinion.   If Bonar Law feared Carson's resignation, Long at least continued to resist his interference with the Reform Bill: (36)

> If you could have got a Home Rule scheme and then secured redis-
> tribution on that basis, that would have been a different matter,
> but you cannot redistribute Ireland now on the present basis and
> then have to do the work all over again.

The intrinsic importance of redistributing Irish constituencies
was very limited in that it gave the Unionists some four or five
extra seats. (37)   Its wider significance in inflicting yet another
humiliation upon the Nationalist Party was to further assist the
erosion of their support in Ireland;   by the autumn of 1917 this was
well underway as was demonstrated by the loss of four seats that
year to the Sinn Fein. (38)   It was therefore a time to conciliate
and shore up the Nationalists if a settlement was still genuinely
sought, not to foster the conditions in which their more extreme
rival flourished.   The progress of the Irish Convention was far
from discouraging in the autumn in that a prospect had opened up of
agreement being reached by a majority comprising the Nationalists,
the Southern Unionists and Labour representatives. (39)   After a
meeting of the Irish Unionist Alliance in September their representatives were reported to be prepared to 'agree with Mr. Redmond's
following to settle a Home Rule Act provided they get certain guarantees for the minority again on the lines of the Amending
Bill'. (40)   In this connection the attempt of the Irish Nationalists in the Commons to extend Proportional Representation to the
towns provided an opportunity for the Government to promote agreement in the Convention;   for a measure of Proportional Representation would both have given the Unionists fairer representation in
the south while saving the Nationalists from the Sinn Fein at the
same time.   Sir Horace Plunkett, the Chairman of the Convention,
who had been President of the Irish Proportional Representation Society since 1912, was keen to have this solution adopted.   Lord Selborne also made much of the usefulness of Proportional Representation as the only means of preventing Sinn Fein from sweeping the
entire country outside the six counties: (41)   with less than 60 per
cent of the vote they would be able to win 82 seats to the Unionists' 23 - a majority, on the face of it, of 59 for total independence.   Yet under Proportional Representation, Selborne believed,

there would be about 50 for independence against 55 Nationalists and
Unionists opposing it.   This forecast drew only a characteristically neutral and evasive reply from Bonar Law, (42) for he, like the
Cabinet itself, had in effect washed his hands of the Convention by
early 1918.   If the Convention produced a plan for Home Rule the
Ulstermen would have to be cajoled into acquiescence; but if it
failed the situation would merely drift towards a General Election
in which the Nationalists would become extinct.   With no one left
on the Irish side with whom to negotiate the problem would be simplified if not solved.

It was not until 17 October 1917 that Sir John Lonsdale raised
the question of Irish redistribution in the Commons; Cave, who knew
all along of the National Union's opinion of the matter, gave every
indication of a man desperately anxious to 'save my Bill' and be
fair to all parties. (43)   He therefore threw out the suggestion
that if the total number of Irish seats was left at 103 they might
still be internally redistributed.   This would leave the Nationalists with the form of a victory - for while the Act of Union remained in force the number of Irish seats could not be reduced.
Yet it would mollify the Unionist malcontents with a concession of
substance in that it would help them towards the extra seven to ten
seats to which they were entitled on the basis of the Protestant
population.   The day after he had aired this plan the Home Secretary advanced to the House the view that it was not reasonable to
extend to Ireland a new franchise without also reforming her constituencies: 'I see no answer on merit to that contention': (44)
they must therefore produce a contingency plan in case the Irish
Convention should fail.   In this way Cave committed himself to a
scheme of redistribution in blithe disregard for the work being done
on this by the Convention.

This turn of events naturally aroused the hitherto somnolent
Irish benches to an angry display which some Unionists privately
regarded as rather contrived. (45)   In several unpleasant debates
on 4, 5 and 6 November the Nationalists made a strong case, with the
help of Herbert Samuel, though it was marred by occasional feuding
between Redmondites and O'Brienites.   To them Cave's innocent
desire so late in the day to remove the admitted anomalies of Irish
constituencies smacked of partisanship incompatible with his role as
guardian of the Reform Bill.   Altogether seven important divisions
took place in which the Irish, assisted by large Liberal and Labour
contingents, held up the Bill on the verge of its Third Reading.
Among these the most crucial were the defeat of Redmond's amendment
to abandon redistribution by 219 to 165 votes, and of Devlin's
amendment to adopt Proportional Representation in the main centres
of population by 183 to 119.   Once it had been demonstrated that
they could no longer get their way Redmond was driven to accept the
compromise offered by Bonar Law on 6 December; (46) they would for-
mulate an agreed Bill embodying a scheme of redistribution which
would be passed simultaneously with the Reform Bill itself.   To
this end a committee was appointed under the Speaker comprising two
Nationalists and two Ulstermen.   This plan had been devised with
the support of Colonel James Craig, (47) the Ulster leader, only
shortly before the debate in which it was announced on 7 December;
the House thereupon rapidly granted a Third Reading of the Bill.

Lowther guided his committee (48) to a successful conclusion (49)
only by using his casting vote after five sittings of deadlock; (50)
they divided evenly on Proportional Representation and the Speaker,
though he favoured the reform, decided that he 'would not impose
P.R. on Ireland by my casting vote'.   In the event the Republic of
Ireland waited only until 1922 for a permanent system of Proportional Representation, Northern Ireland half a century longer.

The seven controversial divisions on Irish aspects of the Bill
reveal the advanced state of the split within both the Liberal and
Labour Parties by the end of 1917.   Members of both parties were
much more reluctant to obstruct the Bill as became obvious when the
Nationalists forced a vote on their motion to recommit the Bill to a
Committee of the whole House;   only 13 Liberals and 2 Labour men
joined 47 Nationalists in support of this.   Leaving exceptional
divisions of this sort aside, however, one can distinguish 88 Liberals and 12 Labour Members who opposed the Government fairly consistently on Irish matters.   Predominant in this group were the habitual radical-pacifist rebels such as R.L. Outhwaite, Philip Morrell,
Arthur Ponsonby, Joseph King, J.A. Baker, D.M. Mason and A. Rown-
tree.   Asquithians like Sir John M'Callum, Augustine Birrell and
John Burns were rather few and seem to have collected in the unhappy
group of 40-odd Members with a patchy and confused voting pattern;
this included E.G. Hemmerde, a radical, John Gulland and Sir John
Fleming, Asquithians, C.T. Needham, a radical and subsequently a
Coalitionist, and those like Percy Harris and Willoughby Dickinson
who faced a real dilemma over their loyalty to the leadership.
Asquithians also figured prominently among the 55 non-voting Members.   The death of the Liberal Party is written plainly in these
figures: the men who staunchly opposed Lloyd George were largely
destined, in the absence of leadership, to drift towards Labour or
out of politics altogether.   It was the sagging mass of doubters
languishing between the left and the Coalition hoping for the end of
the war, who formed the base of the post-war Liberal Party.

The rebels attained their maximum strength over the basic issue
of redistribution on which they had the support of 101 to 34 Liberals and 11 to 7 Labour Members.   However, the pattern of voting
carried a melancholy moral for the Opposition; for while the Liberal and Labour Parties were partly cancelling out their strength the
large Unionist vote was allowed to swamp the smaller Nationalist
Party; this represented a neat reversal of the situation that had
prevailed during the summer when the Liberals had appeared to dominate the House because of the division of the Unionists into two
camps (see Appendix 8).   It was a striking and novel demonstration
of Lloyd George's capacity to survive by dividing and ruling a House
of Commons in which he was so widely disliked.

Of course this exercise in alternating majorities was less simple
than the parliamentary mathematics appear on paper, for the Party
stalwarts could hardly be switched on and off at will.   There existed a simple division, broken by the parliamentary recess, between
the Liberal hegemony of the summer and Unionist predominance in the
autumn and winter; had Irish issues been allowed to come to the
fore in the summer the Government would have risked simultaneous
Carsonite and radical revolts with the temptation for them of coal-
escing to ditch the Bill along with the administration.   Instead

Ireland was wisely delayed until the eleventh hour when the Commons
had completed the bulk of the work on the Bill and many Liberals
were consequently loathe to throw away all their gains.

The behaviour of the Asquithian leaders on the critical Irish
divisions is interesting.   Among those with no recorded votes one
finds McKenna, Hobhouse, Tennant, Simon, who was absent, and Asquith
himself.   Some like Runciman, Gulland and McKinnon Wood, contrived
to cast a single vote for the Government and one against.   But the
nadir of opposition was reached by the two most significant - Samuel
who spoke but avoided voting on the important questions, and Birrell
who voted twice on the Nationalist side but did not speak at all.
This sort of performance reduced Asquithian backbenchers like
Richard Holt to despair.   For Asquith's failure, seen in its context, amounted to a relentless frittering away of his Nationalist
support from September 1914 which reached a climax in July 1916 when
he allowed Lansdowne, Long and Selborne to veto Lloyd George's settlement.   In 1917 he might have repaired some of the damage;
instead, when Redmond attempted to censure the Government in October
for the misconduct of the civil and military authorities in Ireland
a mere 23 Liberals joined him, compared to 57 who supported the Government.   It was a similar story in April 1918 when 65 Liberals
backed the Government over Irish Conscription against the 40 who
opposed them.   In this process Asquith lost both Liberal and Nationalist supporters;   radicals left continually without a frontbench
lead inevitably fell away after the drift into the disastrous 1918
election.   The point is not so much that the War destroyed Liberal
issues or removed the Party's *raison d'être* but rather that Asquith
lost the battle for the party's life through inertia.

On the other side the 63 Liberals who consistently supported the
Government over Ireland were characteristically members of the administration themselves, right-wingers or Welsh Members such as Sir
W.H. Cowan, T. Towyn Jones, Alfred Mond, Gordon Hewart, F.G. Kellaway and General Ivor Phillips.   To these were added 9 Labour Members including C.B. Stanton the pro-war 'Labour' representative for
Keir Hardie's old seat at Merthyr Tydfil.   In the vital vote on
Redmond's motion it was the 34 Liberal and 7 Labour votes provided
by these two groups that accounted for the Government's majority of
54.

The question arises how far Members were voting on the merits of
these issues and how far out of loyalty to their respective leaders.
One can usefully cross-check for this by comparing the voting on
Proportional Representation for Ireland with Proportional Representation for England.   For both Nationalists and Unionists Irish Proportional Representation was virtually a straight party question;
the former supported it by 48 to 0 on the grounds that it could provide them with the necessary protection against Sinn Fein.   The
Unionists rejected Proportional Representation in this instance by
the unusually wide margin of 135 to 9, a clear indication that loyalty to the Government was seen as the real issue.   The Liberals
divided 53 to 44 in favour of Proportional Representation for Ireland, as did Labour by 11 to 3.   Of the 53 Liberals, 43 were among
the group of 88 who took a consistently rebellious line on Irish
issues;   the pattern becomes clearer if one examines Liberal voting
behaviour over Proportional Representation for England in which

groups of 98 Liberal supporters and 82 Liberal opponents of Proportional Representation emerged.   The 98 in general comprised most of
the radical Liberals, while the 82 included many Coalitionists and
uncommitted Members, though both sections were mixed in their affil-
iations.   Among the 98 Proportional Representation men some 38
voted for Irish Proportional Representation and 10 against it;
these 10 prove on examination to be Coalitionists to a man. (51)
Conversely among the 82 anti-Proportional Representation men 5 suddenly switched to support Proportional Representation for Ireland,
in each case in the context of a consistent anti-Government voting
record; (52) of the 24 who opposed Irish Proportional Representation 16 were regular Coalitionists and none firm Asquithians.   In
this way one can see how the effect of crossing a relatively neutral
issue like Proportional Representation with a major political division was further to consolidate allegiances for or against Lloyd
George.

The controversies of the autumn of 1917 went a long way to crys-
tallising the split within the Liberal and Labour Parties.   The
evidence of twelve divisions in which Members' loyalty to the Government was tested showed some 56 Liberals with a markedly Coalitionist voting record, some of whom went out of their way to demonstrate their position - for example, F.G. Kellaway with 11 votes,
and Sir F. Cawley and J.H. Lewis with 10 each.   Lloyd George's
ability to dispense patronage helped here in that 19 of the Liberals
and 7 of the 10 Labour Coalitionists held posts in the administration; in addition 7 more obtained posts subsequently, and 3 were
parliamentary Private Secretaries to Ministers, thus making a total
of 36 out of 56.

Of these 56 Coalitionists on the Reform Bill 42 voted with Lloyd
George in the Maurice Debate, while 13 abstained and 1 only voted
with Asquith,which is an indication that the Maurice controversy
only underlined a split that already existed.   Indeed the work done
by Mr Edward David on Liberal voting from 1915 to 1918 shows that
the Lloyd Georgeites at the time of the Maurice Debate had rarely
revolted against illiberal measures at any time during the war; the
Asquithians, on the other hand, rebelled on occasion before December
1916, but regularly thereafter. (53)   Thus the split, though long
in the making, only became serious because of the formal division
between the two leaders of the party.   As Prime Minister Asquith
had been able to take illiberal measures without disastrous effects
on the parliamentary party, as even the Lloyd George camp admitted. (54)

The numbers of Liberals who fell into the two camps during 1917
and 1918 were of vital importance in determining the circumstances
in which the Liberals entered the General Election in 1918.   Lloyd
George received much advice during the course of 1917 to the effect
that he should put together a party organisation for himself; (55)
it was an open question whether this would be a Liberal one or a
Centre Party designed to attract Unionists.   Milner briefed him on
the sort of prospectus he would need for the latter purpose. (56)
The funds Lloyd George could find, but the candidates were much more
of a problem in view of the fact that he had no organised following
in the country.   As Addison (57) complained in April 1917 Lloyd
George's leverage with the Conservative Party depended very much

upon his ability to place a large number of Liberal candidates, which
at that stage he could not do.   Lloyd George's Liberal Party by the
autumn of 1918 comprised at most a parliamentary group of 25 Liberal Ministers and 73 other Liberal Members with claims on 98 existing constituencies. (58)   Yet one cannot measure the size of his
following by the number of Members who received the 'Coupon', for
many of them either accepted it without enthusiasm or positively re-
pudiated it.   Thanks to the comparatively free run allowed to the
Government by Asquith the Lloyd George Liberal Party attracted just
enough support to make it worthwhile for the Conservatives to make a
pact on generous terms;   a group of twenty or thirty would not have
given Lloyd George a strong enough bargaining position, while a much
larger party would have been incompatible with the Conservatives in
the constituencies.   One hundred and fifty represented both the
limit of Conservative forbearance and the most optimistic interpretation possible of Lloyd George's support.
    On the Asquithian side there was little concerted attempt to
avert the drift of Members to the Government.   Basically the
leadership of the party had broken up, thereby depriving the Liberals
of the great phalanx of oratorical talent that they had enjoyed
before the war.   A fraction of that talent, in the form of Churchill and Montagu, was drawn into the Coalition Government;   the position of these two, who joined in July 1917 after months of doubt and
expectation, remained rather uncomfortable as their voting records
show;   they simply avoided critical divisions as much as possible.
In addition a large slice of the Liberal leadership had disappeared
into the House of Lords for political, health and financial reasons:
Haldane, Harcourt, Grey, Buckmaster and Pease.   As for the remainder they languished in a dismal twilight for nearly two years in the
Commons until extinguished at the election.   From the start of 1917
Asquith gave no lead to his lieutenants even when, like Runciman (59) they sought one;   he voted only five times on the Reform
Bill, and never in any of the twelve critical ones.   The attitude
of Asquithians like McKenna who had at first been disposed to show
some fight in the Commons was strongly deprecated by Harcourt who
feared he would 'upset the applecart altogether if he went on like
this and gave L.G. his excuse for a General Election'. (60)
    Asquith's refusal to organise a normal opposition in the Commons
produced an acute sense of frustration on the backbenches (61) where
the Pringles and Hogges busily attacked Lloyd George;   yet the Coalitionists soon began to move into the vacuum by such means as the
political breakfasts organised by J.W. Pratt at the Hotel Central at
which backbenchers could meet the Coalition leaders.   As McCallum
Scott, who sympathised with the Asquithians despite being PPS to
Churchill, noted rather gloomily: (62)

    The party machine is a soulless thing and very little of a real-
    ity.   It has no popular hold.   The leaders are not in touch
    with the rank and file....   Unless the orthodox leaders stir
    themselves they will find the ground cut from under their feet.
    The mercenaries will inevitably be attracted towards the hand
    that dispenses patronage.   The rank and file will be attracted
    towards those who take the trouble to keep in touch with them.
Towards the end of 1917 some sporadic efforts were made to launch a
real opposition in spite of Asquith;   Richard Holt, still angry over

the disfranchising of Conscientious Objectors, organised a small
group of Members including Leif Jones, Sir Charles Seely, Sir W.
Collins, Godfrey Collins, Haydn Jones, Percy Molteno, Henry Nuttall,
J.F.L. Brunner, Joseph Bliss and Sydney Arnold who desired to see
'intelligent, patriotic and active opposition'; Holt endeavoured to
bring M'Kinnon Wood, Runciman and Pringle into the plan. (63)
These Members were greatly encouraged by the publication in the
'Daily Telegraph' of Lord Lansdowne's letter on the subject of a
negotiated peace, as a result of which a small group of backbenchers
waited on Asquith to persuade him to take the same line. (64)   The
Members followed this up with a debate in the Commons on War Aims
introduced by Sir William Collins. (65)   Unfortunately, in the
absence of frontbench speakers and the reluctance of many Members to
debate the subject at all, the time was filled by such MPs as Arthur
Ponsonby whose views were so unpopular as to draw the Government
spokesmen away from the case made out by Collins; at length Runciman contributed a rather pathetic speech largely devoted to apolo-
gising for having intervened in the discussion at all.   Asquith
was still not to be lured into debating such an issue, though Holt
felt encouraged by a speech he made at Birmingham which went a long
way towards Lansdowne's position.   They therefore kept up the pressure on him during 1918, though with mixed results.   He declined to
intervene over the application of conscription to Ireland - a golden
opportunity in the radicals' view - but perhaps because it would
merely have detracted from his attack over a sound war issue in the
Maurice Debate on 8 May.   Yet the Maurice affair was badly bungled
by Asquith who failed to grasp Bonar Law's unwise offer of a judicial enquiry which would have relieved him of the need to deliver a
partisan speech in the Commons.   In the event Asquith's speech was
so studiously academic and hesitant compared with the responses from
the Government bench that McKenna, Samuel and Runciman sat out the
debate in silence.   Despite this 100 Liberals voted with Asquith
against seventy-one for the Prime Minister; but the debate, instead
of inaugurating a regular opposition again, proved to be an aberration in the general pattern of drift and abdication.   Holt eventually despaired of any action from Asquith: 'I fear he funks Lloyd
George and feels that the venemous, incompetent, clever, plucky
little Welshman is his master in debate.' (66)

Asquith's irresolution arose partly out of a patriotic desire to
see the war through to a conclusion, and partly out of a realisation
that he could not now form a war administration even if Lloyd George
were defeated in Parliament.   In addition he probably shared with
other Liberals an anxiety over the Reform Bill which inhibited him.
Holt himself readily conceded that his fellow plotters, for all
their detestation of Lloyd George, were keen to pass the Reform Bill
before risking a major row. (67)   For it was commonly assumed in
the Liberal and Labour ranks that the Bill contained so much of
benefit to them that it should be helped forward as much as possible; their real fear, as Barnes warned the Cabinet, (68) was that
the Peers intended to delay it.   A special delegation from Labour
waited on the Prime Minister in September 1917 to extract a promise
that the Bill would not be kept waiting until a measure dealing with
the Second Chamber could catch up.

A further consideration in Asquith's thinking and that of his

colleagues was the need to go on preserving the 1910 House of Commons until peacetime.   The other parties, who were less concerned
about this, had allowed the by-election truce to lapse;   and although they did not challenge Liberal seats in by-elections they
ignored Gulland's attempts to commit them to an extension of the
truce. (69)   Fear of a wartime election paralysed Liberal efforts
in parliament, as for example in the debate on the suppression of
foreign editions of the 'Nation' in April 1917, when Holt noted:
'a division was staved off by the loquacity of those who are afraid
of beating the Government and having to face a general election.' (70)   Lloyd George himself had made it clear to Bonar Law
that if he were pushed too hard by the Asquithians his response
would be a dissolution;   when, for example he faced possible defeat
over Irish Conscription in 1918 he announced: 'It should be resignation or dissolution.' (71)
   Behind Liberal fears about an election lay their knowledge that
MPs had allowed the constituency organisation to decay dramatically
during the war.   Members such as Richard Holt and C.P. Trevelyan
virtually severed their connections with their local associations
through complete lack of sympathy with the war effort;   as MacCallum
Scott observed in May 1915, (72) Liberals ought to have kept in
close touch with their constituencies with a view to the next election, but for many of them the formation of the Coalition made them
deeply unhappy about defending the Government on local platforms;
yet as they hesitated to attack it the best course often seemed to
be to avoid contact altogether.   After Asquith's fall from power
Harcourt established himself at 21 Abingdon Street, interviewed the
party agents who came up to London and attempted to overhaul the
party machinery; (73)   but it was probably too late to achieve anything of significance.
   The Labour Party also had good reason not to cause too much
trouble in the House before the Reform Bill was safe, for they
feared not an election, but an *early* election which Henderson suspected the Prime Minister might spring upon them. (74)   Not only
did they require time to organise the new candidates, but they
counted also on the Reform Act being in operation when the election
took place.   Ironically it was Bonar Law who stood between the
radicals and an early appeal to the country which he suspected would
undermine his control of both the party organisation and the parliamentary party.   He would have been compelled to give way to the
Prime Minister's desire for a new House only if the Asquithians had
organised themselves sufficiently to have defeated the Government
over any of the controversial measures of 1917 and 1918.   The re-
percussions of such action by the Opposition would thus have been
the loss of the Reform Bill as well as an election in which Lloyd
George would have been the only real winner.

Chapter 10

THE REGIMENT OF WOMEN

> When one talks to the young sentimental Woman Suffragist he sees
> no relevance in the enquiry whether the great mass of women know
> or care anything about politics.   It is quite enough for him
> that they are human beings.   As such they have a right to vote.
> When we wrote 'Essays On Reform' in 1866 we argued that working
> men were fit for a vote, both parties assuming that fitness had
> to be proved.   (James Bryce to A.V. Dicey (copy), 15 September
> 1917)

In 1917 Mr Asquith caught the bus - the woman suffrage bus as graph-
ically depicted by 'Punch' in a cartoon which simplified unduly the
complex relationship between the Great War and woman suffrage.   It
is possible that Asquith saw the light, that the scales fell from
his eyes, as he said himself, that the experience of war, in short,
changed the attitudes of men towards women as citizens.   It is
also possible that Asquith had already changed his tactics on the
question but had not yet found a suitable opportunity to demonstrate
this;   indeed his friendly reception of Sylvia Pankhurst in 1914 may
well have been the start of an attempt to claw back for Liberalism
the support of politically concerned women already drifting towards
Labour.   This bus Asquith may well have missed altogether.   It is
also more than possible that Mr Asquith, not being at all in the
habit of riding on buses, remained somewhat impervious to the significance of women as bus conductresses; who indeed can doubt that
Asquith, with his fastidious and severe intellect, regarded the idea
that such war service entitled a woman to the rights of political
citizenship as an absurdity?
    In short, although women's votes were won during the Great War
they were not simply a consequence of war;   there existed an indirect connection in that certain accidents and circumstances provoked
by the war situation facilitated their enfranchisement;   and the
pre-war struggle for the franchise generally contributed much to the
1917 reform.   This is not to suggest that the militants had essentially won by 1914;   they in fact had lost by 1910, but the consti-
tutionalist forces had begun to regain ground in the last three
years of peace.   It is also the case that the Conservatives, most
numerous among those who changed position during the war, were

strongly impressed with the narrowness of their escape from damaging
franchise reforms before 1914; they were therefore acutely aware
that a settlement of the whole question ought to be made during the
special circumstances of wartime Coalition.   Indeed the object of
the exercise for some Conservatives was precisely to forestall the
eruption of radical demands in the post-war period.

For the way was paved for woman suffrage by the virtual dis-
appearance of the campaign.   It is true that in the East End of
London Sylvia Pankhurst's followers continued to combine politics
with relief work for the war, and the Women's Freedom League contrived a normal hum of activity; yet it is well to distinguish what
was important in the context of the internal politics of the movement from what assisted the attainment of their objective.   The
main arms of the movement underwent a rapid metamorphosis; the
largest and best organised part, the NUWSS, turned itself into the
'Women's Active Service Corps', and the WSPU simply vanished as a
suffragist body.   The fact that neither pro nor anti-suffragists
launched any appreciable campaign goes a long way to explaining why
in the long history of women's suffrage the vital 1914-18 period has
been neglected.   In the strange hiatus between 1914 and 1916 the
Pankhursts had not just abandoned suffrage but freely subordinated
it to the claims of men.   They therefore played no part in the
final triumph which, by comparison with the earlier story, seems
devoid of the drama which is appropriate for such an historic occasion.   The Pankhursts were denied the sensational triumph for which
they had craved even at the last moment when Lord Curzon's abject
surrender in the House of Lords converted climax into anti-climax in
a matter of moments.

Under the impact of war the women's movement reacted in three
different ways.   Most dramatic, as ever, was Mrs Pankhurst's transformation from public enemy to patriot, not to say chauvinist.   Her
trial of strength with the Home Secretary ceased abruptly; already
on 3 August 1914 McKenna had begun to receive requests - not from
the suffragettes themselves - for the release of political prisoners, (1) and on 7 August he announced an amnesty for those 'who
will undertake not to commit further crimes or outrages'; (2) three
days later this condition was waived both for women and for those
convicted in connection with strikes: (3)

His Majesty is confident that the prisoners ... will respond to
the feelings of their countrymen and countrywomen in this time of
emergency and that they may be trusted not to stain the causes
they have at heart by any further crime or disorder.

Christabel Pankhurst, who perceived that the crisis provided an
opportunity to withdraw without loss of face from the confrontation
with the Government, left her Parisian exile on the outbreak of war
and reappeared a month later at the London Opera House with a speech
on 'the German Peril'; and it was not long before she and her
mother became familiar figures on recruiting platforms, the past
forgotten in the patriotic avalanche of the Pankhursts' powerful
emotions.   'The War has made me feel', Mrs Pankhurst declared, 'how
much there is of nobility in man, in addition to the other thing
which we all deplore.' (4)   As to the events of the last few years,
she reminded her audience:
never throughout the whole of that fight did we for one single

moment forget the love we had for our country, or did we relax
one jot of our patriotism ... one of the mistakes the Kaiser
made, one among many, was that he thought under all circumstances
the British people would continue their internal dissensions.

The 'Suffragette' newspaper also vanished after 7 August, re-
appearing briefly in April 1915, only to be reborn in October as a
war paper entitled 'Britannia' which advocated a policy of military
conscription, internment of aliens and a war of attrition against
Germany.   Soon 'Britannia' was to be found vociferously demanding
the resignation of miscellaneous traitors and scoundrels including
Sir Edward Grey, Lord Robert Cecil and Sir Eyre Crowe of the Foreign
Office, the latter on account of his German connections. (5)   In
1915 the Pankhursts obliged Lloyd George by organising a women's
procession demanding to be given work in the munitions factories,
towards the cost of which Lloyd George had found £3,000 from his
own Ministry.   According to Annie Kenney (6) he had told them: 'I
have such opposition to face among the Cabinet that some pressure is
needed, and you are the only people who can bring that pressure to
bear.'   So anxious were they to play this new role that it was not
until April 1917 that Christabel found time to write a word about
woman suffrage, and even then no comment was offered during that
critical year.   In their frantic search for a new purpose in politics the Pankhursts inevitably overdid their patriotism, so much so
that in January 1917 their premises were raided by the War Office
because of articles attacking General Sir William Robertson.   Eager
now to be of service to Government and country Christabel spent six
months in the United States attempting to persuade Americans to
enter the war; in the summer of 1917 Mrs Pankhurst prepared herself
for a visit to Russia where she was to whip up enthusiasm for the
war thus counteracting Ramsay MacDonald who was also going.   The
Pankhursts' translation into orthodox Conservatism went a stage
further when, in November 1917, the WSPU became the 'Women's Party',
whose programme included opposition to Irish Home Rule, abolition of
Trade Unions, and the elimination of all persons of non-British
descent from Government Departments and essential industries.   In
the General Election Christabel stood at Smethwick, armed with the
Coupon, but though polling well she lost to a Labour candidate; by
this time her politics had degenerated into a diatribe against Bol-
shevism.

In contrast the NUWSS appeared distinctly ambivalent about the
war at first, and even participated in a well-publicised Peace Meeting on 4 August: 'Action of that kind', Lord Robert Cecil reproved
Mrs Fawcett, (7)
    will undoubtedly make it very difficult for the friends of Woman
    Suffrage in both the Unionist and Ministerial parties.   Even to
    me the action seems so unreasonable under the circumstances as to
    shake my belief in the fitness of women to deal with the great
    Imperial questions and I can only console myself by the belief
    that in this matter the National Union do not represent the
    opinions of their fellow country women.
Mrs Fawcett, however, reasserted her leadership once war was underway: 'Let us show ourselves worthy of citizenship whether our claim
to it be recognised or not.' (8)   Thus the National Union, through
its network of branches, embarked upon an extensive programme of

relief work of a fairly traditional type involving the distribution
of scarce goods, help for Belgian refugees, endowing of hospital
beds, purchasing of ambulances, organising concerts and coffee rooms
for soldiers, clubs for their wives, maternity centres, war nurse-
ries and Employment Exchanges for Day Domestic Workers; (9) they
insisted that regular political activity had merely been suspended,
not abandoned, for the time being because 'we know that a War Government cannot busy itself with legislation for franchise
reform'. (10)

In this process, however, several leading members who sympathised
with the attitude of the Union of Democratic Control towards the
war, left the National Union after a running battle lasting for some
months.   The pro-war leadership recognised the danger of the
National Union becoming a medium of propaganda over any war issue
and firmly resisted all invitations to participate in international
gatherings for the promotion of peace on the grounds that women from
the various belligerent countries were no more likely than men to be
able to discuss the war without violent disagreement. (11)   It
proved impossible to contain the anti-war group within the National
Union and in April 1915 eleven members of the Committee including
Catherine Marshall and Miss Courtney resigned.   A similar difficulty faced the WFL in 1917 when their President, Mrs Charlotte Despard, decided to work for the Women's Peace Crusade; her executive
were most anxious to dissociate her individual action from that of
the WFL and especially to postpone her new work until the Reform
Bill had been safely passed into law. (12)

It was greatly to the advantage of the women that during the
first three years of war no major branch of their movement had
become publicly associated with the cause of a negotiated peace,
though many individual members had devoted themselves to it.   Anti-
suffragists in Parliament were only too anxious to deploy the argument that women as voters would hinder Governments from waging war;
indeed during the Boer War Lloyd George himself had used this argument, (13) and the example of the Australian Government's defeat
over conscription - widely attributed to the women's vote - could be
cited in support.   However, by 1917 such a line of argument could
never be made to stick; the moderates had been too diligent in
relief work, the Pankhursts too shrill in summoning young men to the
Army and rooting out half-heartedness in the war effort generally.
Even the ladies of the League For Opposing Woman Suffrage became em-
barrassed at being outdone in patriotism by the Pankhursts; there
grew up a clear sense that the anti-suffragist cause was being
undermined with every patriotic act committed by a woman: 'They sew
and knit comforts for the soldiers', lamented the 'Anti-Suffrage
Review', (14)

but with such a perpetual running accompaniment of suffragist
self-laudation that they might as well embroider the sacred name
of Mrs. Pankhurst or Mrs. Fawcett on every sock and every muf-
fler, so as to give notice to the soldiers as well as to the
country at large that Suffragism alone has the trademark of
thoughtful and benevolent patriotism.

Not all suffragists allowed the war to restrict their normal
activities.   The WFL for instance seems to have taken advantage of
the slackened efforts of its rivals to make up its membership figures.   As one WFL delegate explained in 1915: (15)

> Since the War there has been an absolute dropping of suffrage
> work.   There are many people who meant to go on with Suffrage
> but had nothing to follow.   Even before the War there were tons
> of people who would have liked a W.F.L. in their district, but
> they were afraid to join the W.S.P.U. and so joined the National
> Union.

Thus the WFL launched new membership drives in selected areas from
1915 to 1917 for which they claimed much success.   The ladies also
kept up fairly frequent deputations to Ministers to pester for
action on a wide range of topics including Munitions work, Food Control, Venereal Diseases and the Honours List; on the franchise they
sought Lloyd George's consent to receive a deputation late in 1916
and early in 1917, to which he apparently did not even reply. (16)
This contrasted with his willingness a little later to respond to
Mrs Fawcett's better timed overture; it was rather pointless for
the WFL to pester him before the Speaker's Conference had reported,
or to send its vigilantes to picket the meetings and badger its members with letters and telegrams every Wednesday and Thursday.   In
general the WFL gave every indication of an organisation absorbed
in its regular peacetime activities; not that they made any significant impact at this stage beyond reminding the politicians that
the women were still capable of agitation for the vote.

By 1915 the women's cause was in a state of vaguely optimistic
suspension, and Mrs Fawcett believed they would enjoy extra public
support 'when next we have a chance of demanding the enfranchisement
of women', (17) though when this might be she had no idea.   The
year brought little satisfaction for suffragists, although they
scanned the ranks of the Coalition Government for supporters;   Henderson, Balfour, Bonar Law and Selborne - all suffragists in varying
degrees - came in, while Harcourt, Hobhouse and Samuel - all antis -
went out; but so did suffragists such as Haldane, Montagu and
Emmott, and a formidable trio of opponents - Curzon, Chamberlain and
Lansdowne - joined the Government.   The real gain for the women lay
simply in the multi-party nature of the Ministry, but for the time
being the Coalition, in Mrs Fawcett's view, merely served to underline the futility of suffrage work; she actually cancelled a letter
to the Prime Minister because: (18)

> The necessary preoccupation brought about by the recent Cabinet
> crisis would prevent Mr. Asquith from giving attention to our
> affairs....   Now that there is a coalition Government there is
> practically no chance of a new franchise being introduced.

These sentiments were echoed by the Secretary of the War Emergency
Workers National Committee in a letter to Sylvia Pankhurst later
that year: 'the public mood is far too much centred on war matters
to concern itself very much about suffrage.' (19)   As a result the
women's leaders who were still thinking about the franchise at all
became so resigned to the prospect of a long wait that they were in
danger of failing to see the possibilities of the situation in 1916.

In one sense, of course, Mrs Fawcett was quite right; it was inconceivable that Asquith's Government could have reached agreement
on a franchise Bill.   Yet they had to face the prospect of doing
precisely that, which is what made woman suffrage a live issue once
again in 1916.   As has been shown the women's claim arose through
the wish of the Cabinet to deal with registration for the troops, a

situation to which the women woke up slowly.   In 1916, with a franchise Bill now threatening, even the sceptics of the National Union
deemed it time to send the Prime Minister an open letter on the subject on 4 May, (20) which drew the following characteristic reply
from Asquith: (21)

> No such legislation as you refer to is at present in contempla-
> tion; but if, and when, it should become necessary to undertake
> it you may be assured that the considerations set out in your
> letter will be fully and impartially weighed without any pre-
> judgement from the controversies of the past.

On the basis of this and letters from Grey and Henderson Mrs Fawcett
declared that the anti-suffragist citadel had reached the verge of
capitulation; May 1916 therefore marked the resumption of the on-
slaught on politicians' postbags, and Ministers confessed to being
inundated with letters from moderate suffragists on the subject of
the Registration Bill. (22)   Asquith, however, continued to rebuff
pleas to receive deputations throughout the summer, pleading pressure of business on each occasion.   The pressure being exerted by
Henderson and Cecil at this time served to prolong and exacerbate
the Cabinet debate and thereby to save the women's cause during the
dangerous period in the summer when the Cabinet might otherwise have
got away with a simple Bill dealing with soldiers' registration.

In June a Joint Suffrage Conference adopted the National Union's
policy of offering to stand aside from the controversy only on condition that the Government confined themselves strictly to a Registration Bill and avoided franchise changes.   Tried friends on the
backbenches, Dickinson, Simon, W.C. Anderson and Lord Hugh Cecil,
were requested to see that the women's claim was raised in the
House, to hold meetings of suffragist Members, and to draft a new
women's Bill. (23)   Yet it is clear, despite all this activity,
that the women were very much on the defensive; it was the soldiers' case that demanded attention, and the women asked only to be
allowed a place in their Bill.   By July Mrs Fawcett was anxiously
interviewing Lord Hugh Cecil about Sir Edward Carson's Motion to
make military service a qualification for the franchise, her idea
being to line up Dickinson and Anderson with Cecil to make an all-
party plea for the inclusion of women: 'I still don't think it
probable that such a motion would be adopted', she confessed, 'still
we ought to be prepared for all contingencies.' (24)   On 15 August
a meeting of friendly MPs took place at the Commons under Dickinson's Chairmanship with a view to promoting a separate Bill if the
Government's Registration Bill passed unamended, but at this point
they were overtaken by the decision to hold the Speaker's Conference.

In the event the women launched no public campaign at all as Lord
Northcliffe, a new and eager convert to their cause, complained: (25)

> There is absolutely no movement for Woman Suffrage anywhere.   I
> have made enquiries of a great many women on the subject, but
> they do not take any interest in it.   I cannot explain the psy-
> chology, but it is the fact.   Try and get up a public meeting on
> the subject, and I will support it, and you will soon find out
> whether I am right or wrong.

Mrs Fawcett who was nettled by these remarks as no doubt Northcliffe

intended, nearly allowed herself to be pushed into a resumption of
suffrage work among the public: 'People are already beginning to
say "There is no sign of any movement for W.S. anywhere."' (26)   On
23 December the persistent press baron warned her: (27)

> I do not suggest window-breaking, but I do think that some great
> meeting, or united deputation is necessary.... Public psycho-
> logy is such that the people can only think of one thing at a
> time.   They are now thinking of the war.   And it is quite pos-
> sible that legislation will arrive unnoticed that may be detri-
> mental to the interests not only of women, but to many other sec-
> tions of the community.

Mrs Fawcett replied coolly to these overtures, stressing the danger
of dissipating the goodwill women had recently acquired by hasty
public demands, and indicating her preference for a deputation to
the Prime Minister to whom she wrote on the subject; (28)   in her
mind there was a suspicion that Northcliffe was an *agent provocateur*
whose continued requests for more demonstrative action she frostily
rebuffed.

In spite of Northcliffe's blandishments the women's groups were
on the whole prepared to await the outcome of the Speaker's Conference passively but vigilantly.   Although their two Liberal allies,
Simon and Dickinson, were Conference members the National Union
seems to have remained uninformed about its progress;   this is clear
from a letter of Mrs Fawcett's in December in which she refers to
the 'Manchester Guardian' as her source for saying that the Conference is still at work. (28)   Even after the decision on the women's
question had been taken Dickinson refrained from telling Mrs Fawcett
anything beyond that it was 'something substantial upon which to
build'. (29)   No doubt he wished to break gently the news that
equal suffrage was not going to be recommended and feared a precipi-
tate response from the women: (30)

> please do all you can to induce women to see that it will be bad
> tactics to fall foul of the Conference because it may not have
> done all that they expected.   The whole matter will need the
> most careful handling so as to avoid the risk of the Government
> having an excuse for saying that as it [is] impossible to satisfy
> the advocates of W.S. they refrain from dealing with W.S. at all.

Now Mrs Fawcett was by no means content with the proposals, as her
notes on her copy of the Report show; (31)   but she took Dickinson's
warning to heart as did suffragists generally.   Those who attempted
to exert any leverage with the politicians met little success as is
evident from an exchange between the WFL and the Labour Party in
February 1917.   The WFL sought an undertaking from every Labour MP
to 'vote against any Bill dealing with Electoral Reform which does
not enfranchise women'; (32)   only five Members even replied to
this, all of whom avoided the commitment   sought, though later
Ramsay MacDonald gave the promise.

In a meeting with Walter Long Mrs Fawcett undertook on behalf of
twenty-two suffrage societies to accept the Speaker's proposals, provided the Government agreed to include them in their Bill, and not
to agitate for more. (33)   The Government had to consider the example of the American suffragists who at the start of 1917 had begun
to picket the White House, tactics which were to lead to mob violence, arrests and hunger strikes as the year progressed.   Any

means of averting the re-opening of the campaign in Britain therefore seemed most attractive and the agreement with Mrs Fawcett
helped Long in his efforts to commit his colleagues to a Bill.
However, in view of the antagonism of Curzon and Carson the Cabinet
could agree to offer no more than a free vote on the women's clause.
This seemed adequate for the suffragists were by now growing confident of the mood in parliament, and it was thus a distinctly
friendly occasion when on 29 March Lloyd George met a deputation
representing most of the women's societies. (34)   He made a point
of excluding Sylvia Pankhurst's group because they were much less
amenable politically and insisted on full adult suffrage, a point
which the Prime Minister plainly did not wish to debate with the
deputation.   The rest, however, were happy to compromise: 'we
should greatly prefer an imperfect scheme that can pass', as Mrs
Fawcett put it.   The mood of the meeting reflected her confidence
that the end was now in sight, the only real doubt having been removed by the Prime Minister's assurance that a women's clause would
be inserted into the original Bill before it left the draftsmen.
In this way the Government managed to avoid any public demonstrations by the women in connection with the Reform Bill during the
war.
     The fact that neither the suffragist nor the anti-suffragist
camps launched campaigns to win over opinion during the war renders
it difficult for historians to venture the kind of claim made by
Professor Marwick (35) that there was a collapse of pre-war prejudice against women.   It remains to ascertain whether for instance
the men who granted the vote had lost their prejudice, and if so, to
what extent if any this was due to the experience of war.   It is
important to recall that far from the war awakening men to the need
to incorporate women into the body of citizens, the *first* effect of
the crisis was to elevate manhood above all things;   at the commencement of hostilities the British promptly turned the neglected
Tommy Atkins into the Saviour of the Nation, as Kipling had always
said they would.   From all sides the stay-at-home male was assaul-
ted by the posters of the Parliamentary Recruiting Committee and the
white feathers of patriotic ladies challenging him to prove his manhood or face ridicule and humiliation from his countrymen.   One
political consequence of this glorification of the fighting man was
the desire of some politicians to enfranchise the troops, which, as
has been suggested, threatened by 1916 to enshrine in law the old
anti-suffragist argument that women should not be voters because
they lacked physical force and were therefore unable to contribute
to the defence of their country.   To accept military service as a
qualification for the vote was to erect a hurdle which women could
not hope to cross;   this possibility greatly alarmed suffragists (36) not least because the point was publicly subscribed to by
Mrs Pankhurst who willingly surrendered priority to the troops.
'Could any woman', she asked, (37) 'face the possibility of the
affairs of the country being settled by conscientious objectors,
passive resisters and shirkers?'   In August 1916 she went to the
length of authorising a Conservative MP, Commander Bellairs, to
state on her behalf in the House of Commons that the WSPU would not
use the enfranchisement of soldiers and sailors as a reason for agi-
tating for women's votes. (38)   Fortunately the Pankhursts' will-

ingness to give away their position in this fashion was adequately countered by the resistance of Cecil and Henderson in Cabinet.

On the other hand people did gradually pick up the notion that women were making a special contribution to the war effort. Women's war work was a great boon to the press and therefore easily exaggerated; the number of women working in munitions factories, where the most dramatic rise occurred, increased from 200,000 before the war to 900,000 at the end of it; this accounted for nearly all of the 800,000 increase in the number of women workers employed in industrial occupations. Men had in fact been making use of the labour of women in this way for some considerable period of time, so that there was not likely to be a sudden or profound change in their attitude towards them. For most men the women workers appeared less as saviours than as insidious threats to the jobs and wage rates of the men they replaced. As a result the Government felt compelled not only to give assurances to the Unions that they would return to the old trade practices after the war, but also to live up to them in the panic demobilisation of 1918. Women therefore duly departed from most of their newly won positions, and if fewer returned to domestic service in the interwar years this was because long-term changes in production and commerce created a wider choice of work in offices and factories; the advance of women in certain occupations owed little or nothing to the war, the impact of which was essentially short-term and superficial.

On balance the war probably did more to emphasise the traditional functions of men and women than to demonstrate the equality of their contribution to society. This was especially true with regard to women's prime function - in the eyes of men - as child bearers for the nation; nine months after the outbreak of war when the large numbers of unmarried mothers left behind by the volunteers were discovered, the national press quickly recovered from its shock with the thought that the War Babies represented a vital contribution to the next generation of fighting men. Earl Grey actually detected a link between the rearing of a family and political citizenship in that he urged the Speaker's Conference to give an additional vote to every married man and woman who had produced four children, on the grounds that such people had 'had an additional experience of life and their vote is therefore of more value. Further, they have rendered a service to the state without which the state could not continue to exist.' (39)   Although Grey's somewhat eccentric definition of citizenship did not command complete acceptance it does seem true that politicians felt much happier about the mature family woman as a voter than about the single, the independent or the younger woman; the former was much less likely to have broken new ground during the war, but she made the male politician less uneasy and provided an element of stability in a changing world. It is therefore misleading to see a causal relationship between the wartime emancipation of some women and a realisation by the State that they were too important to be denied citizenship.

In a superficial way the war contributed to the debate on woman suffrage that had been running for decades. For example, the old argument that women were, in the words of A.V. Dicey, 'by nature incapable of taking part either in the defence of the country against foreign enemies or in the maintenance of law and order at home'

appeared distinctly churlish and ungrateful at a time when women
were undertaking heavy and dangerous work in munitions factories.
Some contemporaries hastened to repudiate the physical force idea
though this was more typical of journalists than of politicians.
'In the past', announced the 'Observer' (40) penitently, 'we have
opposed the claim on one ground, and one ground alone - namely that
women, by the fact of their sex were debarred from bearing a share
in national defence. We were wrong.' Such people, as the 'Anti-
Suffrage Review' pointed out, must have been blithely unaware of the
vital role women played in peacetime, 'or they must subscribe to the
hopelessly illogical contention that willingness to serve implies
capacity to rule'. (41) However, the undermining of the physical
force argument had the effect of dividing the anti-suffragists since
some perceived that suffragism occupied the patriotic stance; to
oppose the franchise seemed divisive and unpatriotic and they therefore retreated in confusion to find more defensible ground.
    The war also modified the discussion by giving force to the argu-
ment that women would require political power to defend the industrial role that they had undertaken; although this was widely aired
when the House of Commons came to debate woman suffrage in May and
June 1917 MPs had not the slightest intention of supporting the industrial role of women at the expense of men. However, it was the
kind of point, along with the discrediting of the physical force
theory, that Members liked to raise as a means of lending an air of
topicality to speeches now dog-eared by decades of use. It also
provided a convenient method of covering the retreat from anti-
suffragism that some Members wished to make. Yet hardly any Members actually *advocated* woman suffrage on the grounds of the work
they had performed during the war, though all paid the necessary
tribute to it. The idea of the vote as a reward was rejected on
all sides as well it might, for without repudiating the idea parliament could not consistently have refused to enfranchise the women
under thirty who were largely engaged in munitions work and other
normally male occupations. On the whole then, Members who were in
favour of the reform do not seem to have discovered any positive
reason arising out of the war for their belief.
    In fact the idea that war changed attitudes originated essential-
ly with journalists for whom women's work provided a source of fresh
copy to brighten pages jaded with war news, rather than among politicians. Lord Northcliffe, as we have seen, grew so alarmed at the
lack of interest in the franchise that he actively sought a show of
strength from the women; this would 'give the newspapers the opportunity of dealing with the matter. I shall speak to the Editor of
"The Times" on the question today. I believe he is entirely favourable. P.S. Have done so. He is.' (42) Northcliffe may have
had other reasons for pestering Mrs Fawcett; perhaps Lloyd George,
with whom Northcliffe was in close contact over this question,
wanted some pressure applied by the constitutional suffragists in
order to back him up in Cabinet discussions; if so it clearly flat-
tered Northcliffe to be able to act as go-between. But the whole
correspondence underlines the difficulty of using the press as an
indicator of public opinion; anti-suffragists certainly thought
that editors were refusing to publish their letters owing to a
change in editorial policy in favour of the women which itself re-

flected the desire of newspapermen to promote national unity and
harmony as their best contribution at a time of crisis.   The kind
of process at work in this particular instance began with the Government's initiative which Northcliffe realised was leading rapidly
towards woman suffrage; he then tried to provoke a response from
those suffragists of whom he approved in order to report favourably
upon it in his papers.   The phenomenon thus generated can, if
channelled into the opinion polls of a later generation, be allowed
to masquerade as public opinion; and so in a sense it is, but it
tells the historian more about press barons than about changes in
the attitudes of the people.

This problem should alert one to the fact that the phenomenon of
widespread wartime conversions to woman suffrage among politicians
was more apparent than real; only a few stalwarts were ready to go
down with the anti-suffrage ship; as Ramsay MacDonald observed, the
rest were inclined to change sides without having altered their
opinions.   This precisely described the position taken by the Post-
master-General, Sir Joseph Compton-Rickett. (43)   Walter Long is
another often claimed as a convert; in fact, as his private correspondence shows, (44) Long retained his basic hostility but took
the view that Conservatism should cut its losses by settling the
whole reform question during the war rather than risking something
more radical when peace returned; (45) he felt confident that a
limited franchise for women, given without delay and prevarication,
would, on the precedents set by earlier reform Bills, keep them in a
minority for at least a generation.

Thus it is to the ex-Prime Minister that one has, apparently, to
turn for an example of a prominent convert to woman suffrage.   It
was in May 1916 that Asquith had first dropped a hint of a change of
heart in his letter to Mrs Fawcett, (46) and in August he had declared that he would not be able to deny the women's claim to the
vote after the war was over. (47)   His speech on the Speaker's
Report was therefore awaited eagerly.   'Why, and in what sense, the
House may ask, have I changed my views?' Asquith posed himself the
question and promptly resorted to a classical anecdote by way of an
answer; (48) he continued:

My opposition to woman suffrage has always been based, and based
solely, on considerations of public expediency.   I think that
some years ago I ventured to use the expression 'Let the women
work out their own salvation'.   Well, Sir, they have worked it
out during this War.   How could we have carried on the War without them?...   But what I confess moves me still more in this
matter is the problem of reconstruction when the War is over.
The questions which will then necessarily arise in regard to
women's labour and women's functions and activities ... are questions in regard to which I, for my part, feel it impossible consistently either with justice or with expediency, to withold from
women the power and the right of making their voice directly
heard.   And let me add that, since the War began, now nearly
three years ago, we have had no recurrence of that detestable
campaign which disfigured the annals of political agitation in
this country, and no one can now contend that we are yielding to
violence what we refused to concede to argument.

In short Asquith was saying that while he had remained fixed in his

position the women had changed, thus allowing him to climb down
without admitting defeat.   Yet one must remember that his antagonism to woman suffrage went back a long way before the onset of
militancy in 1905; as early as 1892 he had gone out of his way to
secure the defeat of woman suffrage Bills, (49) and in later years
as Prime Minister his persistence in thwarting the women indicates a
hardening of his antipathy towards women in politics.   The question
is, at what point did he modify his obstructionism?   The evidence
suggests that it was 1912-14 rather than 1914-17.   For the Cabinet
had agreed to allow their 1912 Franchise Bill to be amended, and
subsequently to provide time for a Private Member's Bill; and the
Prime Minister had been unusually courteous in 1914 when receiving a
deputation of suffragettes from the East End of London. (50)

Yet although Asquith's handling of the issue had changed his
views persisted for some years to come.   In 1920 he remarked of the
women voters of Paisley where he was fighting a by-election: (51)

There are about fifteen thousand women on the Register - a dim,
impenetrable, for the most part ungettable element - of whom all
that one knows is that they are for the most part hopelessly ig-
norant of politics, credulous to the last degree, and flickering
with gusts of sentiment like a candle in the wind.

Yet he went on to say of the (presumably male) electors of Paisley:
'They are among the most intelligent audiences I have ever had....
Violet [his daughter] is a marvellous success as a speaker.'   These
remarks indicate how mixed Asquith's feelings had become by this
time.   Always a man who took considerable pleasure in the company
of women he none the less resented their presence in politics; for
Asquith, though a twentieth-century Prime Minister, had had a mid-
Victorian upbringing in the West Riding of Yorkshire, followed by
Oxford, the Bar and the House of Commons.   Life for him had been a
series of male clubs; his conception of the proper role of women
would not therefore be lightly abandoned.   Women as known to Asquith, inhabited one of three categories; first the small group
with whom he was at one time or another on close and intimate terms
including his mother, his two wives, Helen and Margot, his daughter
Violet, and Venetia Stanley; second, a less distinct group of
ladies with whom one played bridge at weekends as a relief from the
pressure of work; third, the 'dim impenetrable' mass that comprised
the rest of the sex and from whom Asquith was largely cut off.
These relationships did not, on the whole, lead him to modify his
early prejudice.   Helen's distaste for the political life (52) no
doubt confirmed his own feelings, while Margot, with her insatiable
appetite for tactless interference, may well have had the same
effect in spite of the energy and shrewdness with which she attempted to shore up her husband's position whenever it was threatened.
Miss Stanley seems to have provided a sympathetic ear for a Prime
Minister under pressure rather than a critic or advisor, and it was
not until after her marriage in 1915 that Asquith became more dependent upon an intellectual relationship with his daughter whom he
valued even more after the death of his eldest son Raymond.   Moreover, Violet - and Asquith obviously took pride in the fact - was a
very political animal and would have made an excellent Member of
Parliament.   As Violet's political talent emerged in the post-war
years perhaps a genuine change came about in his attitude.   But it

would be misleading to think of him as a wartime convert to woman
suffrage, for the evidence, in so far as it permits a conclusion,
suggests that he changed tactics before the war and his opinions
later, if at all; the point is that the war made it easier to
recant publicly.

For the House of Commons as a whole the divisions on woman suffrage Bills provide some interesting evidence. The issue was
effectively settled on 19 June 1917 when Members approved Clause
Four of the' Representation of the People Bill by 387 votes to 57
(including tellers); this clause embodied the Speaker's proposal
with an age limit of thirty years. Such a massive vote cannot be
explained away by saying that the radicals and pacifists granted the
franchise while the Unionists were away at the war. Each Party
registered a clear majority in favour of the reform:

	Liberals	Unionists	Nationalists	Labour
For	184	140	33	30
Against	12	45	–	–

In order to measure the extent of the change in Members' positions
one may examine the previous voting, in 1913 and 1911, of the 444
Members who voted in 1917 (see Appendix 4). To consider first the
1913 vote on Dickinson's Bill: of the 387 'suffragists' of 1917
some 240 had voted in 1913, 151 for and 87 against woman suffrage;
of the 57 'antis' of 1917, 43 had voted in 1913, all against. Thus
a net total of 87 Members in 281, or 30.9 per cent had changed
sides. One can specify the areas of change more precisely. The
Labour Party, as usual, gave no anti-suffrage votes. The Nationalists, on the other hand, show a complete reversal; in 1913 they
had voted against the women by 21 to 5, and their switch to suffragism in 1917 accounts for a quarter of the total gains in the House.
Of course the reason for their behaviour had only an indirect connection with the war; woman suffrage had always been of comparatively minor importance to them and in 1913 they had simply not
wished to add to Asquith's troubles by supporting women's Bills.
But by 1917 the Asquithian alliance had withered away, Asquith had
himself left office and abandoned his opposition, and there was
therefore no inhibition about backing the Bill. Among the Liberals
some 32 out of 196 had switched in favour of the women, and among
Unionists 35 out of 185. In each case the hostile votes of 1913
owed something to suffragette outrages, then reaching their climax,
especially on the Liberal side where the women were seen by some to
have wrecked the Government's own Bill; the Unionists at that time
were concerned to prevent the passage of anything more than the Conciliation Bill which enfranchised only one-fifth of the numbers in
Dickinson's Bill. These various considerations no longer applied
in 1917.

However, the question arises as to how fair a comparison the 1913
division provides, for in that year the suffragette outrages clouded
the issue, whereas in 1917 the women were basking in favourable if
less extensive publicity. A truer basis for comparison would be
1911, a time when the militants suspended hostilities in order to

give a fair chance to the Conciliation Bill.   Taking the 444 Members in the 1917 division one finds among the 'suffragists' 151 for and 18 against the 1911 Bill;   while the 'antis' show 4 for the Bill and 21 against it.   There was thus a net change of 14 (18-4) in favour of the women in a total of 192 which is 7.2 per cent.   This figure reminds one of two important points;   first the shift to woman suffrage was not all one way in that a few Unionists who approved the Conciliation Bill would not go as far as the 1917 Bill; second the 1911 vote was much more typical of the attitude of the Commons over a long period of time than the aberration of 1912 to 1914.   The figure of 7 per cent, while in no sense a precise measure of the change, does provide a realistic indication of the impact of the war years on politicians.   According to Party the proportion of Members who changed was nil for Labour, 6 per cent for the Unionists, nearly 9 per cent for the Liberals and 10 per cent for the Nationalists.   What explains this?   The Liberal vote in 1911 and 1917 reflected largely the difference in the two Bills;   the one million women covered by the Conciliation Bill were suspected of being wealthy and liable to increase the preponderance of upper-class Conservatives among the electorate.   The age limit in the 1917 Bill was not open to this objection, though the fact that the women's parliamentary franchise was tied to the local government qualification was a restricting factor;   in practice it proved wide enough to include over eight million women, clearly not a privileged stratum.

The Unionist reaction is less clear because of the considerable difference in turnout from 1911 to 1917.   The fact that less than 100 voted in 1911 suggests a shrewd indifference, for while the brunt of controversy broke upon Liberal heads it was wise not to draw off any suffragette fury by taking too prominent a role in the opposition.   However the combination of militancy and Dickinson's Liberal Bill in 1913 clearly provoked many more Unionists to vote against the women.   This voting trend actually runs against the feeling, much believed in if not measured, that anti-suffragism was weakening in the party before 1914 as the electoral gains from the Conciliation Bill became apparent.   What is clear is that the Unionists did not fear that women voters as such would alter the balance of the electorate to their disadvantage;   it was the working class vote of either sex which made them apprehensive, largely because the other parties professed their confidence in them.   Thus once the Unionists had come to accept adult male suffrage there was no reason for holding out against the women.   In 1916 the 'Conservative Agents' Journal' had begun to suggest that the claims of the women could no longer be resisted; (53)   and among all the dire warnings about the Speaker's proposals issued by the Central Office in that year and in 1917 woman suffrage was hardly mentioned. When it was raised a highly phlegmatic attitude was displayed. None of the members of the National Union's sub-committee were 'very much afraid of the women's vote, as it is possible very few of them will exercise it judging by the attitude they take up in Municipal and County elections, in which very few of them take the trouble to vote'. (54)   W.A. Gales of Central Office commented sagely, 'the granting of a vote to the wives of duly qualified male electors would as a rule increase the majority of the opinions of the male

voters'. (55)   Thus when the Unionists came to deal with a serious
proposal for women's suffrage in 1917 it is less surprising than
their past record would lead one to suppose that they should have
accepted it by a margin of three to one.

The massive vote for the women's franchise must be qualified in
one or two other respects.   For example the division did exaggerate
the suffragist preponderance somewhat in that anti-suffragists were
disproportionately Unionist and Unionists were disproportionately
absent on Military Service; however, though the absent Members
would have boosted the opposition vote, the result was clearly not
in doubt.   Some Members who still disliked the reform held back out
of opportunism as is clear from those who abstained in the first
vote and then supported the women's clause in the second vote after
a history of anti-suffragism.   As Sir Henry Dalziel was reported to
have observed cynically: (56)

> All the men who hope to be returned at the next election vote in
> this lobby.   In the other lobby you will find all the men who
> don't intend to return to Parliament, all the men who are certain
> of Peerages, and the few honest men in the House.

It must also be emphasised that the women's clause benefited from
being part of the general reform scheme which the Government regarded as essential; many Members were really acquiescing in various
clauses of which they disapproved for the sake of the measure as a
whole, which helps to account for the remarkably small number who
voted against the women's clause.   Whether such large numbers would
have supported a separate women's Bill remains rather doubtful.
However, the point is that the Government would not have promoted or
supported a special Bill, which is why the women behaved so meekly
in the face of a Bill which offered the vote to boys of nineteen
while denying it to women of twenty-nine; 'we recognised that the
Government were saving face and offering a sop to masculine vanity
at the same time', as one of the suffragettes said. (57)   Despite
the insult being offered to their sex at the moment of triumph the
women realised that the public might not look sympathetically upon a
renewal of agitation for equal franchise with men at this time.
Thus Sylvia Pankhurst was practically alone in wanting to hold out
for equal suffrage, and regarded with disdain the other suffrage
leaders including her mother and sister who were to be found 'in the
lobby of the House of Commons, asking Members of Parliament what
sort of suffrage they should ask for, and whether they should accede
to the age limit of thirty or thirty-five'. (58)

Indeed what has to be explained is the fact that a majority of
seven to one in favour of woman suffrage was not converted into a
vote for equal suffrage with men.   For although the tactics of the
Government were to cling fast to the letter of the Speaker's Report,
the scheme was liable to be amended where a general consensus of
opinion emerged even in respect of the women's franchise.   For
example, an anomaly had arisen in the Bill, based on the Report, in
the form of women parliamentary electors who were without a municipal franchise themselves.   In June 1917 Charles Roberts proposed to
include the five million married women affected, and as his amendment was not pressed at that time the women's organisations spent
the next few months endeavouring to demonstrate to MPs the existence
of a general demand for the local government franchise.   They were

pushing at an open door, for in November when Cave allowed a free
vote on the question no division was necessary; it was not surprising that the anti-suffragists let it pass, for they had long argued
that women should be given a local government vote as a preparation
for the parliamentary franchise.

Thus the argument about not contravening what was in the Report
was a convenient excuse when the House did not wish to do so.   In
fact an amendment to abandon the age limit was hatched by a group of
diehard opponents of the Bill in the hope of disrupting the majority.   The ensuing debate (59) provided the novel spectacle of Lord
Hugh Cecil and Sir Frederick Banbury gathering the mantle of radi-
calism around them while Sir John Simon and Philip Snowden made uncomfortable speeches against adult suffrage.   Naturally advocates
of the amendment had a field day extolling the young female munitions workers who were being deprived of the vote; some like Sir
Henry Craik told the House very gallantly that they knew when they
were beaten and accepted the verdict for woman suffrage: where then
was the need for, let alone the logic in, an age limit?   Two Liberal diehards, MacCallum Scott and Sir Charles Hobhouse, hinted
darkly that the age limit was all a Tory ploy to exclude working-
class women.   No one would defend the clause on its merits, yet the
House stuck to it with what Cecil called a 'sort of lust of irra-
tionality'.   In fact the only logic behind the law was political.
The House believed they were enfranchising about six million, a
solid gesture but not a capitulation which would deliver the male
minority into the hands of the female majority.   This compromise
maximised support for the women's clause where a more rational and
radical proposal would, if passed, have begun to undo the ramshackle
majority for the Bill as a whole; for the merit of the measure was
that everyone had something to be grateful for even if he was not
getting everything he wanted.   Thus the motives behind the amendment were transparently obvious, and Sir George Cave routed it with
a warning that its passage would cause the Government to reconsider
the Bill; this explains the fact that the radicals conspicuously
voted against the amendment among whose twenty-five supporters only
four Liberal suffragists were to be found.

One last consideration may have induced the women and their
allies to play for safety: the House of Lords. (60)   In fact there
is abundant evidence that their Lordships' resistance was crumbling
well before they came to deal with the Bill.   Back in August 1916
Lord Salisbury (61) had confessed: 'I am inclined to think it on
the whole a change for the worse, but if the women turn out really
to demand it I hardly think it can be refused.'   Though some anti-
suffragists like Lord Bryce (62) remained adamant, the less stub-
born Peers grew very doubtful about their proper course of action,
as Lord Balfour of Burleigh admitted:

> To some extent I have changed my views, and I think also the dice
> are loaded against those of us who even yet mistrust the change.
> The latter consideration makes me resolved to put up the best
> fight possible.   Now to be quite candid I cannot and never will
> forgive those who burnt our Churches and buildings....   I do not
> think this Parliament is morally entitled to make this tremendous
> change behind the backs of everyone.   M.P.'s are afraid to vote
> against the possible new votes....   Now please this is private.

I have refused to move the rejection of the clause.   I need not
go into reasons but to save my conscience I think I shall go for
a Referendum on it. (63)
This remarkably defeatist talk shows how the Peers were just as concerned as MPs to save face if they could;   yet the Upper House was
not yet a broken reed, for they chose to exert their strength on the
Reform Bill though not on woman suffrage.   They repeatedly rejected
the Alternative Vote and reintroduced schemes for Proportional Representation against the wishes of the Commons, but that was a conflict in which they were defending Unionist interests as they understood them without offending public opinion, which would not have
been the case with woman suffrage.   Another consideration making
for a careful response was the Bryce Committee on the future of the
Upper House which in January 1918 was only half-way through its
work;   it would not have been wise to have prejudiced the reception
of its recommendations by too much high-handed action on parliamentary reform.
      One man personified the Peers' dilemma over the women: for the
Leader of the House was also the President of the League For Opposing Woman Suffrage - Lord Curzon.   He played thoroughly true to
character.   Although the League had ten months between the Government's decision to implement the Report in March 1917 and the Lords'
debate in January 1918 they did not launch any serious campaign
either in public or in private.   Arnold Ward, MP, had been willing
to give up his Army post in order to return to take up the fight at
home, but only on condition that the League's Committee was unanimous for resistance and would make available the money in the Reserve Fund, now nearly £8,000, for this purpose. (64)   By April the
Committee felt that it was time to start spending the money before
it was too late, (65) but Curzon objected;   indeed, as late as December 1917 he was still arguing that the real crisis would not come
until the Peers had rejected the women's clause or added provision
for a Referendum to it. (66)   This was patently insincere advice in
view of his own intention to abstain which he had intimated to the
Committee through Mrs Mary Ward. (67)
      Yet the Committee could hardly have regarded his attitude as a
surprise, because they had been fighting a losing battle for the co-
operation of their leaders for some time;   in March Arnold Ward had
been anxious to organise meetings in order to stiffen resistance
among MPs since 'many are cowed by the attitude of the Government
and the Press'. (68)   But it was not easy to find speakers to address them: Bryce was away in Scotland, and he was frantically
trying to get Loreburn and Lansdowne instead.   Curzon, though expected to assist in such tasks, refused to do so with the result
that the League's case largely went by default.
      The situation thus drifted towards the debate in the Commons in
June after which Ward warned that if nothing was done the fifty-
seven surviving anti-suffragists in the Commons would inevitably go
down to their constituencies and declare their acceptance of the
verdict so as to make peace with the new electors. (69)   By July
Curzon had stopped attending meetings of the Committee, and by November the Treasurer reported that subscriptions, not surprisingly,
were drying up.   Indeed the League at this stage seemed chiefly
absorbed with the problem of the disposal of their investments, and

Mrs Ward begged Curzon to agree to spend the remainder of the money before the League broke up, as she anticipated it would as soon as the Reform Bill had been passed. (70)   Curzon's position grew ever more uncomfortable: 'It is I am told impossible to hang up the Women's part of the Bill pending a referendum.... It is of course possible to hang up the whole Bill.   But such a course would provoke very great feeling outside.' (71)   Yet in December he agreed to the circulation of an article by Mrs Ward among the Peers, saying, 'It is no use hammering at the public at the moment - that may come later'. (72)   In retrospect this ambivalence irritated the Committee but at the time it served to keep their hope alive.   Mrs Ward appealed vainly for short interviews with Curzon who was now determined to escape from the last ditch in which she was endeavouring to organise a final stand.   By January she was reduced to the plea: 'I do hope you will speak strongly for us tomorrow! We all look to you.' (73)

In vain.   When the critical debate took place on 9 January Curzon could not quietly keep his seat as his Committee expected; instead, after boldly flourishing a catalogue of reasons for opposing woman suffrage, thereby raising both hopes and fears, he subsided abruptly into ignominious anti-climax by urging the Peers to abstain despite everything he had said, since rejection of the clause 'may involve us in a struggle from which the House of Commons is not likely to desist'. (74)   His behaviour throughout provided the League with the opportunity to blame him for the size of the vote - 134 to 71 - for woman suffrage, though the result was surely a foregone conclusion.

With the anti-suffragist forces routed so decisively in both Houses it remained only to crown the victory by enabling women to take their seats as MPs in the Commons.   For this purpose a Bill seemed necessary because, according to Herbert Samuel who introduced a motion urging the Government to act, (75) it would otherwise rest with each Returning Officer to decide whether to accept a nomination paper on behalf of a woman candidate.   The House made no protest about the ensuing Bill which was rushed through just in time for the General Election.   At the same time the Commons also voted to instruct the Speaker to throw open all the galleries of the House to men and women equally. (76)   The women's triumph was, for the present, complete.

What conclusions may one draw from this about woman suffrage and the Great War?   If there was a general collapse of anti-suffragism in British society during this period the kind of evidence provided in the press is too muddied with editorial and proprietorial motivation to provide a clear reflection of it.   Moreover, the definite evidence on the politicians suggests that there was no more than a marginal improvement in the longstanding suffragist majority, and this due more to tactical considerations than to genuine conversions.   However, the point is that comparatively little was said and heard publicly on either side of the controversy after 1914, which enabled anti-suffragists in Parliament to claim that women in general were still showing no desire for the franchise.   It was the Government itself which awakened the women's slumbering cause with their dilemma over the Register in 1916, by which time the movement had partly disintegrated and partly run down.   As a result the women lost the initiative to the politicians and Parliament found itself unusually free from outside pressure on electoral reform in 1917.   If the Representation of the People Bill was a war measure it was far from being essentially a women's measure; they had, in fact, to swallow the very mixture that had been considered so un-palatable when offered in 1912: a large dose of male suffrage in combination with a limited franchise for women.   In 1917, however, nearly all the women's organisations meekly accepted what was offer-ed to them, and this was the most noticeable effect of the war upon their cause.   Such a situation would not,.of course, have lasted long; hence the speed with which politicians like Walter Long acted in pushing the Speaker's Report through Cabinet.   They knew that a post-war settlement would have given the women a chance to mobilise, focus attention upon themselves again, and hold out for equal suf-frage.

What the war really did for woman suffrage was to establish a multi-party Government in May 1915.   Although this seemed at first too divided to handle electoral reform it was precisely the quarrel-someness of Cabinet and Parliament that forced Asquith to appoint a Speaker's Conference, thereby facilitating a far more comprehensive scheme of reform than the Government could envisage.   It was a for-tunate accident that the ensuing Report fell into Lloyd George's hands: 'We know that you are our friend as no previous Prime Mini-ster has ever been', Mrs Fawcett told him, 'and we feel that you have the power to show your friendship as never before.' (77)   None the less Lloyd George could not have forced a woman suffrage Bill onto his colleagues, and there is no indication that he was in any case concerned about the franchise except in so far as it affected the troops.   However, he did make the most of the circumstances that had placed a ready-made reform Bill in his hands only six weeks after coming to power.   The women benefited from this arrangement to the extent of being assured a place in the original Bill, though they had to be abandoned to a free vote in the House.   In this way the suffragist majority of what was still the Parliament of 1910 was at last harnessed to a measure which the Government wanted to enact. Woman suffrage thus gained a large measure of immunity from the depredations of the House of Lords, though the price to be paid was the illogical thirty-year age limit.   In short the circumstances of war proved inhibiting for the suffragists almost as much as for their opponents and led them at last to an unspectacular victory.

Chapter 11

THE PEERS AND PROPORTIONAL REPRESENTATION

> The Tadpoles and Tapers of the [Conservative] Party are opposed
> to [P.R.] because they believe the next Khaki Election will
> return them by a large majority.   (Earl Grey to Wilson-Fox
> (copy), 26 March 1917, Grey Papers, 236/7)

It was not to be expected that the House of Lords would throw out
the Reform Bill; to have provoked a constitutional conflict in 1918
would hardly have endeared them even to their own party.   Thus,
though the Peers throughout the war did nothing in particular they
worked with commendable speed on parliamentary reform, accomplishing
their task of revision between December 1917 and February 1918
during which time many amendments of a minor improving nature were
added, while others seemed essentially gestures of defiance not
persisted in.

There was, however, one exception to this: they fought very
stubbornly to retain some form of Proportional Representation in
the Bill and to eliminate the Alternative Vote.   In the latter
objective they were ultimately successful in defeating the wishes of
the Lower Chamber.   It was the efforts made in this connection that
brought the whole Bill to the verge of failure for a week at the
beginning of February 1918 and left the final form of the measure in
doubt for several months afterwards.   Now the Peers' behaviour was
not simply 'a tactical move against the alternative vote rather
than a sincere acceptance of the principles of P.R.', as Dr
Butler (1) has suggested.   For although party interests influenced
some Peers, we now know that many Unionist politicians had become
Proportional Representation supporters before the war and were not
just adopting it for tactical reasons in 1918.   Moreover, the Proportional Representation issue exposed the natural difference between Unionist MPs and Unionist Peers in that though the latter
shared an interest in elections they were not so obsessed with the
immediate General Election expected during or after the war.   The
Peers represented the sentiments of elderly, independently-minded
Unionists, free from the shackles of ambition and discipline which
inhibited many of their counterparts in the Commons; as such they
tended to regard Proportional Representation in quite a different
light.

At this time the Peers had two related considerations to weigh; one concerned the Bryce Committee which was deliberating on the future of their own chamber, and the other was that a General Election would probably intervene before the passage of legislation to give effect to whatever recommendations Bryce might make.   To many Peers the Coalition Government seemed to provide the best hope of rescuing them from the debilitated condition in which the 1911 Parliament Act had left them;   unless it acted within the next few years there would sooner or later come another election on the lines of 1906 which would leave them at the mercy of a radical House of Commons flourishing a mandate from the adult male electorate in their faces.   For many Peers the virtue of Proportional Representation was that it would tend to make vast swings of the electoral pendulum and subsequent extremist programmes, unlikely.

Although there existed the possibility of a grand bargain between the Government and the Peers over Electoral Reform and Second Chamber reform, there was a fatal time lag between the two which could not be overcome.   Back in August 1917 Lord Bryce, a Liberal so out of sympathy with democratic reform as to be more acceptable to the Peers than Unionists like Lowther, had been invited to chair the new Committee.   However, the first meeting did not take place until October, and the Report was not available until March 1918 by which time the Reform Bill was safely out of the way.   Now Lloyd George had given his consent for the appointment of this Committee in March 1917, and the delay in settling the details looks suspiciously like a deliberate attempt to avoid giving the Peers a bargaining weapon later;   this at least was the effect if not the intention.

Altogether some thirty-two members sat on the Bryce Committee, half of them Peers, and half MPs, (2) among whom were a large proportion of eminent men such as Crewe and Loreburn on the Liberal side and Lansdowne, Chamberlain, Cecil and Selborne for the Unionists.   This excess of elder statesmen and independent notables made it far more difficult for Bryce to exercise the firm control which Lowther had done at the Speaker's Conference.   Their task was to report upon the legislative powers of the Second Chamber, possible methods of adjusting its differences with the Commons, and changes in its composition.   Agreement was difficult to reach not only because many of the radicals felt no great desire to reform the powers of the Lords, but also because the Unionists themselves could not be persuaded to work together before the Conference met. (3)   Opinion ranged between Austen Chamberlain who was generally ready to meet the Liberals half way, to Hugh Cecil who rather agreed with radicals like J.M. Robertson that the Committee might as well be allowed to fail for all the good that was likely to come of it.   On the central problem of powers two solutions emerged, one favouring some intermediate body designed to stand between the two Houses, and the other a Referendum procedure for contentious matters.   So intractable was this problem that members found it more congenial to devote their time to devising a multitude of ingenious schemes for the selection of the members of the reformed chamber;   nearly everyone had his own manifesto on this topic as the papers of Bryce and Selborne show.   Order began to emerge from the chaos in the first week of December when Chamberlain approached the Liberals with a compromise (4) to which Lord Crewe formally replied with a set of propo-

sals representing the views of nine of the radical members; (5)
these were: 1, the Second Chamber should be elected by the Commons;
2, there should be 200 members, a quarter of whom could be selected
by the Peers; 3, their term should be ten years, with half retiring
every five years; 4, they should receive a salary; 5, Proportional
Representation should be the method of election.   This brought a
favourable response from Chamberlain, though his colleagues were
very hostile to the payment of members which had to be dropped.
The largest group of Unionist compromisers coalesced around the
figure of Selborne, since Lansdowne and Cecil were feeling far too
disgruntled to negotiate on such terms.   Selborne thus offered
Crewe counter-proposals on behalf of eight Unionists who included
Lords Burnham and Stuart of Wortley, Evelyn Cecil, R.A. Sanders,
and, by implication, Chamberlain and the Duke of Rutland. (6)   The
proposals of the Crewe-Selborne groups which represented the lowest
common denominator, made a report just possible in a very quarrel-
some committee, though not without a further three months of talks.
Ultimately the Report was signed by all the members but four among
whom were Lords Sydenham and Loreburn; it was decided to foster an
appearance of unity by avoiding the usual practice of allowing dissenting members to record their views in the Report.

The Report (7) envisaged a new House comprising two groups, one
of 246 members elected by MPs grouped in territorial areas and using
the single transferable vote, the second of 81 to be chosen by a
Joint Standing Committee of both Houses from among hereditary Peers
and Bishops in the first instance, but thereafter from commoners as
well.   All the members would serve for twelve years with one third
retiring every four.   On the subject of powers the Report accepted
the Commons' control of finance but proposed using a Finance Committee of seven members of each House to determine what was a finance
Bill.   All other disputed legislation would be considered in private by a 'Free Conference' comprising a few of the 'most experienced, most trusted and most judicious' members of each House chosen
at the start of every Parliament.   If one House still disagreed
with their proposals the Free Conference would consider the Bill a
second time; if it failed to agree on a second revision the Bill
would lapse, but if they made further suggestions it would then rest
solely with the Commons to accept or reject them; without the
Commons' approval the Bill would lapse.

From the Unionist view this Report threw away their party majority without restoring the powers of the House, while in the Liberals' judgment it rendered the passage of legislation more difficult
than at present; consequently the Government felt very reluctant to
attempt to legislate on Bryce's proposals.   When a deputation from
the National Union of Conservative and Unionist Associations urged
Lloyd George and Bonar Law to implement the Report they were told it
could not be done before the autumn General Election; it would however, form part of the Coalition programme and might be dealt with
by the new parliament. (8)   Of course it never was.

However, when the House of Lords received the Reform Bill on 11
December 1917 the Bryce Committee was still four months away from a
conclusion, and the promoters of Proportional Representation had
therefore little to bargain with.   The experimental Proportional
Representation scheme, though a unanimous recommendation of the

Speaker's Conference, had been put to a free vote by the Government
and thrice defeated in the Commons.   Ministerial supporters of the
change included F.E. Smith, Lord Robert Cecil, A.J. Balfour, Dr
Addison, Sir Alfred Mond, and, though they were rather lukewarm,
H.A.L. Fisher and Lord Milner; against them were Lloyd George,
Austen Chamberlain, Walter Long, Sir George Cave and Hayes Fisher.
Since there were no existing party commitments on Proportional Representation the role of the leaders was crucial.   Bonar Law, when
confronted with the new and disruptive issue made the characteristic
plea: 'On this question I have no decided view (perhaps I ought to
have) but I should like if it were possible to see the experiment
tried on a small scale.' (9)   He was careful to add that he would
not wish to coerce a constituency unwilling to be experimented upon;
in practice Bonar Law voted against Proportional Representation.

Lloyd George's initial reaction had been that he would apply
Proportional Representation 'all round or not at all'. (10)   Unhappily he was never a particularly numerate politician and the
mathematical subtleties of Proportional Representation quotas cannot
have appealed to his mind.   To be convinced of such schemes Lloyd
George always needed the constant attendance of a persistent advocate, a function which C.P. Scott attempted to perform; but after
their first discussion on the subject in January 1917 the Prime
Minister hardened against Proportional Representation, referring to
it as 'a device for defeating democracy[,] the principle of which
was that the majority should rule[,] and for bringing faddists of
all kinds into Parliament and establishing groups and disintegrating
parties'. (11)   Behind all these 'usual commonplaces' as Scott
called them, lay the obvious electoral threat to the Welsh Liberals
whose seats, held at the expense of thousands of unrepresented Conservative and Labour voters, he did not wish to jeopardise.   'You
can readily understand', wrote E.T. John, a Welsh Liberal MP, 'that
it does seem extraordinarily quixotic for Welsh radicals to go much
out of their way to alter the present arrangement.' (12)   It was no
surprise then that the Prime Minister announced in the Commons that
he had no opinion on the subject and no intention of studying it
during the war 'unless forced to do so'. (13)

Even before the handicap of Government disapproval became apparent the parliamentary committee of the Proportional Representation
Society had decided to accept the limited experiment offered in the
Speaker's Report as the maximum attainable. (14)   Much propaganda
was sent out to MPs, and the arguments disseminated through the
sober press, nationally and provincially, the 'Manchester Guardian'
'The Times' and the 'Daily Telegraph' being the main supporters.
To counter this there sprang up the Anti-Proportional Representation Committee under the leadership of William Burdett-Coutts, MP
for Westminster. (15)

Proportional Representation was three times defeated before the
Reform Bill went to the Lords, the first occasion being the defeat
by seven votes after the unexpected debate on 11 and 12 June. This
verdict arose out of the heavy Unionist opposition of over two to
one which outweighed the small but favourable majorities of the
three other Parties.   On 4 July when Proportional Representation
was defeated a second time the majority of 31 had been swollen by
extra Unionist Members, anxious to maximise dual voting.   Although

the Irish Members doubled their turnout they had still mobilised
only half their full strength.   A mere 88 Liberals voted for Proportional Representation for which some rather flaccid speaking
from the leaders was partly to blame.   Thus when Aneurin Williams
pressed the Proportional Representation clause for a third time on
22 November it was thrown out decisively by 76 votes with the Liberal Party split almost evenly in two.   This killed Proportional
Representation in the Commons for the time being.

The explanation for this course of events lies to some extent in
the general feeling of MPs against the scheme regardless of Party
interests.   Thus the speeches often concealed the natural aversion
of sitting Members to losing their constituencies in the unknown
hazard of multi-member sears in which the local contacts and credit
built up over the years might count for little.   Indeed many Members discussed Proportional Representation primarily in terms of
their own convenience: there was the difficulty of canvassing a
whole county, the prospect of rivalry between candidates of the same
party, and the loss of contact with the larger electorate.   Such
sentiments were common currency among the party organisers on both
sides.   The Liberal agents, always hostile to Proportional Representation saw it as a threat to their own professional position in
that it would reduce their usefulness to candidates;   moreover, the
simplified registration procedure was expected to deprive agents of
a large part of their work.   On the Unionist side too the agents
jumped to the conclusion that they were under attack, (16) as Archibald Salvidge, the Liverpool Unionist boss complained to Lord Derby:
'there is on foot an attempt not only to ignore but to destroy the
influence of our Party Organisation.   Members of Parliament are
being deluded into the belief that they can do without organisation.' (17)   This of course was only true in the sense that agents
would not have to produce the extra handful of votes for victory in
the marginal seats;   and the party unity so beloved by the organisers would be shattered by rebel candidates appealing to the voters
over the heads of the leadership.   Salvidge, obviously infuriated
by the pro-Proportional Representation attitude of some of the
Liverpool Unionist Members, epitomised the classic arrogance of the
party boss towards his candidates: 'Scott's speech is disgraceful.
He was never heard of until I brought forward his name for the Exchange Division.'   In addition to this, the effect of Proportional
Representation would have been to deprive the Unionists of the monopoly of Liverpool seats that they enjoyed (apart from the Scotland
Division represented by T.P. O'Connor).

Critics such as Walter Long often advanced contradictory arguments by claiming both that Proportional Representation would serve
to introduce cranks and independents into the House and that it
would increase the power of the party organisation.   In some cases
such views arose from genuine misunderstanding about the meaning of
the Single Transferable Vote system;   for example Members often
thought it was the same as the block vote as formerly used in School
Board Elections, or the limited vote system which had been used in
three-Member boroughs between 1867 and 1885.   These methods had
also been designed to give minority representation, but could be
condemned for having given rise to the 'caucus' in Birmingham politics.   If politicians found Proportional Representation confusing,

Members were fond of arguing, how much more so would the electorate; for the British were commonly held to relish simple elections
with straightforward results rather than the Continental subtleties
involved in the use of quotas and the redistribution of votes involved in a Proportional Representation count.

Among the particular causes of the defeat of Proportional Representation must be mentioned the conspicuous hostility of the London
Members who had rejected it by thirty-seven to eight on the first
vote in June. (18)   As far back as April the London Unionist Members had unanimously resolved that Proportional Representation would
not suit London, and took steps to enlist the co-operation of the
London Liberal and Labour Members in order to secure its
defeat; (19) in Unionist circles attention was drawn to the party's
poor results in the large constituencies which existed before the
redistribution of 1885 - the gains of the last thirty years could be
thrown away by abandoning the single-Member seats, it was claimed.
The Proportional Representation Society attempted to counter this by
cultivating Lord Claude Hamilton, the Chairman of the London Unionist Members and an opponent of Proportional Representation. (20)
Earl Grey adopted the tactics of playing off the fears of one party
against the other by suggesting to Hamilton that the radicals feared
Proportional Representation because it would limit their ability to
win sweeping majorities. (21)   Indeed the London Liberal Federation, after their sudden acceptance of Proportional Representation
in 1913 following some poor results in the local elections of that
year, returned to their previous opposition.   After the Speaker's
Report the Federation lost little time in issuing 'The Case Against
Proportional Representation', which drew a considered reply from
H.G. Chancellor (Liberal, Shoreditch) and Aneurin Williams; (22)
and in April a Conference of Liberal Agents was treated to a catalogue of the drawbacks of Proportional Representation. (23)   According to J.M. Robertson it was the memory of 1906, when the Liberal-
Labour forces had won forty-two to the Unionists' nineteen seats,
that kept the party so hostile; (24) their suspicions were further
exacerbated by the support for Proportional Representation shown by
some sections of the Tory Party, for it seemed odd that the Cecils
should be united with Joseph King and Philip Snowden on electoral
reform.   Once the hostility of London became clear, however, the
Proportional Representation Society took a tactical decision to
accept the exclusion of London from the clause, which was probably
an unwise confession of weakness for it did nothing to mollify the
London Members and encouraged representatives of other cities to
try for exemption. (25)   Special canvassers were appointed to
approach their respective party comrades with a view to converting
them, (26) and A.J. Balfour was enlisted as a speaker for the second
debate on Proportional Representation, though to little effect.   On
the first vote some Members had supported Proportional Representation as part of the Speaker's Report, but once it had been defeated
without apparently endangering the Bill, they were disinclined to
encourage attempts to reintroduce it.

In view of the assumption made at the Speaker's Conference that
Proportional Representation was a safeguard for the Unionists, the
hostility of the MPs towards it was remarkable.   From the three
early divisions one can distinguish some forty-eight Unionist sup-

porters of Proportional Representation, a very mixed group of no
pronounced political character.   Among them were only nine of the
right-wing rebels, including Banbury, who may have seen it partly as
a means of obstructing the Bill.   There were also the remnants of
the Cecil cause for whom Proportional Representation provided insurance against the Tariff Reformers.   Others, like Major J.R.P.
Newman (and Selborne in the Lords), saw it as a means to a moderate
settlement in Ireland, a point much stressed in Proportional Representation propaganda for Unionists; (27) the social imperialists
often saw Proportional Representation even more widely as a way of
promoting 'the cardinal policy of the Unionist Party', by which was
meant national union in each of the self-governing dominions and the
closer union of the Empire as a whole. (28)
    However, neither the constructive nor the negative case weighed
with most Unionists;   172 of them appeared as opponents of Proportional Representation among whom forty-eight were habitual rebels on
the Reform Bill who disapproved of the democratic, innovating, un-
English character of Proportional Representation.   To Earl Grey
and Lord Burnham the Unionist attitude seemed a 'continual surprise'
and an 'unfathomable mystery', yet their motives are plain enough.
The invitation to increase dual voting by dropping Proportional Representation drew out extra Unionist Members who had at first abstained.   There was a multiplicity of local objections where existing boroughs would have to be merged into multi-Member county seats,
and in places such as Birmingham and Liverpool Members had a vested
interest in not sharing the representation proportionately with the
other parties.   Grey and other Peers tried hard to convince the
Unionists that they really stood in need of protection from elections like 1906 which would be much more common under the new franchise; (29) however confident they might feel about popular support
in the circumstances of war, 'it will not take long before the
country returns to normal conditions when organised labour in every
constituency will have it in its power to sweep the board'. (30)
But politicians look to the next election - the anticipated 'khaki'
election in this case - rather than to subsequent ones, and it is
thus no surprise that Grey's warnings fell on deaf ears.   With the
Liberal-Labour Pact disintegrating, the Nationalists collapsing and
the soldiers safely on the register the Unionists could feel their
much delayed victory in their grasp.
    Conversely the Liberals should have been inclined to value Pro-
portional Representation partly as a safeguard in a 'khaki' election
and also as a means of curbing dual voting.   Yet although the Party
supported Proportional Representation it was never by a margin of
more than three to two.   Some 83 Liberals voted against Proportional Representation at least once in the three initial divisions of
whom 53 were Coalition supporters.   These Members were clearly influenced by the known hostility of Lloyd George towards Proportional
Representation, and Coalitionists like Cecil Harmsworth were prevailed upon by him not to speak on the subject at all. (31)   In the
100 Liberals who voted for Proportional Representation one or more
times, there were far fewer Coalitionists, but many radicals, some
of the old-fashioned variety like Richard Holt and A.J. Sherwell,
Lib-Lab radicals such as Edward Hemmerde and H.G. Chancellor, and
the anti-war rebels like Arthur Ponsonby, Joseph King and H.B. Lees-

Smith.   Among them too were Asquithian leaders including Simon,
Samuel, McKenna, Birrell and Gulland, but they leant neither conviction nor leadership to the cause;   Samuel, for example, spoke as
though he were really opposed to the reform despite his vote for it;
at best his contributions were attempts to balance the arguments
for and against so finely as to baffle those who looked for a lead
on the question.   Even Simon and Asquith dammed Proportional Representation with the faintest of praise by emphasising that a limited
experiment was the most that they wanted. (32)   Many Members were
consequently left genuinely undecided and liable to be influenced by
those who did speak in the House.   Unhappily for the Liberals one
of the finest orators, Lord Hugh Cecil, was also an advocate of Proportional Representation and his contribution on 12 June gave them
plenty to think about;   for it contained an eloquent appeal to
Unionists to recall the electorate's dislike for many Liberal policies;   a proportionately elected Parliament, Cecil reasoned, would
never have passed the 1909 Budget, the Parliament Act, Home Rule or
Welsh Disestablishment. (33)   The effect of this argument, according to one observer (34) was to drive 'the [Liberal] waverers into
the division lobby against [Proportional Representation]'.   Since
no leading Liberal contradicted Cecil's view of the effect of Proportional Representation the reform began to look increasingly like
a Tory ploy for hamstringing legislative programmes.

This suspicion about Tory motives gained further credence from
the Unionists' total hostility to the Alternative Vote which survived in the House of Commons because the three radical Parties
united in its support.   Not only had the Alternative Vote presented
itself to the Liberal Cabinet before 1914 as a means of blunting a
Labour attack, but it now seemed to Arthur Henderson too as a necessary method of preventing losses due to three-cornered contests.
This fondness for the Alternative Vote clearly reduced their interest in Proportional Representation even though a majority of the
Labour Members approved of it.   However, now that Labour's hopes
were so high it was not difficult to play upon their fears;   in particular, as MacDonald argued, (35) Labour organisation could be very
severely stretched in coping with a three-Member constituency in
which they needed 26 per cent of the votes to be sure of returning a
Member.   It was tempting, therefore, to stick to the single-Member
seats with the Alternative Vote as a safeguard.   So long as this
was in the Reform Bill radicals felt disinclined to look seriously
at Proportional Representation.

For the Irish Nationalists Proportional Representation was an
opportunity missed.   Before 1914 they had been somewhat cool towards it because over the years they had perfected their organisation and mastered the techniques of arranging swallow voters and
registers;   as a result they had a vested interest in maintaining
the existing single-Member seats most of which went uncontested anyway.   By 1917, however, they had begun to revise their attitude in
the face of the undermining of their position by the Sinn Fein.
Yet there was no provision in the Bill for Proportional Representation in Irish constituencies, and so, on the first division only
fourteen Members bothered to support the Proportional Representation
clause;   the Irish votes could easily have prevented its initial
defeat by seven votes.   It was not until November 1917 that full

Irish support for Proportional Representation was mobilised, but by
then it was too late, for support amongst the other parties had been
overwhelmed.

In the autumn of 1917 the second phase of the fight to save Proportional Representation began when the Peers took a hand.   A House
of Lords Committee for Proportional Representation had been formed
in July (36) and circulated propaganda in both Houses of Parliament;
special canvassers were appointed to deal with each party separately, (37) Unionists in particular were to be lured into the Carlton
Club by Proportional Representation Peers hoping to convert
them. (38)   The immediate objective was to raise a head of steam
for a third debate in the Commons on Report Stage as a prelude to
intervention by the Peers later;   for in Lord Salisbury's view his
colleagues might be diffident about altering a franchise Bill unless
a serious stand had already been made in the Commons. (39)   Unfortunately this activity among the Peers was not altogether welcomed
by radicals such as H.G. Chancellor who feared that the reinsertion
of Proportional Representation by the Upper House might endanger the
Bill. (40)   This did not mean that radicals saw the Peers' initiative simply as an attempt to sabotage the Bill, indeed the 'Manchester Guardian' (41) welcomed their efforts to put Proportional Representation back in the Bill again.

When Lord Selborne moved the adoption of a Proportional Representation scheme in the Lords on 21 January (42) it became clear that
they were proposing to include more than 90 per cent of the constituencies in a framework of multi-Member seats.   This dealt with the
objection that the experimental scheme was partial, but it did unite
all the 'victims' in opposition.   Another factor in Selborne's mind
was the urgent need to contain Sinn Fein;   indeed John Humphries,
the Secretary of the Proportional Representation Society, believed
that the by-elections at East Clare and Roscommon would 'compel the
Prime Minister to look into P.R.' (43)   A further consideration
driving them towards a near universal scheme was the recent surge of
interest among the farming community (44) who were worried about
the loss of agricultural representation through redistribution.
During the winter 'petitions have come up from almost every chamber
of agriculture in the Kingdom' (45) with the result that their
voice was heard at the special conference convened by the National
Union of Conservative Associations in November 1917;   complete Proportional Representation, as Major Newman reminded the Conference, (46) would satisfy the farmers and remove the Alternative Vote
at the same time.   Sir Charles Bathurst, MP, formally petitioned
the Proportional Representation Peers on behalf of the chambers of
agriculture to reinsert Proportional Representation into the Reform
Bill, (47) thereby providing them with a plea that touched Unionist
Members at a sensitive point (48) when used by Selborne to support
his case.

As a result, when the Lords voted on his amendment after a two
day debate a pro-Proportional Representation majority of 132 to
forty-two emerged;   this reflected massive approval by the Unionists, while the Liberals split fairly evenly;   their leading
figures, Crewe, Harcourt, Gainford, Haldane and Buckmaster, regarded
it with great suspicion and voted with the minority.   Two days
later, on 24 January the Cabinet discussed the situation thus

arising. (49)   Bonar Law objected that the amendment would prevent
the passage of the Bill that Session since the Boundary Commissioners would have to conduct fresh investigations, but Selborne (50)
hastened to assure the Prime Minister that this was not the case;
he proposed simply to take the constituencies already worked out and
amalgamate them into three, four and five-Member seats so that virtually no delay would be necessary.   By 26 January he had a new
schedule ready for the English constituencies involving 25 five-
Member, 42 four-Member and 50 three-Member constituencies.

The alternative to this, suggested by Balfour, (51) was to separate the whole question of Redistribution and make another Bill,
though the Cabinet feared that such a course would be badly received
in the Commons.   It would certainly have given the Peers a lever
and a useful delaying period while the Bryce Committee moved towards
the conclusion of their work.   However, Selborne was not interested
in this sort of strategy, for his object was not to obstruct the
Bill but to improve it according to his genuine belief in Proportional Representation.   For the Cabinet the wisest course, as
Curzon pointed out, was to wait and see what view the Commons would
take now;   they agreed that while Sir George Cave should refrain
from discussing the merits of the issue he should 'point out the
effect that any inclusion of P.R. would have on the fate of the
bill'. (52)

In the Commons William Burdett-Coutts and Austen Chamberlain
launched a passionate attack upon the Peers for having abandoned
their proper role of defending the country against untried
changes, (53) spurred on, in Chamberlain's case, by fear of losing
the Unionist monopoly of Birmingham.   An element of personal antagonism entered here, for Salisbury had been very active in promoting
Proportional Representation;   after seeing his own family pitch-
forked out of their constituencies by the Tariff Reformers before
1914 he doubtless relished the opportunity of tossing this explosive
device into Chamberlain's own backyard.   Not that this was his
chief motive, but it did add edge to the controversy.   However, it
did not help to have the issue personalised by the House of Cecil:
'I don't quite understand the system', confessed Herbert Nield, MP,
'but I don't trust the judgement of the Cecils in these matters.' (54)

Thus the Unionists conducted a debate of their own with Long and
Cave supporting Chamberlain, and Lord Robert Cecil and Balfour
taking the side of the Peers.   For Labour Snowden spoke for and
William Adamson against the amendment.   On the Liberal benches
several former Proportional Representation supporters now changed
sides, notably Asquith who took his stand on East Fife;   he simply
did not want a multi-Member seat comprising the County of Fife, an
arrangement that would have saved him from a humiliating defeat ten
months later.   As a result the Lords' amendment was rejected by a
majority of 100, a division which concealed an interesting reversal
in the positions of the parties.   For this time the Unionists
opposed Proportional Representation by only 96 to 61, while the
Liberals, as if working on the principle that whatever the Peers
wanted must be undesirable, rejected it by 111 to 43;   Labour followed suit with 15 votes to 7.   As for the Nationalists they were
reduced to baffled incoherence by this subtle turn of English poli-

tics and only 7 of them bothered to vote.   Altogether some 31
Unionists seem to have been inspired to support Proportional Representation by the Peers, of whom 19 had previously voted against it
and 11 had abstained.   Earlier on a shift of opinion on such a
scale would have been enough to preserve Proportional Representation
in the Bill.   By January 1918, however, it was entirely cancelled
out by the much bigger reaction produced among the radical parties.
Among the Liberals 29 former supporters of Proportional Representation changed sides, and 16 abstainers and 9 Labour Proportional Representation supporters joined them.   Thus a total of 54 Liberal and
Labour Members had been alienated by the Peers' tactics.

Everything the Peers did served to confirm Labour suspicions
about a plot to delay the Bill;   Curzon had denied this when challenged in Cabinet by Barnes (55) but ventured the suggestion that
some Peers might desire to be given guarantees as to the proposed
reform of their own chamber.   What told particularly with Labour
and Liberal Members was the persistent refusal of the Peers to
accept the Alternative Vote, even to the extent of refusing an experiment simultaneously with Proportional Representation.   This
began to reduce the dispute to a struggle between the radicals' Alternative Vote and the Peers' Proportional Representation.   Yet
although some MPs such as Cecil, Sanders and Younger were intent
upon eliminating the Alternative Vote above all things, Selborne,
the leader of the Proportional Representation cause in the Lords was
not;   he desired Proportional Representation for its own merits not
as a tactical device, (56) and the Peers in general were induced to
oppose the Alternative Vote only by strong pressure from Younger,
the party chairman. (57)   There was indeed an interesting conflict
within the Unionist Party between the MPs and Peers, arising from
the fact that the latter were less obsessed with the next election,
less concerned about the convenience and comfort of parliamentary
candidates and more sympathetic to the rural interests.   They had
the interests of their party no less at heart but simply took a more
detached and longer-term view of them.

Moreover the Peers, far from delaying the Reform Bill, sought to
expedite its passage.   Selborne dramatically telegraphed Henderson
about their plans (58) and wrote to the Prime Minister to explain
them;   (59)   what they intended was that the Bill should go ahead
into law and registration work proceed with a provisional schedule
of constituencies;   this could be revised by the Commissioners and
the results sanctioned by an Order in Council presented to Parliament in the usual way. (60)   However, these hopes were dashed by
the Commons' emphatic rejection of the amendment;   the Peers promptly climbed down one step and Curzon asked the Cabinet for a compromise.   At their meeting on 1 February the Cabinet decided to
offer a Commission to frame an experimental scheme for using Proportional Representation in up to 100 constituencies, (61) which,
unwisely, the Peers felt disinclined to accept at this stage.

Then began a hectic week in which amendments were shuttled
rapidly back and forth between the two Houses.   The Commons, after
rejecting the full Proportional Representation scheme, reinserted
the Alternative Vote on 31 January.   This division proved a close
one with 172 Unionists being outnumbered by 155 Liberals, 19 Labour
and 6 Nationalist Members.   When the Lords met on 4 February to re-

consider their position Selborne proposed to revert to something like the Speaker's original scheme based upon Proportional Representation for three-Member boroughs. (62)   As before the idea was that the Commissioners' Report for such a scheme could simply be presented to Parliament and become law within twenty-one days unless nullified by resolution of either House.   The new amendment gained approval by 86 to 35 votes, and the Peers went on to delete the Alternative Vote again after an extremely short debate.

The next day, 5 February, the Commons replied briskly.   The Cabinet declined a compromise suggested by Sir Ryland Adkins on behalf of Asquith and Gulland to accept the Peers' Proportional Representation scheme on condition that the Alternative Vote was tried in a similar number of constituencies, (63) and considered instead three possibilities; (64)   Proportional Representation might be applied to three, four, and five-Member boroughs; or Proportional Representation might be applied with the proviso that any constituency should be exempt if 5,000 of its electors petitioned against the change within a thirty-day period; or finally a Royal Commission might be appointed to select 100 borough and county seats for the experiment. It was agreed, meanwhile, that the Commons should be urged to reject the Peers' latest Proportional Representation amendment but to accept the loss of the Alternative Vote.

Thus later that day the Lords' main amendment was duly defeated; but over the Alternative Vote a tricky procedural problem had developed for Lowther ruled that if the House refused to accept the Lords' view the Bill would be lost and unable to join the list of measures now awaiting the Royal Assent.   However, Dickinson got around this by moving a different amendment which applied the Alternative Vote only to parliamentary boroughs.   In the subsequent divisions this proposal was carried though five non-Unionists (65) obliged the Government by opposing it.   Thus on 6 February their Lordships found that their bluff had been called.   If they were to avoid the responsibility of overthrowing the Reform Bill they would have to content themselves with the Government's offer of a Royal Commission which would endeavour to produce an acceptable experimental scheme of Proportional Representation.   The question was whether the Government would take responsibility for enacting such a scheme once produced.   Curzon (66) promised that if it obtained the support of both Houses it would be placed under the charge of a Minister and treated like the Speaker's Report.   This undertaking did not amount to very much in view of the obvious reluctance of the various parties in the Commons.   The plan, (67) which covered 149 constituencies, was debated in the Commons in May 1918 and flatly rejected.

However, the Peers acquiesced reluctantly in the proposal, though they threw out the altered amendment for the Alternative Vote which Dickinson had inserted.   Within minutes these decisions were communicated to an expectant House of Commons.   For a second time Members were solemnly warned that the Alternative Vote must be surrendered or the Bill would be lost.   Cave therefore urged the House to settle the Bill at once by accepting the plan for a Royal Commission on Proportional Representation after which a free vote on the Report would be allowed. (68)   Asquith and Henderson took up the idea of conducting a similar experiment with the Alternative Vote in

100 constituencies, but Cave refused and the House rejected their amendment by 186 votes to 168, which represented a marked change compared to the vote of the previous day.   On 5 February the Liberal turnout in favour of the Alternative Vote fell by 22, Labour by 6, and the Nationalists by 2.   Moreover 4 Liberal, 1 Labour and 1 Nationalist voted with the Unionists; (69)   in addition 13 Liberals who abstained on this division but voted two minutes later on the Government's proposal were Coalitionists to a man. (70)   These 19 Members saved the Bill by tipping the vote in the Government's favour.   The House thereupon approved Cave's amendment, gave a Third Reading and despatched the Representation of the People Bill to receive the Royal Assent.

Part four

Chapter 12

REFORM AND THE
COUPON ELECTION

> When I said that none of the political parties wanted an Election
> now ... he [Lloyd George] gave a mischievous look and said, 'You
> have forgotten one party' and, as I pointed at him, 'perhaps the
> most important'.   Clearly ... he felt the need of a mandate.
> (C.P. Scott's Diary, 8 August 1918)

The timing of the Coupon Election of 1918 was determined essentially
by the Parliamentary Reform Act of that year in that Lloyd George
had resisted a very natural temptation to seek a mandate in 1917 in
the full knowledge that a franchise measure would limit his options
for a year or more.   That no election took place until December
1918 did not mean that the Prime Minister had entirely forfeited the
right to dissolve, but rather that in the intervening period his
opponents never forced him into a position in which he had to use
it;   further, the realisation that a wartime election would elevate
Lloyd George and destroy his critics on the left served to emascu-
late an Opposition which under Asquith gladly took refuge in the
patriotic view that the Government ought not to be obstructed in its
efforts to bring the war to a successful military conclusion.   Yet
despite being allowed a nearly free run by Parliament, Lloyd George
grew alarmed in the months between the passage of the Reform Act in
February and the completion of the new register in the autumn, for
now that the soldiers' franchise was so near to realisation even his
Conservative allies felt disinclined to rush an election.   This is
why the Prime Minister became so agitated in April and May over the
opposition to Irish Conscription and the Maurice Debate, each of
which could have led to his replacement by an Asquithian Government.
Though such a Government would not have been allowed by the House of
Lords to survive for long without going to the country it would have
enjoyed a few precious months of military success in the summer of
1918.
  Lloyd George's plans hinged on the assumption that the war would
continue through 1919 and possibly into 1920, so that the election
to be fought on the new register would be a wartime one in which he
would seek a simple mandate to fight on to victory.   As early as
March Lloyd George had determined to protect himself from a normal
election fought on party lines by cobbling together a broad front of

Lloyd George Liberals, 'Patriotic Labour' and the Conservative
Party.   At this stage, with the German offensive threatening to
split the British and French armies apart, he seemed the indispensable leader, though even now, in the absence of any organised
Lloyd George party in the country, there was no question of his
making an independent appeal to the electorate.   However it was
unavoidable that when the fighting on the Western Front began to
turn in the Allies' favour in August and victory suddenly loomed
ahead, Lloyd George's usefulness in the eyes of the Conservative
Party began to ebb.   For several years the belief remained among
Conservatives that the Prime Minister was a necessary draw with the
large new electorate, but he appreciated himself that if he were to
exploit his prestige and popularity the General Election must follow
very closely upon the cessation of hostilities.   Despite the swiftly changing military situation the political arrangements for the
election were by no means chaotic, for the agreement to allow a free
run to 150 Lloyd George Liberals had been reached by F.E. Guest and
Sir George Younger in July. (1)   Though this plan involved the
deliberate proscription of most of the Liberal Party, Lloyd George
was still keeping his options open as far as the radicals were concerned.   What finally closed his options for him was the Armistice
on 11 November, the withdrawal of the Labour Party from the Coalition on 14 November, and the continued refusal of Asquith to join
the Government as Lord Chancellor.   This left the Prime Minister
high and dry on a little hump of parliamentary support; he had not
only to fight the election with Bonar Law's co-operation, but to
avoid delay lest the Conservatives should wake up to the fact that
they could win an election without him.

   The argument against a quick election, much used by Liberal candidates, centred on the inaccuracy of the register now being hastily
prepared, and on the inability of thousands of soldiers to participate in it.   Lloyd George, as a leading advocate of the soldiers'
franchise, felt acutely vulnerable to this criticism and worked off
his irritation upon the President of the Local Government Board who
spent the summer on the preparation of the register.   It fell to
the lot of Hayes Fisher to provide for the registration of all soldiers over nineteen years of age who had seen active service and to
arrange for them to vote either by post or by proxy according to
their geographical location - a practical impossibility.   As always
Lloyd George showed no appreciation of the practical problems involved and as time wore on he increasingly cast Fisher as the scapegoat for his own determination to rush into an election before an
accurate register could be produced.

   Quite apart from the problem of registering the troops the preparation of the new register was bound to take longer than usual
because the Registration Officers had virtually to scrap the old one
and start from scratch.   In February Hayes Fisher decided that the
six-month qualifying period for residence should run up to 15 April
and the new register come into force on 1 October; (2) however, it
soon transpired that the process would take longer than this and he
was obliged to ask for an extension of Parliament's life for a final
six months until 31 January 1919. (3)   The original intention had
been to send out postcards to all the men in the Forces through the
Army Council, the Admiralty and the Air Council, a method that was

neatly disrupted by the German offensive in March.   The military
situation on the Western Front so impeded the circulation of the
postcards that it rapidly became clear that for many men there was
little chance of returning the information to the Returning Officers
in time for the publication of the electors' lists on 15 June. (4)
This date was therefore put back by two weeks, but it was still
found that large numbers of cards continued to arrive after 29 June,
which were treated as claims, which could be made up to 25 July, and
thus registered.   This haphazard system was largely superceded by
the departments whose official records showed the qualifying addresses for each man which they passed on to the Registration Officers. (5)   The Board of Trade sent out cards to merchant seamen and
the Board of Agriculture supplied them for fishermen.   At the same
time all the forms left with householders required an entry of the
names of all persons who would normally have been resident but for
the war.   By these diverse means the names of some 3,900,000 naval
and military electors found their way onto the new parliamentary
register, and at the election over 2,700,000 ballot papers were
issued for voters in England, Scotland and Wales. (6)   Under the
Act it had been left to the discretion of the Local Government Board
to decide which soldiers would vote by post and which by proxy.
Plainly many ballot papers sent out after nominations had closed
would fail to reach men whose position was changing rapidly, and in
the eight days between the poll and the count many would fail to
reach the Returning Officers.   For these reasons the Count was delayed for two weeks over the Christmas period, and postal voting was
restricted to troops stationed in the United Kingdom, the Isle of
Man, the Channel Islands, France and Belgium. (7)   Even so only a
third of the ballot papers despatched were included in the count.
Perhaps the 900,000 men who thus participated justified the efforts
made on their behalf by the politicians, but Lloyd George had laid
the blame for the shortfall in advance by summarily dismissing Hayes
Fisher in October for his 'lack of judgement and want of efficiency'. (8)
     The impact of the fourth Reform Act upon the election of 1918 is
so large a question that it cannot be treated here in more than a
superficial way.   There were some 21,400,000 electors on the 1918
Register (see Appendix 10) a figure equivalent to 78 per cent of the
population over twenty-one on the basis of the 1919 Census.   The
total was swollen by the inclusion of nineteen-year-olds; and the
franchise fell short of the male suffrage ideal through the conditions attaching to removals particularly the geographical one which
required a voter to keep within the same parliamentary unit or a
contiguous one in order to retain his vote.   The Register was generally accepted to have been very inaccurate; many soldiers were
not registered while some were listed twice as a result of the dual
method of enquiry through households and through the Armed Forces;
Conscientious Objectors were on the Register since their disfranchisement did not become operative until 1921 after peace had been
declared.   Even then few were actually struck off the lists apart
from well-known men like Fenner Brockway who was able to contest a
parliamentary election but not to vote.   Women remained predominant
among the non-voters, though the 8,400,000 of them on the register
formed 40 per cent of the total.   The number of dual voters was

surprisingly low; with only 159,000 business electors and 68,000 University electors they formed a little over 1 per cent of the total electorate.   Moreover the exercise of these franchises was restricted by one day polling, though ironically Members of Parliament were perhaps the hardest hit group; for example Richard Holt, with his residence in London, his business in Liverpool and his constituency in Northumberland became effectively disfranchised.

The turnout of voters at the election was only 58.9 per cent, a considerable drop on the 81.1 per cent poll recorded in December 1910 by an electorate one third the size.   No doubt this is partly to be explained by the poor state of the party organisations after four years of decay, but the major single reason must be the low rate of participation among the men still on active military service.   The fact that only one third of those who received ballot papers succeeded in returning them in time for the Count cannot be blamed upon poor organisation.   In fact the average soldier, contrary to all the assumptions made by the politicians, was too apathetic to take the trouble of filling up forms for the appointment of proxies or to cast a vote for a candidate of whom he knew nothing. (9)   Most concentrated on surviving until the declaration of peace released them from the trenches; a vote in a General Election, represented by pieces of paper, cannot have seemed anything but an irritating distraction to men facing death each day.   Certainly the low participation of the troops suggests that the 'khaki' vote that swept the Coalition back to office was essentially a civilian one; no doubt for the men and women who had stayed at home throughout the war a vote for a tough peace settlement was the only way of working off their anti-German emotions.

Party Agents were inclined to adopt an attitude of severity mingled with resignation about the whole business of registration and electioneering in 1918.   This was partly due to the difficulty of gathering the resources to cope with the election and also to a personal sense of loss; for once deprived of their central role as interpreters of the seven-franchise tangle the agents inevitably suffered a check to the rising status which they had been fostering before 1914.   To some extent also, the diminished standing of the agents reflected the collapse of the Liberal professional cadre from the First World War onwards; the prospects for careers in the political parties now became distinctly unattractive on the left at least.

Yet the simplification of registration and the franchise by no means destroyed the need for party agents.   With an electorate of more than two and a half times the pre-war size it became even less likely that the Member of Parliament could make extensive personal contact with his voters; it thus became even more important than before to produce large teams of canvassers to approach the voters on his behalf and to establish between elections a full network of branches throughout the constituency.   By the 1922 election the return to normal conditions was such that some 71.3 per cent of the electorate turned out to vote; and for the next half century participation was to remain within the 70-80 per cent range, only in 1950 and 1951 did it exceed 80 per cent as it had done in the Edwardian period.

The shortage of resources and materials in 1918 prepared the

agents for a time of greater economy in election expenditure.   The
new scale of expenses which allowed 7d. per county elector and 5d.
per borough elector would have reduced expenditure by two-thirds
under the old electorate; (10)   even though the swollen numbers restored something like the previous level there was clearly far less
money to be spent per voter than before.   In compensation for this
the candidates were granted under the 1918 Act a free postal deliv-
ery of half an ounce of material per voter, and the free use of
school rooms for meetings.   One final cost was, however, imposed
upon the candidates - the £150 deposit.   This had been seen as a
means of deterring independents, cranks and rebels - as defined by
orthodox politicians - from contesting elections, and was generally
glossed over with the argument that one had to deter the unscrupu-
lous from seeking election now that a tempting salary of £400 came
with a seat in Parliament.   That this change went unopposed in the
House of Commons was some indication of the fear of non-party candidates who had done so well during wartime by-elections;   they
wanted to be certain of a return to a regular confrontation between
two or three parties.   In 1918, £150 was a serious obstacle but one
which inflation rapidly diminished.

The results of the election bore out the view that the circumstances of war could only benefit the Conservative Party whose candidates were triumphant in 383 out of the 707 constituencies and
would almost certainly have won more but for the withdrawal of candidates in favour of Lloyd George Liberals.   On the other hand the
Conservative poll was only 38.2 per cent, well below the disastrous
1906 poll of 43.6 per cent which had yielded them a mere 157 seats.
Clearly the Conservatives had not suffered badly from the new electorate, but a poll of 38 per cent, repeated in 1922 and in 1923,
would, under the conditions of Edwardian politics, have confined the
party to the position of a minority force once again.   In this
sense the fears expressed by the Central Office during the war were
vindicated.   However the vital conditions of Edwardian politics did
not obtain any longer.   For the Independent Liberals had only 253
candidates in the field and the Labour Party 388 with no electoral
pact to stave off the menace of a split radical vote.   Thus the two
parties with more than one-third of the votes won only one-eighth of
the seats between them.   This made for the Conservative hegemony of
1918 to 1939 and serves to emphasise the crucial failure to obtain
a reform of the electoral system through the 1918 Act.   However,
though Proportional Representation would clearly have helped the
Labour Party as well as the Liberals in 1918 its effect thereafter
is more problematical.   For it would have limited Labour's expansion in the industrial strongholds and, by holding up the Liberal
representation in Parliament, would have made it easier for the Liberals to return as a governing party especially in 1923 when the two
parties were polling evenly in the country.

The timing of the 1918 election was doubly unfortunate for the
Liberal Party.   In the first place the huge new electorate were
voting for the first time when the Liberals were divided at the top,
when large sections of the parliamentary party were edging towards
the other two parties, and when their constituency organisation was
too weak to contest every seat.   In the second place the Reform Act
indirectly damaged the Liberals simply by delaying the election

until the autumn of 1918.   This had crucial consequences for the
decline of the party because an election early in 1917, for example,
would not have found the Liberals clearly divided between Lloyd
George and Asquith.   At that stage all, apart from a few pacifists,
were willing to support the Government and a 'coupon' arrangement
directed against the Liberals would have been highly unlikely.
This is not to say that many Liberals would not have fallen at the
polls; the point is that their chances of effecting a recovery
would have been quite different.

With Asquith and some of his henchmen out of Parliament and
sobered by electoral setbacks the ex-Ministers that remained would
no longer have felt obliged to ignore Lloyd George's offers of posts
in the Government; in this way the Liberal Party would have become
more rapidly Lloyd George's and would have been spared the worst
effects of the Maurice Debate and of similar formal divisions.
Divisive debates would still have taken place, of course, but they
would not have carried the same implications if no alternative Government stood behind the rebels.   This is why Asquith's position
was quite impossible from 1916 to 1918, for however much he might
avoid dividing the House against the Government he could not stop
his followers doing so in the certain knowledge that if they were
successful he would have to step forward as the alternative Prime
Minister.

Moreover, the presence of the majority of the Liberal forces in
the Lloyd George camp would have rescued him from isolation and
hence dependence upon the Unionists.   Indeed, an extra hundred or
even fifty Liberals on the Government side would have rendered a
distribution of coupons impossible from the Conservative side and
ruled out the continuation of the Coalition after 1918.

An early election in the middle of the war would also have deci-
mated the Labour Party whose condition until mid-1917 was as bad as
that of the Liberals; although Labour would doubtless have used the
latter part of the war to organise in the country they could hardly
have emerged as the largest Opposition party at the end.   Although
Labour had great expectations of an election fought on the new
franchise and with the protection of the Alternative Vote, they
rightly dreaded a dissolution in the middle of the war and feared to
provoke the Government into that action.   In short the timing of
certain decisions over the Reform Bill and the election moulded the
fate of the Liberal and Labour Parties during the war and after;
though the Liberal disaster may have had long term causes it could
not have occurred *in 1918* but for several avoidable mistakes made by
Asquith and Lloyd George.   A bad electoral defeat of some kind was
probably unavoidable, given the military failure of the Allies; the
radical politicians had so strong an impression of the last 'khaki'
election in 1900 that they did their best to avoid one altogether.
It is only with hindsight that one can see clearly that the Liberals
should have given the voters an opportunity in 1916 or 1917 to vote
against Germany; there would then have been a breathing space at
the end of the war for emotions to settle and for the party to re-
group to fight a Reconstruction Election.   This is the essential
difference between the elections of 1918 and 1945; in the latter
case the voters' attention had shifted decisively to domestic questions because they had had several years during which looming vic-

tory had taken the edge out of war; in 1918 they had feared the worst until the late summer of that year so that the pent up force of chauvinism had not spent itself by polling day.

Chapter 13

WAR, REFORM AND THE DECLINE OF PARLIAMENT

> We showed characteristic British phlegm when in the midst of a
> great war, we deliberately decided to have a Reform Bill.   (Sir
> William Bull, H.C. Deb., 29 February 1924)

Since 1945 the study of war by historians and social scientists has
changed in emphasis from the strictly military to the examination of
war's impact upon society as a whole.   Among the most stimulating
suggestions has been Stanislas Andreski's concept of the Military
Participation Ratio (1) which hypothesises that the greater the proportion of the population whose co-operation is necessary in wartime, the greater is the tendency towards social levelling in society, an idea which was taken up and deployed attractively by Professor Titmuss (2) with regard to social policy in Britain.   However, the facts of a situation rarely fit into neat theoretical explanations, and some writers have made the relationship between war
and society so mechanical as to produce rather bad history.   Andreski claimed, inaccurately, that the First World War brought universal adult suffrage and that the Second World War brought the
Labour Party to power to 'soak the rich'!   Titmuss wrote of the
First World War as a mere repeat of the Boer War in terms of its
effect upon social change;   and Arthur Marwick fell further into the
trap with his attempt to fit the impact of twentieth-century wars to
a 'model'.   Not only are models no substitute for *explanations*
based upon research, they can also lead, as in Marwick's case, to
the historian brushing aside evidence which does not seem to fit the
prescribed scheme. (3)
   The first difficulty in examining the relationship between war
and society is the tendency to ignore all the other causes apart
from war which contribute to social and political change.   As Dr
Pelling has observed, (4) it is easy to forget that societies that
contrived to avoid the total wars of the twentieth century have created their own equivalents of the Welfare State, as fast or as
slowly, as the belligerents.   And it seems unlikely that Britain's
long and peculiar approach to modern democracy was vitally affected
by war in the twentieth century.
   A second pitfall is the exaggeration of the changes which occur in
wartime and the failure to see them in historical perspective.   Dr

Abrams (5) has pointed out how slight were the actual legislative
consequences of the First World War for social reform; and to retreat from measurable to 'unguided' social change as Marwick has
done invites vague generalisation; it is not compatible with Andreski's participation theory which hinges upon a definite and conscious response by the ruling groups who control society.   Third,
even mass-participation wars do not simply promote social levelling;
they may do more to retard it.   No doubt the Whiggish historians of
the 1920s exaggerated the negative aspects of the war; but we now
appreciate the advance of social and economic policy in the Edwardian period which left a far deeper impression than the dramatic,
but ephemeral, expedients of 1914-18.   Historians have too quickly
forgotten R.H. Tawney's remarks on the abandonment of economic controls by governments after 1918; (6) each measure of control was
taken *ad hoc* to meet a crisis; there had been no intellectual commitment to state control.   From the Liberal and Labour point of
view the prospect of social reform during the war represented no
more than a continuation of pre-war policy conducted under greater
difficulties.   Moreover, it is arguable that the war did more to
disrupt and delay British social policy especially in the hostile
reaction it produced in the Conservative Party towards the extended
role of wartime governments as personified by Lloyd George.   The
history of 1918 to 1939 can hardly be adequately explained except as
a Conservative reaction against the trend of social and economic
policy in the Edwardian and war years.   Because Conservatives were
keen on conscription and all kinds of action by the Government designed to win the war it is easy to run away with the notion that
they were converted to interventionism while the Liberals clung to a
defunct *laissez-faire* philosophy; the reverse is closer to the
truth as both the Edwardian and post-war periods show.   Similarly
wars do not necessarily lead to new social policies by the state
through the higher expenditure they generate; the Napoleonic Wars
led to the prompt abandonment of the income tax, the Boer War killed
Chamberlain's plans for Old Age Pensions, and the First World War
put Governments in the same dilemma of trying to reduce taxation
while paying off the interest on war debts.   Not until after 1945
do we find a Government committed to higher expenditure for social
reasons, and only then because they were inspired by the experience
of the 1930s and fortified by the new Keynsian orthodoxy.
     If one considers the specific case of the relationship between
the Great War and the fourth Reform Act one must see the problem in
its proper perspective.   This involves, first, a consideration of
the contribution of pre-war conditions; second, an explanation of
the indirect political effects of the war upon reform; third, an
examination of the extent to which the war experience directly fur-
thered or retarded reform; and fourth, an attempt to put the 1918
Act in proper perspective within the wider history of reform and the
development of Parliament in Britain.
     There was an obvious and strong element of continuity with Edwar-
dian politics in that the Liberals certainly regarded parliamentary
reform as unfinished business.   The franchise and registration details of the Act were essentially a reflection of pre-war Liberal
policy tempered by the need to compromise with the Conservatives on
many points.   Here one must distinguish the fact of a compromise

Bill which clearly arose out of the war from the specific items
which, apart from the disfranchisement of Conscientious Objectors
and the franchise for nineteen-year-olds, owed nothing to the war.
During 1914-18 the Liberals' position was fixed both by their
ideological pretensions as democrats and by the calculation of the
party organisation that one-man-one-vote would be to their advantage
electorally; to some extent these long-standing assumptions blinded
the Liberals to the fact that a future election fought on a democratic franchise would be of greater benefit to their rivals than to
themselves.   Neither they nor the Labour Party underwent any obvious change of attitude on male suffrage; and even on the female
suffrage they achieved precisely the package laid down by the Edwardian Governments, namely, a measure of woman suffrage that both followed a Bill for adult male suffrage and was large enough to deny
the Conservatives any advantage.   It is significant that the radicals resolutely refused to be drawn into enfranchising the women
under thirty, for the very good reason that such women, especially
where they were domestic servants, had always been considered too
susceptible to the influence of their Conservative employers.

Labour and the Liberals were also working on pre-war assumptions
in their attachment to the Alternative Vote; indeed Labour's electoral strategy had been based upon this reform.   The political
circumstances of the war merely confused them here by detaching some
of the radical forces to the Coalition which, for the Liberals particularly, both obscured their longer term electoral interest and
paralysed the Asquithian leadership so that no clear guide on electoral reform was given at the time when it was most needed.   Both
Parties, but the Liberals especially, entirely missed the need for
and the opportunity for achieving Proportional Representation in
1917; this again was essentially because pre-war conditions had led
them to neglect Proportional Representation in favour of the Alternative Vote as an immediate solution.

Similarly the Conservatives were reacting to Edwardian conditions
in two senses; first, the party organisation continued to go
through the motions of opposing reforms lest too much were conceded
to the Liberals; their behaviour in other words, was often instinc-
tive rather than a rational reflection of their best interests;
second, they appreciated keenly how narrow had been their escape
from various Liberal-inspired reforms before 1914 so that it seemed
to the leadership only prudent to undertake reform during the war
when they were in a position to influence it and thus forestall any
post-war Liberal attempts which could only damage them.   Thus the
magnitude of the political reform generated during the Great War can
be explained in the first instance by the politicians' sense of previously missed opportunities and the lessons they drew from Edwardian politics, rather than by their reaction to mass participation
in war.

Of course the wartime situation affected the cause of reform in
purely indirect ways.   Initially it checked the course of domestic
reform and replaced the Liberal Government with a Coalition: there
thus seemed little chance at first of parliamentary reform being
rescuscitated by a Government which considered it a disruptive and
grotesquely inappropriate pursuit.   Indeed nothing is more striking
than the way in which the Asquith Coalition stumbled eventually upon

the idea of the Speaker's Conference in 1916 as a result of their
desperate efforts to avoid having to devise a Reform Bill of their
own.   Had it not been for the fact that Parliament's life ran out
in 1915 there can be no doubt that they would simply have resisted
any pressure for tackling the registration problems arising out of
war service.   In view of its origins the Act of 1918 can hardly be
represented as a war measure in inspiration but rather as an accident of wartime which none of the three war administrations would
deliberately have conceived.

Another vital accident was that Lloyd George's replacement of
Asquith coincided with the Speaker's Conference so that its Report
was delivered to the new Government early in its life at the only
stage between 1914 and 1918 when it was politically feasible.

More generally the war had the effect of severely restricting
popular politics and the activity of pressure groups which allowed
Parliament to thrash out the reform question in relative isolation.
Even when the proposals for the Bill became public they failed to
arouse much interest, although the issue had served to stimulate
the flagging cause of woman suffrage in 1916.   However, while the
leading suffragettes had already abandoned the cause, the suffragists never attempted to mobilise their support in the country -
perhaps because they doubted how much they would find during the
war - and contented themselves instead with what the politicians
would willingly offer.   Thus the war period both helped the women
towards their goal and, by restoring the initiative temporarily to
Parliament, limited their achievement strictly to the deal offered
earlier by Liberal Governments.

If the political accidents of 1914-18 explain the timing of
reform and pre-war politics explain most of the substance, what
remains to be accounted for?   Was there in addition a change in
attitude on the part of the ruling classes towards the masses that
made them willing to raise their status in society?   The evidence
that one is dealing in 1914-18 with some fundamental change is elu-
sive and easily exaggerated.   It is for instance hard to see a
change of principle on the male franchise; after all the old system
for all its complexity, theoretically included a majority of the
male population under one of the seven franchises; it was merely
the mechanics of the registration system that kept 30 per cent of
them in practice off the Register.   In 1918 there were no new
classes of people waiting to be enfranchised as in 1832, 1867 or
1884.   Consequently the politicians steadfastly refused to discuss
the issue in terms of principles or theories of representation as
Lord Hugh Cecil urged them to do; it is true that the new legislation went a long way to abandoning the traditional idea that a man
enjoyed a vote on the basis of his stake in a particular community,
and moved some distance towards the democratic view that each man as
such was entitled to one vote and no more.   But while the old was
not completely rejected the new was not entirely accepted, and Parliament refused to debate reform in these terms.

Now this tells us something about the Conservative approach to
reform.   Before 1914 the Conservative opposition to Liberal Bills
had not taken the form of opposition to male suffrage, but to the
practice of tinkering with the franchise, particularly plural
voting, while ignoring anomalies such as Irish over-representation

which were helpful to the Liberals.   There was some danger that as
in 1866 the Conservatives would be manoeuvred into an anti-reform
position by the double strategy in which the popular wing of Liberalism clamoured for one-man-one-vote while Liberal Governments produced rather limited Bills whose effect was to damage the Conservatives electorally.   The attachment of many Conservatives to plural
voting was separate to their attitude to the extension of the franchise.   Though they would not undertake it out of choice, when they
found themselves in a position in which some measure of reform had
become a political necessity, in 1917 and in 1867, their leaders did
not hesitate to be bold rather than cautious in extending the popular franchise.   This was for two reasons; the first was that to
enfranchise merely the top layer of the unenfranchised would be more
likely to assist the Liberals, whereas dipping down deeper would
bring in workers who, as Ramsay MacDonald recognised, were often
less politically conscious, more dependent upon their employers, and
thus more amenable to Conservative influence.   The second consideration was purely tactical; in 1917 as in 1867 the Conservatives
did not feel threatened by the movement in the country, but rather
by the use to which demagogic Liberal leaders might put it.   Just
as Gladstone in 1867 would sooner or later have stumped the country
for reform had not Disraeli managed to forestall him, so there was
the prospect in 1918 of Lloyd George fighting a Reconstruction Election in which 'votes for heroes' would be a demand the Conservatives
could not resist.   That was the very prospect that Walter Long
strove to avoid.   His and Bonar Law's approach to the whole question of reform was careful and calculated; the inevitable protests
put up by the party organisation did not deflect Law so long as he
had the backing or acquiescence of his leading colleagues, and the
attempts to amend the Bill by Conservative backbenchers were important to the leadership not so much for their intrinsic value as for
their contribution to party management.

The point is that none of this necessarily involved the Conservatives in a radical reappraisal of the men to whom they were granting
the vote.   Some Conservatives, as we have seen, took encouragement
from the response of the workers to the call to fight for their
country, but this arose from their own desire for a General Election
which they were bound to win and from a misapprehension that the
troops of 1914-18 were in the Conservative tradition of the professional Army.   Those Conservatives who set up the demand for soldiers' franchise during the first two years of the war succeeded
rather better than they had wished in that Asquith was driven to
open up a comprehensive reform scheme into which they fell by their
own momentum; thus ensnared they were implicated in a compromise
measure that was far more radical than they had wanted.   It was not
easy subsequently to attack a Bill designed to enfranchise the
troops except on the grounds that it did not do so adequately.

The idea that military necessity revolutionised the attitude of
such politicians towards extending the bounds of citizenship is only
superficially attractive.   For it hinges upon two things: the
nature of participation and the size of it.   It is surely clear
that there was a world of difference between the volunteer recruits
of the first part of the war and the conscripted, and increasingly
reluctant, soldiers of 1916-18.   Would not the volunteers' response

merely serve to confirm the ruling classes in their confidence in
the loyalty of the masses without therefore leading to any reappraisal of their social policies?   Certainly the different sense and
degree of participation under voluntaryism and under conscription
has to be taken into account by the MPR theory.   Again if one asks
the question what was the size of participation that was *necessary*
in the First World War, one realises that there were various answers
to it.   The Liberals tried to fight the war on a comparatively
limited base of volunteer soldiers.   What raised the 'necessary'
number of troops by several millions was the political force represented by Lloyd George and the Unionists.   Their capacity to control and ultimately overthrow Asquith was the force that increased
participation in the war and simultaneously imposed rigid limitations upon the social and political consequences.   For it was the
same Coalition that choked off social reform after 1918;   and it is
most unlikely that the Coalition would have enacted a Reform Bill
after the Coupon Election.   A radical reconstruction of society
could only have come through a continuation of the pre-war Liberal-
Labour alliance;   social reform failed because that alliance disintegrated.   To the extent that social and political reform succeeded, this was due to the survival at the top of the anti-war politicians until 1916 and to Lloyd George's dependence upon Liberal support thereafter.   Now this hardly suggests a straightforward link
between reform and military participation;   in fact in the case of
Britain in 1914-18 there appears to be an *inverse* relationship between the social size of the war and the process of social and political levelling in that the forces which generated one militated
against the other.

Finally one must consider the 1918 Act within the context of the
long history of parliamentary reform in Britain.   That there was a
remarkable absence of controversy over the franchise in 1917-18 is
not to be ascribed merely to the spirit of unity engendered by the
war but also to the fact that the fire was already departing from
the issue.   This is why the Speaker's Conference became a permanent
device for twentieth-century reform, and why 1918 marks the end of
the great Reform Acts.   As early as March 1918 it was being hailed
as the 'Greatest' of the Reform Acts, (7) a view which really cannot
be justified except in terms of the sheer numbers of new voters
which exceeded both in total and as a proportion, that of any previous measure.   However there was no drastic new departure in 1918;
the addition of new electors, simplification of registration and
equalisation of constituencies were changes in degree along well-
established lines.   With 1918, in short, one enters a period in
which marginal electoral reforms are effected without controversy by
means of Speakers' Conferences.   All this is a reflection of the
vastly altered place of constitutional and electoral issues in British public affairs during the twentieth century.   By 1918 it mattered very much less who had a vote than it had in 1832 because it
was becoming less important to sit in Parliament whose Members were
increasingly spectators in the drama of politics.

The waning of both Parliament and of parliamentary reform is emphasised by the defeat in 1917 of Proportional Representation, the
one proposal which would have been a change in kind not merely of
degree, and which consequently attracted most controversy during the

war.   The strength of the support for Proportional Representation
reflected a long period of perceived decline for Parliament and MPs
against the Cabinet and the party organisations.   As the 'Manchester Guardian' (8) aptly commented in 1917:

   The House of Commons has lost, not its ultimate power, but its
   will to control affairs, and if the Commons does not control
   affairs it does not so very much matter who elects it.   In rejecting P.R. a House willing to be weak has refused the remedy
   that might make it strong.

In the midst of the Great War the House of Commons induced itself
to accept a modest role which it would not have tolerated in peacetime, and one which it was not to recover since so many of those who
valued the traditional strength of the legislature were by now
approaching the end of their political careers tired and dispirited.
Apart from the Liberal, Labour and Free Trade Conservative groups
who had advocated Proportional Representation before 1914 there was
now one special group with interests in the reform - the Coalition
Liberals and Unionists of the stamp of Milner and Amery.   These
politicians, drawn together by the leadership of Lloyd George and by
their contempt for what they regarded as the blinkered narrowness of
the orthodox party leaders, badly needed to maintain the fluidity
that the war situation had introduced into politics; for them Proportional Representation was a natural panacea.   Multi-Member constituencies alone would have allowed those who straddled more than
one party and gave their loyalty to none to have sought election on
their own terms and retained their independence in the House of Commons.   But ironically these men were ill-disposed in most cases to
Proportional Representation by reason of another basic characteristic; they exhibited a strong Governmental mentality and a dislike
of legislatures in general which seemed to them merely a drag on
efficient Government.   Lloyd George and Milner therefore gave no
lead to their followers.   The opportunity for Proportional Representation was allowed to pass; within four years Lloyd George was
out of office and the lines of regular party conflict began to close
in again.   Thus it was that with the achievement of democracy in a
formal sense, the British Parliament and its Members resumed their
steady decline for half a century.

PROPORTIONAL REPRESENTATION, THE SECOND BALLOT, THE ALTERNATIVE VOTE AND THE NANSEN METHOD

Among the many variations of PR the two main types are the Single Transferable Vote, always favoured by the British society, and the List System, used on the Continent and in Israel. In both cases the essential ingredient is multi-member constituencies.

There are different methods of calculating quotas. The idea seems to have originated with Thomas Hare in England and Professor Andrae in Denmark in the 1850s. Hare envisaged that the entire country would form a single constituency and a quota would be calculated simply by dividing the number of valid votes by the number of vacancies to be filled. An improvement on the 'Hare quota' is the 'Droop quota', according to which, if there are four vacancies and 100 votes a candidate needs

$$\frac{100}{4 + 1} + 1 = 21 \text{ votes to be elected}$$

These systems are commonly confused with the Second Ballot and Alternative Vote which are not proportional systems and cannot be since they operate under single-member constituencies. They simply prevent the election of a member in any constituency by a minority of votes by effectively reducing the candidates to two, the Alternative Vote allows this to be done on one ballot paper instead of a re-election at a later date.

The Nansen Method was invented by a Professor Nansen, a mathematician of Melbourne, Australia; it is a different method of counting under the Alternative Vote system.

It seeks to overcome the difficulty encountered in Australia that many voters defeat the object of the Alternative Vote by failing to express a second preference; this is done by assuming that such electors are indifferent to all remaining candidates and therefore share their second preference equally between them.

It seeks, secondly, to avoid the defect that a result is determined by the second preferences of the last candidate only, and to permit the election of the most generally acceptable candidate who may in fact be the one with fewest first preference votes; he would be eliminated at once under the normal method of counting.

Thus one would count all the preferences of every elector but give a weighting to each one; the total 'poll' thus arrived at would in effect produce the same result as would be obtained from

conducting three dual contests between three candidates: the most
acceptable person would emerge the winner.

WOMAN SUFFRAGE IN THE HOUSE OF COMMONS 1910

An analysis prepared by the League For Opposing Woman Suffrage in December 1910 (Curzon Papers, D/1/6).

	Unionist	Lib	Nat	Lab
Anti-Suffragists: 189	121	58	4	2
Suffragists: 283				
i Advocates of a limited franchise: 129	63	60	4	2
ii Same terms as men: 184	20	77	13	24
iii Adult suffrage: 20	-	9	-	11
Unknown views: 175	46	58	64	7

This was based on the following assumptions:

1 that those who voted against the Conciliation Bill were anti-suffragist except those who said it was not sufficiently democratic: they were advocates of suffrage for women on equal terms with men;

2 that Members who voted for the Conciliation Bill but also for keeping it in a Committee of the Whole House were advocates of a limited franchise;

3 that Members who voted for the Conciliation Bill but also for sending it into Committee upstairs favoured woman suffrage on equal terms with men.

PARTY VOTING ON WOMAN SUFFRAGE 1911-17

*Figures in brackets indicate paired Members

1911 Conciliation Bill: Sir George Kemp

	Con	Lib	Lab	Nat	Total
For	53(25)	145(25)	26(5)	31	255
Against	43(43)	36(12)	-	9	88

1912 Conciliation Bill: Agg-Gardener

	Con	Lib	Lab	Nat	Total
For	63(13)	117(18	25(2)	3	208
Against	114(24)	73(8)	0	35(1)	222

1913 Representation of the People Bill: Dickinson

	Con	Lib	Lab	Nat	Total
For	28(12)	146(9)	34(3)	13	221
Against	140(19)	74(5)	0	54	268

1917 Representation of the People Bill

	Con	Lib	Lab	Nat	Total
For	140	184	30	33	387
Against	45	12	0	0	57

WOMAN SUFFRAGE: THE VOTING RECORD OF THE 1917 HOUSE OF COMMONS

	MPs who *supported* woman suffrage, 19 June 1917		MPs who *opposed* woman suffrage, 19 June 1917	
	For	Against	For	Against
1908	101	8	1	14
	Net suffragist gain 5.6%			
1910	152	44	4	32
	Net suffragist gain 17.2%			
1911	151	18	4	21
	Net suffragist gain 7.2%			
1912	136	69	1	36
	Net suffragist gain 24%			
1913	151	87	0	43
	Net suffragist gain 30.9%			

ELECTION EXPENSES OF WILLOUGHBY H. DICKINSON 1892-1918

Expenditure on Public Work, Dickinson Papers

		£			£
1892	Election expenses	155	1907	Election	20
1895	Election expenses	247	1907	Registration	84
1895	Election expenses	411	1908	Registration	91
1898	Registration	50	1909	Registration	67
1899	Registration	50	1910	Registration	52
1900	Registration	40	1910	Election expenses	657
1900	Election expenses	463	1911	Registration	91
1901	Registration	45	1912	Registration	198
1901	Election	20	1913	Registration	210
1902	Registration	78	1914	Registration	237
1903	Registration	87	1915	Registration	208
1904	Election	10	1916	Registration	126
1904	Registration	90	1917	Registration	147
1905	Registration	63	1918	Registration	115
1906	Registration	60	1918	Election expenses	571
1906	Election	549			5292

THE UNIONIST VIEW OF REDISTRIBUTION 1916

From a 'private and confidential' memorandum by Arthur Steel-Maitland, October 1916, prepared for the Unionist members of the Conference; Steel-Maitland Papers, vol. 202

Effect of Redistribution:

England:

Unionist loss	4	
with University seats	5	= 9

Wales:

Unionist loss	5

Scotland:

Unionist loss	3	
with University seats	2	= 5
total loss in Britain for Unionists		19 seats

Ireland:

Unionist gain	31	
University losses	2	= 29 net gains
Net United Kingdom gain for Unionists		10 seats

THE PROPOSALS OF THE SPEAKER'S CONFERENCE 1917

A Registration
1 Reduce the qualifying period to six months.
2 Revise the Register every six months.
3 The qualifying period should end on 15 January and 15 July each year.
4 Reduce the time between the preparation and the coming into force of the Register.
5 Resolutions 2, 3 and 4 not to apply to Ireland.
6 Registration Officers to be Town Clerks in boroughs and Clerks to the County Council in counties.
7 Appeals from the decisions of Registration Officers to go to the County Court.
8 Registration to be paid out of local rates with a 50 per cent subsidy from the state.

B Franchise
9 Residence in any premises during the qualifying period or occupation for business or professional purposes of any premises of £10 yearly value to entitle a man to be registered.
10 The qualification not to be lost through removal to different premises in the same constituency, or in the same borough or county (including London), or in a contiguous county or borough.
11 No one may vote more than once except as either a business voter or a University voter.

C Redistribution of Seats
14-21 Redistribution on the basis of a 70,000 population unit for new constituencies and 50,000 for remainders of counties or boroughs. Old seats under 50,000 to lose separate representation. Two-member seats to lose one seat if the population was below 120,000. Ireland was not considered from the point of view of redistribution.

D University Representation
22 Oxford and Cambridge to continue as two-member seats but each elector to have one vote only. The English and Welsh Universities to be grouped with London to form a three-member seat using

Single Transferable Vote; the four Scottish Universities to
form a three-member seat using STV.   The qualification to be
simply the obtaining of a degree.

E   Methods and Costs of Elections
23   All boroughs returning three or more Members to be formed into
three, four, or five-member seats using STV.
24   All polls to be held on the same day.
25   Payment of Returning Officers on a fixed scale by the Treasury.
26   Duties of Returning Officers to be performed by Town Clerks and
Clerks to County Councils.
27   Every candidate to place a deposit of £150 to be forfeited to
the Treasury if he fails to poll one eighth of the votes.
28   Maximum expenses of 7d. per elector in county seats and 5d. in
boroughs.
29   The financing of public meetings, publications or advertisements
in support of a candidate to be a corrupt offence unless the
expenditure is returned on the candidate's official list of
expenses.

F   Local Government Franchise
31   Anyone with six months occupation either as owner or tenant of
any land or premises in any Local Government area to qualify in
that area; all other franchise abolished, but no recommendation
made for Scotland and Ireland.

G   Soldiers and Sailors
32   Returning Officers' duty is to ascertain the names of men normally resident in his area but serving in the Forces; those
serving in the Forces during the qualifying period to qualify
on the basis of one month's residence immediately preceding 15
January or 15 July.

NB   All the above resolutions were *unanimous*.

H   Woman Suffrage
33   Any woman who is on the Local Government Register or whose husband is on it may also vote in Parliamentary Elections; an age
limit should operate, and thirty and thirty-five were the most
favoured.   This was agreed by a majority.

J   Miscellaneous
35   No person who has received Poor Relief, other than medical
relief, for less than thirty days during the qualifying period
should be disqualified.
36   The Alternative Vote should be used at all elections in single-
member seats where more than two candidates are nominated.
37   Any registered elector who can satisfy the Registration Officer
that the nature of his employment makes it probable that he will
be absent from his constituency on the day of the poll may have
his name entered on a list of Absent Voters.   Such persons will
receive a ballot paper by post to be returned by polling day
with a statutory declaration of identity.

THE PARTY COMPOSITION
THE MAJORITY SUPPORTING
THE REFORM BILL

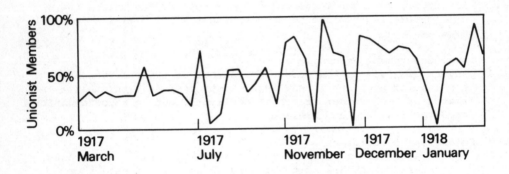

PARLIAMENTARY CONSTITUENCIES 1885-1918

		1885	1918
England:	London	59	62
	boroughs	166	193
	counties	231	230
	Universities	5	7
	Total	461	492
Wales:	boroughs	12	11
	counties	22	24
	University	-	1
	Total	34	36
Scotland:	boroughs	31	33
	counties	39	38
	Universities	2	3
	Total	72	74
Ireland:	boroughs	16	21
	counties	85	80
	Universities	2	4
	Total	103	105
	TOTAL	670	707

THE 1918 ELECTORATE

House of Commons Papers 1918 (138), XIX, 925

	Men	Women	Total
England and Wales	10,281,054	6,941,929	17,222,983
Scotland	1,392,119	840,547	2,232,666
Ireland	1,239,993	696,680	1,930,673
Total	12,913,166	8,479,156	21,392,322

Naval and Military Voters (included above)

	Men	Women	Total
England and Wales	3,359,280	2,748	3,362,028
Scotland	428,307	389	428,696
Ireland	107,176	235	107,411
Total	3,896,763	3,372	3,900,135

Business Franchise 159,013   University Franchise 68,091

Turnout 1918

Average 57%
England   55.5%
Wales   65.9%
Scotland   54.9%
University 60.2%
Ireland   69.5%

NOTES

CHAPTER 1   THE PARTIES AND THE SYSTEM 1906-14

1   N. Blewett, The Franchise in the United Kingdom 1885-1918, 'Past and Present', vol. 32, 1965.
2   H.C.G. Matthew, R.I. McKibbin and J.A. Kay, The Franchise Factor in the Rise of the Labour Party, 'English Historical Review', October 1976.
3   Blewett, op. cit.
4   'Nation', 22 June 1912.
5   H. Pelling, 'Social Geography of British Elections 1885-1910' (1967), Macmillan, pp. 6-14.
6   L. Courtney, 'A Plea for Real Representation' (1905), The Proportional Representation Society, and 'The Regeneration of Parliaments' (1905), The Proportional Representation Society.
7   M. Ostrogorski, 'Democracy and the Organisation of Political Parties' (1902), Macmillan; G. Wallas, 'Human Nature in Politics' (1908), Constable.
8   H. Belloc and C. Chesterton, 'The Party System' (1910), Swift; A.L. Lowell, 'The Government of England' (1908), Macmillan.
9   M.D. Pugh, The Background to the 1918 Representation of the People Act, Bristol University PhD thesis, 1974.
10 J.R. Corbett, 'Recent Electoral Statistics' (1910), Manchester Statistical Society.
11 'Nation', 21 May 1910.
12 J.A.R. Marriott in 'Nineteenth Century', vol. 75, January 1914.
13 N. Blewett, 'The Peers, the Parties and the People' (1972), Macmillan, chapter 12.
14 Minutes of Evidence of the Royal Commission on Electoral Systems, Cd 5352 (1910).
15 Cecil to J.H. Humphreys, 4 April 1905, ERS.
16 A.K. Russell, 'Liberal Landslide' (1973), David and Charles, chapter 3; R. Rempel, 'Unionists Divided' (1972), David and Charles; P. Fraser, Unionism and Tariff Reform: the Crisis of 1906, 'Historical Journal', V, 1963; N. Blewett, Free Fooders, Balfourites, Whole Hoggers: Factionalism within the Unionist Party 1906-1910, 'Historical Journal, XI, 1968.
17 PR Pamphlets, nos 4, 10, 16, 21, 23.

18   M.D. Pugh, New Light on Edwardian Voters: the Model Elections of 1906-1912, 'Bulletin of the Institute of Historical Research', May 1978.
19   Harold Cox, The Denial of Self-Government, 'Nineteenth Century and After', vol. 67, March 1910.
20   Strachey Papers, S/4/4/1.
21   Cecil to Strachey, 10 November 1909, Strachey Papers, S/4/3/17.
22   Strachey to Cecil (copy), 11 November 1909, Strachey Papers, S/4/3/17.
23   Cox, op. cit.
24   J. Westlake to J.H. Humphreys, 3 July 1911, ERS.
25   Ibid.
26   Labour Party Conference Reports 1914-17, 27 January 1914, p. 105.
27   NEC Minutes, 9 October 1913.
28   'The Labour Party and Electoral Reform' (1913), The Labour Party.
29   NEC Minutes, 24 January 1914.
30   Labour Party Conference Reports, 27 January 1914, pp. 104-8.
31   PR Pamphlet, no. 24, P.R. from a Labour Standpoint, by P. Snowden (1913).
32   'The Labour Party and Electoral Reform', op. cit.
33   'Labour Leader', 9 January 1913.
34   'Labour Leader', 18 July 1912.
35   Conference Reports, p. 104.
36   NEC Minutes, 1 December 1909, 9 March 1910, 5 August 1911.
37   NEC Minutes, 27, 28, 31 January 1913.
38   Ibid.
39   NEC Minutes, 19 June 1913.
40   NEC Minutes, 23 June 1913.
41   R.I. McKibbin, 'The Evolution of the Labour Party 1910-1924' (1974), Oxford University Press, pp. 73-6.
42   'The Labour Party and Electoral Reform', op. cit.
43   J.M. Robertson to J.H. Humphreys, 9 July 1906, ERS.
44   Royal Commission on Electoral Systems, Minutes of Evidence, Cd 5352 (1910).
45   Ibid.
46   PR Society, Executive Minutes, 15 April 1907.
47   PR Society, Executive Minutes, 24 March 1914; also PR Pamphlet, no. 26 (1914).
48   Minutes of the PR Parliamentary Committee, 15 June 1914.
49   Cd 3501, Miscellaneous no. 3 (1907).
50   Cd 3875, Miscellaneous no. 2 (1908).
51   PR Society, Executive Minutes, 22 June 1908.
52   Cd 5352.
53   Cd 5163 (1910).
54   HC Deb., 30 March 1910, c. 1387-1430.
55   PR Society, Executive Minutes, 14 June 1912.
56   Hugh Cecil to L. Courtney, 18 November 1911, ERS.
57   'Liberal Magazine', XVI, December 1908; PR Pamphlets, nos 3 (1906), 12 (1909).
58   Asquith Papers, vol. 46, 6 December 1912.
59   G. Younger to J.H. Humphries, 26 July 1912, ERS.
60   J. Gulland to J.H. Humphries, 4 June 1909, ERS.

61 E.T. John to J.H. Humphries, 30 March 1914, ERS.
62 Blewett, op. cit., chapter 12.
63 W.S. Churchill to J.H. Humphries, 8 February 1905, ERS.
64 J. Robertson to J.H. Humphries, 27 May 1907, ERS.
65 J. Robertson to J.H. Humphries, 24 April 1907, ERS.
66 Cockermouth, 1906; Newcastle and Pudsey, 1908; Bermondsey, 1909; Oldham, 1911; Crewe, 1912; Midlothian and South Lanark, 1913; South West Bethnal Green and Leith District, 1914.
67 Cd 5352, on Attercliffe; H. Pelling, 'Popular Politics and Society in Late Victorian England' (1968), Macmillan, pp. 130-46.
68 'Labour Leader', 18 July 1912.
69 'Representation', June 1914; 'Liberal Agent', XVII, July 1914.
70 'Liberal Agent', XVII, July 1914.
71 'Liberal Agent', IX, October 1906, XI, October 1908, XIV, January 1912, XV, October 1912; 'Manchester Guardian', 6 August 1906; 'Nation', 13 July 1907; 'Tribune', 6 July 1907; 'Labour Leader', 12 September 1912.
72 'Liberal Agent', XI, July 1908, October 1908, XVII, July 1914; 'Nation', 21 May 1910.
73 Notes for the Cabinet, January 1912, Gainford Papers, 68; Memorandum for the Cabinet, 30 March 1910; J.A. Pease to Elibank (copy), 17 August 1911; H. Samuel to J.A. Pease, 18 December 1911; E. Montagu to J.A. Pease, 2 January 1912; Memorandum of the Cabinet Committee on Franchise and Registration, 1912 - all in Gainford Papers, 112.
74 'Labour Leader', 18 July 1912.
75 McKibbin, op. cit., pp. 82-4.
76 P.F. Clarke, The Liberal and Labour Parties 1910-1914, 'English Historical Review', July 1975.
77 'Labour Leader', 1 August 1912.

CHAPTER 2 WOMAN SUFFRAGE 1906-14: THE FRUITS OF MODERATION

 1 See A. Raeburn, 'The Militant Suffragettes' (1973), Michael Joseph, and M. McKenzie, 'Shoulder to Shoulder' (1975), Penguin Books.
 2 A. Rosen, 'Rise Up Women!' (1975), Routledge & Kegan Paul.
 3 C.P. Scott's Diary, 2 December 1911.
 4 C.P. Scott's Diary, 23 January 1912.
 5 Asquith to Churchill, 23 December 1911; R. Churchill, 'Winston S. Churchill 1901-14', Companion vol. III, (1967), Heinemann, p. 1477.
 6 C.P. Scott's Diary, 26 October 1911.
 7 'Suffragette', 6 February 1911.
 8 See K.O. Morgan, 'Keir Hardie' (1975), Weidenfeld & Nicolson, pp. 249-50.
 9 Rosen, op. cit., p. 105.
10 Churchill, op. cit., p. 1437.
11 Churchill to Asquith, 21 December 1911; Churchill, op. cit., p. 1475.
12 'Anti-Suffrage Review', August 1911.
13 Women's Freedom League Reports, 1914, pp. 61-3.

14   'Anti-Suffrage Review', February 1914.
15   Eleanor Rathbone to C. Marshall, 23 May 1912, Marshall Papers.
16   I am grateful to Dr W.A. Speck of Newcastle University for draw-
     ing my attention to the Catherine Marshall Papers at Carlisle
     Record Office.
17   Catherine Marshall to F.D. Acland (draft), 4 November 1913,
     Marshall Papers.
18   Hanley, Holmfirth, Leith Burghs, Crewe, Midlothian, Houghton-le-
     Spring, South Lanark, North West Durham.
19   C. Marshall to A. Henderson, 14 October 1912, Marshall Papers.
20   Report of the Election Fighting Fund Committee, 12 July 1912,
     Marshall Papers.
21   C. Marshall to Henderson, 14 October 1912, Marshall Papers.
22   EFF Council Meeting Report, 1914 (?).
23   C. Marshall to Lady Selborne, 13 November 1913, Marshall Papers.
24   Ibid.
25   Undated 'Absolutely confidential' Memorandum, Marshall Papers.
26   Memoranda by Cecil, 20 January 1914, and Selborne, 1 May 1914,
     Bonar Law Papers, 31/2/50 and 32/3/1.
27   Curzon Papers, D/1/11.
28   Maud Selborne to C. Marshall, 15 October 1913, Marshall Papers.
29   Cromer to Curzon, 8 February 1912, Curzon Papers, D/1/7.
30   Cromer to Curzon, 18 January 1912, Curzon Papers, D/1/7.
31   Cromer to Curzon, 5 February 1912, Curzon Papers, D/1/7.
32   Ward to Curzon, 5 February 1913, Curzon Papers, D/1/8.
33   'Nation', 9 May 1914.
34   C. Marshall to Lady Selborne, 13 November 1913, Marshall Papers.
35   Margaret Robertson and C.M. Gordon to C. Marshall, 25 November
     1913, Marshall Papers.
36   C. Marshall to Francis Acland, 4 November 1913, Marshall Papers.
37   F.D. Acland to C. Marshall, 9 November 1913, Marshall Papers.
38   C. Marshall to Eleanor Acland (copy), 25 April 1913, Marshall
     Papers.
39   Asquith Papers, vol. 89, pp. 127-52 ff.

CHAPTER 3   THE GOVERNMENT AND FRANCHISE REFORM 1906-14

 1   N. Blewett, The Franchise in the United Kingdom 1885-1918, 'Past
     and Present', vol. 32, 1965, pp. 27-56.
 2   P.F. Clarke, 'Lancashire and the New Liberalism' (1971), Cam-
     bridge University Press, p. 399.
 3   A.K. Russell, 'Liberal Landslide' (1973), David & Charles, p.
     65.
 4   See Election Addresses at the National Liberal Club.
 5   HC Deb., 19 March 1909, c. 1385.
 6   'Nation', 22 June 1912.
 7   H. Pelling, The Labour Unrest 1911-14, 'Popular Politics and
     Society in Late Victorian Britain' (1968), Macmillan.
 8   'Labour Leader', 18 July 1912.
 9   See H.L. Morris, 'Parliamentary Franchise Reform in England
     1885-1918' (1921), Columbia University Press.
10   Blewett, op. cit.;   G.A. Jones, Further Thoughts on the Fran-
     chise, 'Past and Present', no. 34, 1966;   Clarke, op. cit., pp.
     116-17.

11   'Westminster Gazette', 30 December 1910.
12   Cabinet Papers 37/102/13, 8 April 1910.
13   Private and Confidential Memorandum, October 1916, Steel-Mait-
     land Papers, 202.
14   'Liberal Magazine', XIV, March 1906; 'Liberal Agent', X, no.
     51, January 1908, no. 52, April 1908, no. 56, April 1909.
15   CAB 37/108/148, 16 November 1911.
16   CAB 37/114/4, 7 January 1913.
17   CAB 37/114/12, 1913.
18   CAB 37/108/148, 16 November 1911.
19   CAB 41/30/48, 14 March 1906.
20   C. Rover, 'Women's Suffrage and Party Politics in Britain'
     (1967), Routledge & Kegan Paul, pp. 103, 117-18, 181.
21   C.P. Scott's Diary, 2 February 1911.
22   Rover, cop. cit., p. 134.
23   CAB 37/108/148.
24   'Nation', 6 May 1911.
25   CAB 37/108/148.
26   Speech on woman suffrage, 25 March 1918, Dickinson Papers.
27   CAB 41/32/61, 62, 63, 8, 15 and 23 June 1910.
28   CAB 41/33/15, 17 May 1911.
29   Ibid.
30   C.P. Scott's Diary, 26 October 1911.
31   Harcourt to Pease, 3 February 1911, Gainford Papers, 63.
32   Simon to Pease, 30 May 1911, Gainford Papers, 63.
33   CAB 37/108/181, 14 December 1911.
34   CAB 37/109/3, January 1912.
35   Harcourt to Pease, 27 December 1911, and Pease to Asquith
     (copy), 28 December 1911, Gainford Papers, 63.
36   Churchill to Elibank, 18 December 1911; Randolf Churchill,
     'Winston S. Churchill', vol. II, Companion vol. iii, p. 1473.
37   Asquith to Pease, 29 December 1911, Gainford Papers, 63; also,
     Asquith to Churchill, 23 December 1911; Churchill, op. cit.,
     vols II and III, p. 1477.
38   Necessity for a Bill this Session - notes for the Cabinet, 25
     April 1912, Gainford Papers, 68.
39   CAB 41/33/47, 25 April 1912.
40   Pease to Sir A. Thring (copy), 25 April 1912, Gainford Papers,
     112.
41   J.S. Higham to Pease, 4 July 1912, Gainford Papers, 65/1; W.
     Webster to Pease, 27 December 1912, and Memorandum on the Fran-
     chise Bill, Gainford Papers, 64.
42   CAB 37/111/88, July 1912.
43   Ibid.
44   CAB 37/114/9, January 1913.
45   NEC Minutes, 2 July 1912 and 15 October 1912.
46   NEC Minutes, 27, 28, 31 January 1913.
47   C.P. Scott's Diary, 20 January 1913.
48   C.P. Scott's Diary, 15 January 1913.
49   Cromer to Curzon, 28 September 1910, Curzon Papers, D/1/6.
50   Lady Jersey to Curzon, 21 September 1910, Curzon Papers, D/1/6.
51   Cromer to Curzon, 13 October 1910, Curzon Papers, D/1/6.
52   Cromer to Curzon, 18 July 1910, Curzon Papers, D/1/6.
53   Harcourt to Curzon, 7 July 1910, Curzon Papers, D/1/6.

54 Mrs Harcourt to Curzon, 5 August 1910, Curzon Papers, D/1/6.
55 Cromer to Curzon, 27 July 1910, Curzon Papers, D/1/6.
56 Cromer to Curzon, 18 December 1911, Curzon Papers, D/1/6.
57 Asquith to Churchill, 23 December 1911; Churchill, op. cit.,
    vols II and III, p. 1477.
58 C.P. Scott's Diary, 16 March 1911.
59 Cromer to Curzon, 20 January 1912, Cutzon Papers, D/1/7.
60 Smith to Bonar Law, 27 December 1912, Bonar Law Papers,
    24/5/157.
61 Asquith to Churchill, 23 December 1911; Churchill, op. cit.,
    vols II and III, p. 1477.
62 C.P. Scott's Diary, 15 June 1911.
63 CAB 37/109/3, January 1912.
64 Memorandum, 28 November 1912, Gainford Papers, 65/1.
65 Secret Memorandum of Cabinet decisions, 18 December 1912, and an
    undated Memo on the Bill by Pease, in the Gainford Papers, 68;
    also a typed memorandum by the Cabinet Committee, 18 December
    1912, Gainford Papers, 112.
66 CAB 41/34/3, 22 January 1913.
67 Pease to Curzon, 3 January 1913, Curzon Papers, D/1/8.
68 J.W. Lowther, 'A Speaker's Commentaries' (1925), Edward Arnold,
    vol. II, p. 136.
69 HC Deb., 23 January 1913, c. 643-4.
70 Lowther, op. cit., p. 137.
71 HC Deb., 27 January 1913, c. 1020-2.
72 CAB 41/34/4, 25 January 1913.
73 CAB 41/34/5, 28 January 1913.
74 CAB 41/34/9, 13 March 1913.
75 'Labour Leader', 6 February 1913.
76 C.P. Scott's Diary, 3 February 1913 (a conversation with Grey).
77 HC Deb., 30 May 1913, c. 1249.

CHAPTER 4   WAR IS UNDECLARED

 1 Trevor Wilson, 'The Downfall of the Liberal Party 1914-1935'
    (1966), Collins, pp. 23-68.
 2 Quoted in Jenkins, 'Asquith' (1964), Collins, p. 374.
 3 'The Times', 11 August 1914; The Political Transformation,
    'Fortnightly Review', 1 September 1914.
 4 HC Deb., 30 July 1914, c. 1601.
 5 HC Deb., 15 August 1914, c. 882-93.
 6 Memo by Curzon, 27 January 1915, Balfour Papers, 49693.
 7 Memo by Long, 27 January 1915, Balfour Papers, 49693.
 8 'The Times', 9, 11 January 1915, 3 February 1915 and 3, 4 May
    1915; also correspondence between Crewe and Bonar Law in the
    BLP, 36/1/12, 14, 18.
 9 HC Deb., 3 February 1915, c. 71.
10 National Union Executive Minutes, 18 February 1915.
11 Meeting of the Manchester Conservative and Unionist Association,
    11 May 1916, Derby Papers, 2/21.
12 NEC Minutes, 7 January 1915.
13 NEC Minutes, 26 April 1915.
14 HC Deb., 23 July 1915, c. 1865.

15 Hugh Cecil to Lord Robert Cecil, 10 January 1915, Cecil of Chelwood Papers, 51157.
16 'Liberal Agent', XVII, no. 78, October 1914.
17 Ibid.
18 See Asquith Papers, vol. 26.
19 Steel-Maitland to Bonar Law, 28 September 1915, BLP, 51/3/23.
20 See E.I. David, Charles Masterman and the Swansea District By-Election, 1915, 'Welsh History Review', vol. 5, no. 1, 1970.
21 'Liberal Agent', XVIII, no. 81, July 1915.
22 'Liberal Agent', XVIII, no. 82, October 1915.
23 CAB 37/126/23, 24 March 1915.
24 'Liberal Agent', XVII, no. 78, October 1914: 'We may state the effect of this Act thus:- a man absent from home on actual Naval or Military Service is relieved from residency or inhabitancy, and the pauper disqualification only.... It is abundantly clear then, that nothing in this Act reserves the vote next year if the tenancy lapses before 15th July 1915. If business premises are given up, or wife or family give up the House and go into lodgings, or if the lodger's contract ceases, the vote lapses irrevocably.
25 HC Deb., 6 August 1914, c. 2108-10.
26 Sir Henry Wilson to Colonel Page-Croft, 30 August 1916, Page-Croft Papers, 1/20.
27 Arthur Murray's Diary, 17 June 1916, Elibank Papers, 8814.
28 Lloyd George to Asquith, 17 June 1916, LGP, D/18/2/18.
29 Lord Riddell's 'War Diary' (1933), Nicholson & Watson, p. 193.
30 CAB 37/126/23, 24 March 1915.
31 CAB 37/126/31, 27 March 1915.
32 CAB 37/127/14, 8 April 1915.
33 CAB 37/128/18, 15 May 1915.
34 National Union Executive Minutes, 13 May 1915.
35 M.D. Pugh, Asquith, Bonar Law and the First Coalition, 'Historical Journal', XVII, no. 4, 1974.
36 HC Deb., 14 December 1915, c. 1969.
37 Oliver to St Loe Strachey, 14 March 1916, Strachey Papers, 18/3/10.
38 Law to Curzon, 29 January 1915 (copy), Balfour Papers, 49693.
39 Memo by Long 27 January 1915, Balfour Papers, 49693.
40 Chamberlain to Law, 17 May 1915, BLP, 37/2/37.
41 Memo by Curzon, 27 January 1915, Balfour Papers, 49693.
42 Balfour to Bonar Law (copy), 30 January 1915, Balfour Papers, 49693.
43 Hugh Cecil to Lord Robert Cecil, 10 January 1915, Cecil of Chelwood Papers, 51157.
44 Viscount Long, 'Memories' (1923), Hutchinson, pp. 220-1.
45 Bonar Law to Asquith (copy), 21 May 1915, BLP, 53/6/3.
46 Sir Charles Petrie, 'Life and Letters of Sir Austen Chamberlain' (1940), Cassell, vol. II, p. 25.
47 Ibid.
48 Chamberlain to Law, 17 May 1915, BLP, 37/2/37.
49 'The Times', 4 May 1915.
50 A.J.P. Taylor, Politics in the First World War, in 'Politics In Wartime' (1964), Hamish Hamilton.
51 Conversation with Bonar Law, 15 March 1916, Spender Papers, 46388.

52   Asquith to Balfour, 20 May 1915, Balfour Papers, 49692.
53   A.J.P. Taylor's 'Beaverbrook' (1972), Penguin Books, p. 92.
54   S.E. Koss and Lord Haldane, 'Scapegoat For Liberalism' (1969),
     University of Columbia Press, p. 186; C. Hazlehurst, 'Politi-
     cians at War' (1971), p. 238.
55   W.S. Churchill, 'The World Crisis 1911-1918' (1968 edition),
     Mentor Books, vol. II, p. 524.
56   David Lloyd George, 'War Memoirs' (1938 edition), Oldhams, vol.
     I, p. 136.
57   Petrie, op. cit., vol. II, p. 21.
58   MacCallum Scott's Diary, 19 May 1915.
59   Steel-Maitland to Bonar Law, 13 June 1916, BLP, 64/G/8.

CHAPTER 5   VOTES FOR HEROES?

1   Frances Stevenson's Diary, pp. 99-100.
2   P.B. Johnson, 'Land Fit For Heroes' (1968), University of
    Chicago Press, pp. 10-35.
3   National Union Executive Minutes, 10 June 1915.
4   CAB 37/130/10, 16 June 1915.
5   HC Deb., 23 July 1915, c. 1833-6.
6   Ibid., c. 1845-72.
7   CAB 37/136/25, 20 October 1915.
8   HC Deb., 9 December 1915, c. 1615.
9   Harcourt to J.A. Pease, 20 November 1915, Gainford Papers, 93.
10 Steel-Maitland to Bonar Law, 25 November 1915, BLP, 51/5/52.
11 Simon to Bonar Law, 29 November 1915, BLP, 51/5/61.
12 Dated 2 December 1915, BLP, 52/1/6.
13 HC Deb., 9 December 1915, c. 1611.
14 HC Deb., 14 December 1915, c. 1967-73.
15 Ibid., c. 1945.
16 'The Times', 16 December 1915; also Pease to Asquith (draft),
    8 November 1915, Gainford Papers, 93.
17 HC Deb., 14 December 1915, c. 1967-73.
18 Ibid., c. 1973-82.
19 Ibid., c. 2022.
20 In a note from 10 Downing Street, BLP, 64/G/16.
21 HC Deb., 6 January 1916, c. 823.
22 Ibid., c. 842, and 18 January 1916, c. 947.
23 CAB 37/144/24, 9 March 1916.
24 Ibid.
25 'Englishwoman', XXI, no. 92, August 1916.
26 CAB 37/148/44, 30 May 1916.
27 CAB 37/150/29, 29 June 1916.
28 CAB 37/152/9, 20 July 1916.
29 Steel-Maitland to Bonar Law, 22 May 1915, BLP, 64/G/2.
30 CAB 37/126/23, 24 March 1915.
31 Steel-Maitland to Bonar Law, 13 June 1916, BLP, 64/G/8.
32 Ibid.
33 Ibid.
34 Gulland to Bonar Law, 26 July 1916, BLP, 64/G/13.
35 Christopher Addison, 'Four And A Half Years' (1934), vol. II,
    p. 215.

36   CAB 37/144/24, 9 March 1916.
37   Ibid.
38   CAB 37/148/2, 16 May 1916.
39   CAB 41/37/22, 1 June 1916.
40   NEC Minutes, 26 April 1915.
41   NEC Minutes, 28 March 1916.
42   CAB 37/147/31, 12 May 1916.
43   Cecil to Asquith, 18 May 1916, Asquith Papers, vol. 16.
44   Cecil and Henderson to Asquith, 22 November 1916, Asquith
     Papers, vol. 17.
45   HC Deb., 16 August 1916, c. 1898-1903.
46   CAB 37/149/3, 2 June 1916.
47   CAB 37/149/10, 7 June 1916.
48   CAB 37/149/38, 15 June 1916.
49   CAB 37/153/22, 7 August 1916.
50   'Most secret' Memorandum, 22 May 1916, 'Strachey Papers',
     S/18/3/18.
51   HC Deb., 19 July 1916, c. 1039.
52   Ibid., c. 1045-52.
53   The victory of C.B. Stanton (pro-war Labour) in Keir Hardie's
     old seat at Merthyr Tydvil in November 1915 was the first sign.
     In January 1916 Pemberton Billing polled well at Mile End and
     went on to win at Hertford in March; this was followed by some
     close results where independents attacked Liberal seats (Har-
     borough and Hyde), and the Unionist seat at Wimbledon in the
     spring. However, the elections during the summer and early
     autumn in Tewkesbury, South Londonderry County, Berwick and
     Mansfield showed some falling off in the rebel vote, and their
     polls at Ayr County North and Winchester in October were very
     small.
54   CAB 37/152/21, 26 July 1916.
55   CAB 37/153/2, 1 August 1916.
56   CAB 37/153/16, 4 August 1916.
57   CAB 37/154/37, August 1916.
58   CAB 37/153/22, 7 August 1916.
59   Ibid.
60   CAB 37/153/24, 8 August 1916.
61   CAB 41/37/30, 11 August 1916.
62   Long to Asquith, 10 August 1916, Asquith Papers, vol. 17.
63   Ibid.
64   'The Times', 15 August 1916.
65   HC Deb., 14 August 1916, c. 1447-58.
66   HC Deb., 16 August 1916, c. 1959-60.
67   HL Deb., 22 August 1916, c. 185-98.
68   HC Deb., 14 August 1916, c. 1447-58.
69   'War Workers' were defined as all those in the Army and Navy or
     working under their discretion, ambulance men, prisoners of war,
     internees in Germany, and those who had lost their homes through
     destruction or for home defence.
70   HC Deb., 16 August 1916, c. 1891-2.
71   Introduced into the House of Lords, 22 August 1916, c. 225.
72   HC Deb., 16 August 1916, c. 1900.
73   Ibid., c. 1916-21.
74   Ibid., c. 1904-6.

75   Ibid.
76   Ibid.
77   Steel-Maitland to Bonar Law, 13 June 1916, BLP, 64/G/8.
78   Salisbury to Selborne, 23 August 1916, Selborne Papers, vol. 6.
79   HC Deb., 16 August 1916, c. 1948-50.
80   CAB 37/157/12, 5 October 1916.
81   Long to Lloyd George, 17 October 1916, LGP, E/2/18/2; CAB
     37/158/11, 24 October 1916.
82   CAB 37/158/23, 31 October 1916.
83   Lowther to Asquith, October 1916, Asquith Papers, vol. 17.
84   Newman to J.H. Humphreys, 19 August 1916, ERS.

CHAPTER 6   MR LOWTHER'S TRIUMPH

1   CAB 24/6/1, 13 February 1917.
2   Salisbury to Selborne, 23 August 1916, Selborne Papers, vol. 6.
3   Salisbury to Selborne, 30 August 1916, Selborne Papers, vol. 6.
4   Long to Asquith, 18 August 1916, Asquith Papers, vol. 17.
5   Letter to H.J. Mackinder (copy), 22 August 1916, ERS.
6   Lady Courtney's Diary, 17 October 1916, Courtney Papers, vol.
    XXXVII.
7   Long to Bonar Law, 8 September 1916, BLP, 64/G/19.
8   'Manchester Guardian', 19 January 1917.
9   'The Times', 22 August 1916.
10 Memorandum by Long, 23 August 1916, Asquith Papers, vol. 17.
11 Long to Asquith, 18 August 1916, Asquith Papers, vol. 17.
12 Montagu to Bonham Carter, 13 September 1916, Asquith Papers,
    vol. 17.
13 Montagu to Long (copy), 11 September 1916, Asquith Papers, vol.
    17.
14 Long to Montagu, 12 September 1916; Asquith Papers, vol. 17.
15 Gulland to Asquith (copy), 15 September 1916, BLP, 64/G/20.
16 Long to Asquith, 17 September 1916, Asquith Papers, vol. 17.
17 Dated 18 September 1916, Asquith Papers, vol. 17.
18 Lowther to Asquith, 1 October 1916, Asquith Papers, vol. 17.
19 J.W. Lowther, 'A Speaker's Commentaries' (1925), Edward Arnold,
    vol. 2, p. 196.
20 Gulland to Asquith (copy), 15 September 1916, BLP, 64/G/20.
21 Letter to Newman (copy) 23 August 1916, ERS.
22 Proportional Representation Society Executive Minutes, 15 Sep-
    tember 1916.
23 CAB 37/155/14, 8 September 1916.
24 'Vote', XIV, no. 358, 1 September 1916.
25 Letter from the Speaker to the Prime Minister, CD 8463 (1917).
26 Lowther, op. cit., p. 196.
27 'Common Cause', VIII, no. 392, 13 October 1916.
28 Salisbury to Selborne, 4 September 1916, Selborne Papers, vol.
    6.
29 Suffragists: Sir J. Simon, W.H. Dickinson, Earl Grey, Ellis
    Davies, Sir John Bethell, A. Williams, Lord Southwark (Liberal),
    Lord Burnham, Sir W. Bull, Colonel J. Craig (Conservative),
    G.J. Wardle, Stephen Walsh, Frank Goldstone (Labour), T.P.
    O'Connor, P.J. Brady, Maurice Healy, T. Scanlan (Nationalist).

Anti-suffragists: A. McCallum Scott, Viscount Gladstone (Liberal), Sir F. Banbury, Sir R. Williams, Salisbury, Colonel Page-Croft, Sir Harry Samuel, Sir Robert Finlay, Basil Peto, Donald MacMaster (Conservative).

30 W.M. R. Pringle, Sir Ryland Adkins, George Lambert (Liberal); E.R. Turton and Sir Joseph Larmor (Conservative).
31 HC Deb., 16 August 1916, c. 1938.
32 'Manchester Guardian', 18 April 1917.
33 Lowther, op. cit., p. 199, 205.
34 Ibid.
35 'Vote', XIV, no. 364, 13 October 1916.
36 Lowther, op. cit., p. 196.
37 Ibid., p. 199.
38 HC Deb., 23 May 1917, c. 2364.
39 Cd 8463 (1917).
40 Grey to Bryce (copy), 13 October 1916, Grey Papers, 236/5.
41 'Manchester Dispatch', 31 January 1917.
42 Memorandum on Electoral Reform and Redistribution, probably written in the summer of 1916, attached to Labour Party NEC Minutes, 27 January 1917.
43 W.H. Dickinson, Parliamentary Franchise: the present and future Position, 'Contemporary Review', vol. 110, October 1916.
44 Memorandum on the Speaker's Conference, Dickinson Papers.
45 HC Deb., 22 November 1917, c. 1302.
46 Lowther to Bryce, 26 August 1917, Bryce Papers, UB 40.
47 Lowther to Lloyd George, 14 December 1916, LGP, F/46/12/1.
48 R.A. Sanders' Diary, 10 June 1917.
49 Draft Resolution dated 16 November 1916, Asquith Papers, vol. 133; also a typed copy in the Steel-Maitland Papers, vol. 202.
50 Cd 2602, LXII, 359; also the Report of a Committee of Enquiry, Parliamentary Papers, 1906 (79), XCVI, 113.
51 See the evidence of Sir John Boraston and W.A. Gales to the Royal Commission on Electoral Systems, Cd 5352, 1910.
52 The House of Commons to Scale, March 1914.
53 Memorandum dated October 1916, Steel-Maitland Papers, vol. 202.
54 Memorandum on the Speaker's Conference, 1918, Dickinson Papers.
55 Private and Confidential Memorandum, October 1916, Steel-Maitland Papers, vol. 202.
56 Ibid.
57. Ibid.
58 'Suggestions on behalf of the Unionist Members' (copy), 4 December 1916, Grey Papers, 246/8.
59 Selborne to Salisbury, 12 September 1916, Selborne Papers, vol. 6.
60 Ibid.
61 S. Andreski, 'Military Organisation and Society' (1954), Routledge & Kegan Paul.
62 Salisbury to Selborne, 23 August 1916, Selborne Papers, vol. 6.
63 J.O. Stubbs, Lord Milner and Patriotic Labour, 'English Historical Review' (1972).
64 Long to Asquith, 23 September 1916, Asquith Papers, vol, 17.
65 Lowther, op. cit., p. 205.
66 G.P. Gooch, 'Life of Lord Courtney' (1920), Macmillan, p. 608.
67 Burnham to Grey, 1 February 1917, Grey Papers, 236/7.

68 Aneurin Williams, The Reform Bill and the New Era, 'Contemporary Review', 112, July 1917.
69 Minutes of the Parliamentary Committee for Proportional Representation, 27 March 1917.
70 'The Times', 31 March 1917.
71 'The Times', 2 April 1917.
72 Lowther to Lloyd George, 14 December 1916, LDP, F/46/12/1.
73 Ibid.
74 Lowther, op. cit., p. 203.
75 Lowther to Lloyd George, 22 December 1916, LGP, F/46/12/2.
76 Lowther, op. cit., p. 198.
77 Mrs Fawcett to Miss E. Atkinson, 21 December 1916, FLP.
78 Lowther, op. cit., p. 198.
79 Lowther to Lloyd George, 22 December 1916, LGP, F/46/12/2.
80 Lord Dickinson to Miss Barry, 20/1/43, Dickinson Papers.
81 HC Deb., 22 May 1917, c. 2213-14.
82 Lowther, op. cit., p. 204.
83 Ibid., p. 216.

CHAPTER 7   LLOYD GEORGE'S DILEMMA

1 'Western Daily Press', 16 January 1917.
2 'New Statesman', 3 February 1917.
3 'The Times', 1 February 1917.
4 'Liberal Magazine', April 1917.
5 'Liberal Agent', XIX, no. 88, April 1917.
6 'Westminster Gazette', 7 March 1917.
7 NEC Minutes, 7 February 1917.
8 NEC Minutes, 18 April 1917; also 'The Times', 21 March 1917.
9 'Conservative Agents Journal', no. 44, April 1917; also R.A. Sanders' Diary, 27 May 1917.
10 Minutes of the Executive of the National Union, 8 May 1917:

	The Report For Against	Not during the War	Against PR	Women's vote: For Against
Associations	4 81	56	15	9 6
Chairmen	5 9	3	4	6 1
Agents	23 169	24	41	83 37

11 Ibid.
12 Secretary of the Bridgewater Association to Sir John Boraston, 13 February 1917, Steel-Maitland Papers, vol. 202.
13 Memorandum for the Cabinet by Long, 2 February 1917, Long Papers.
14 C.P. Scott's Diary, 28 January 1917.
15 C. Addison, 'Four and a Half Years' (1934), Barrie & Jenkins, vol. II, p. 288.
16 Memorandum of a conversation between Mr Lloyd George and certain Unionist ex-Ministers, 7 December 1916, Chamberlain Papers, 15/3/6.
17 C.P. Scott's Diary, 28 January 1917.

18 Lord Riddell's 'War Diary' (1933), Nicholson & Watson, 1 April 1917.
19 Addison, op. cit., p. 352.
20 Frances Stevenson's Diary, 25 April 1917.
21 C.P. Scott's Diary, 28 January 1917.
22 C.P. Scott's Diary, 20 October 1917.
23 Under the Parliament and Local Elections Bill (1916), as amended in the House of Lords.
24 Typed memorandum, 2 February 1917, Long Papers.
25 Sir Hugh Thornton's Diary, 3 February 1917, Milner Papers, vol. 301.
26 Long to Steel-Maitland, 4 February 1917, Steel-Maitland Papers, vol. 202.
27 Steel-Maitland to Long (draft), 3 February 1917, Steel-Maitland Papers, vol. 202.
28 Sir Hugh Thornton's Diary, 2 March 1917, Milner Papers, vol. 301.
29 Sir Hugh Thornton's Diary, 7 February 1917, Milner Papers, vol. 301.
30 Lloyd George, 'War Memoirs' (1938), Oldhams, vol. II, pp. 1169-70.
31 Notes on the Report of the Speaker's Conference, 3 February 1917, Steel-Maitland Papers, vol. 202.
32 Ibid.
33 W.A. Gales to Steel-Maitland, 26 February 1917, Steel-Maitland Papers, vol. 202.
34 Speaker's Registration Conference Report regarded from the point of view of the future, 21 February 1917, Steel-Maitland Papers, vol. 202.
35 Notes on the Report of the Speaker's Conference.
36 Minutes of the Council of the National Union, 8 June 1917.
37 Carson to Selborne (copy), 22 March 1917, Bonar Law Papers, 81/4/25.
38 Sir Hugh Thornton's Diary, 15 February 1917, 26 March 1917, Milner Papers, vol. 301.
39 Sir Hugh Thornton's Diary, 12, 27 March 1917, Milner Papers, vol. 301.
40 Bonar Law to Long, 6 February 1917, Long Papers.
41 Long to Bonar Law (copy), 5 February 1917, Long Papers.
42 Addison's Diary, 1 March 1917, Addison Papers, vol. 98.
43 CAB 24/6/1, 13 February 1917.
44 Ibid.
45 Memorandum for the Cabinet by Long (draft), 2 February 1917, Long Papers.
46 Memorandum for the Cabinet on Franchise and Registration, undated (probably March-April 1917), Long Papers,
47 HC Deb., 20 February 1917, c. 1159-60.
48 James Lowther, 'A Speaker's Commentaries' (1925), Edward Arnold, vol. II, p. 205.
49 Richard Holt's Diary, 18 February 1917.
50 MacCallum Scott's Diary, 19 February 1917.
51 C.P. Scott's Diary, 26 February 1917.
52 Spender and Asquith, 'Life of Herbert Henry Asquith' (1932), Hutchinson, vol. II, pp. 279-97; R. Jenkins, 'Asquith' (1964), Collins, pp. 524-46; S.E. Koss, 'Asquith' (1975), Allen Lane.

53 E.I. David, The Liberal Party during the First World War, chapter VI, Cambridge MLitt thesis, 1968; also Trevor Wilson, 'Downfall of the Liberal Party' (1966), Collins, pp. 112-21.
54 Lloyd George, 'War Memoirs', vol. II, p. 1169.
55 Cabinet Minutes, 23/2/105, 16 April 1917.
56 Lloyd George to Churchill (copy), 30 March 1917, LGP, I/2/2/70.
57 C. Addison, 'Four and a Half Years' (1934), Hutchinson, vol. II, p. 348.
58 Frances Stevenson's Diary, 2 April 1917.
59 Sir Hugh Thornton's Diary, 26 March 1917, Milner Papers, vol. 301.
60 Cabinet Minutes, 23/2/105, 26 March 1917.
61 'The Times', 28 March 1917.
62 Typed note by Steel-Maitland, 29 March 1917, Steel-Maitland Papers, vol. 202.
63 Ibid.
64 Bonar Law to Steel-Maitland, 28 March 1917, Steel-Maitland Papers, vol. 202.
65 Lord Riddell, op. cit., p. 246.
66 'The Times', 30 March 1917.
67 Minutes of the National Union Executive, 13 March 1917 and the Council Minutes, 8 June 1917.
68 Younger to Long, 30 March 1917, Long Papers.
69 Ibid.
70 Long to Younger (copy), 30 March 1917, Long Papers.
71 Long to Lloyd George (copy), 30 March 1917, Long Papers.
72 The 1917 Deputation to Lloyd George, copy in the London Museum's collection of Suffragette Papers, Z6065.

CHAPTER 8   THE UNIONIST REVOLT

1 Milner's Papers amply confirm Hankey's view.
2 Sir Charles Mallett, 'Lord Cave: a Memoir' (1931), Hutchinson, pp. 184-5, 190-9; Lord Riddell's 'War Diary' (1933), Nicholson & Watson, p. 232.
3 Lady Cave to Bonar Law, 11 April 1917, BLP, 78/3/7.
4 Bonar Law to Long (copy), 14 April 1917, BLP, 78/3/9a.
5 Hayes Fisher to Bonar Law, 13 April 1917, BLP, 78/3/9.
6 CAB 24/12/655, 5 May 1917.
7 Derby to Percy Woodhouse, 8 May 1917, Derby Papers, 2/31; Derby to Bonar Law, 15 May 1917, BLP, 81/6/13.
8 National Union Executive Minutes, 22 May 1917.
9 National Union Executive Minutes, 7 June 1917.
10 Salvidge to Derby, 2 June 1917, Derby Papers, 1/29.
11 Ibid.
12 Colonel Sanders' Diary, 27 May 1917.
13 Long to Talbot (copy), 9 May 1917, BLP, 81/6/12.
14 Long to Bonar Law, 26 May 1917, BLP, 81/6/18.
15 Sir Hugh Thornton's Diary, 23 January 1917, Milner Papers, vol. 301.
16 Harcourt to John Gulland (copy), 29 May 1917, Harcourt Papers, 27/3; Asquith to Crewe, 2 June 1917, Crewe Papers, C/40.
17 HC Deb., 6 June 1917, c. 162.

18 Long to Cave (copy), 1 June 1917, Long to Charles Bathurst (copy), 4 June 1917, and Rowland Hunt to Long, 15 June 1917, Long Papers.
19 Colonel Sanders' Diary, 10 June 1917.
20 Colonel Sanders' Diary, 15 June 1917.
21 Colonel Sanders' Diary, 20 July 1917.
22 Memorandum on seats by Long (copy), 19 January 1918, Long Papers.
23 Long to Walter Jerred (copy), 14 June 1917, Long Papers.
24 HC Deb., 11 June 1917, c. 684.
25 Sub-committee Report, National Union Council Minutes, 8 June 1917.
26 HC Deb., 7 June 1917, c. 459.
27 HC Deb., 6 June 1917, c. 219.
28 'Private and Confidential' Memorandum on swallow votes by Long, undated, Long Papers.
29 HC Deb., 7 June 1917, c. 376.
30 Ibid., c. 404.
31 Ibid., c. 419.
32 Ibid., c. 424.
33 Ibid., c. 444.
34 Ibid., c. 459.
35 Ibid., c. 472-9.
36 HC Deb., 18 June 1917, c. 1497.
37 Labour Party NEC Minutes, 5 June 1917.
38 HC Deb., 18 June 1917, c. 1513.
39 HC Deb., 20 June 1917, c. 1914.
40 HC Deb., 25 June 1917, c. 60.
41 Selborne to Salisbury (copy), 25 August 1916, Selborne Papers, vol. 6.
42 HC Deb., 25 June 1917, c. 69.
43 Ibid., c. 68.
44 Ibid., c. 63.
45 Cabinet Minutes, 23/4/274, 15 November 1917; CAB 24/31, 13 November 1917.
46 HC Deb., 26 June 1917, c. 307.
47 Ibid., c. 315-21.
48 Lord Hugh Cecil and John Cator.
49 'Conservative Agents' Journal', no. 45, July 1917.
50 Memorandum (copy) by Long, 20 April 1917, Long Papers.
51 Colonel Sanders' Diary, 20 July 1917.
52 HC Deb., 15 August 1917, c. 1213-18.
53 HC Deb., 26 June 1917, c. 258-60.
54 Ibid., c. 282-5.
55 HC Deb., 9 August 1917, c. 653.
56 National Union Council Minutes, 8 June 1917.
57 National Union Council and Executive Minutes, 10 July 1917.
58 Lloyd George to Long (copy), 30 March 1917, LGP, F/32/4/59.
59 Asquith to Crewe, 28 July 1917, Crewe Papers, C/40.
60 National Union Council Minutes, 10 July 1917.

CHAPTER 9   WAITING FOR ASQUITH

1   See J.M. McEwen, The Liberal Party and the Irish Question during
    the First World War, 'Journal of British Studies', XII, no. 1,
    November 1972.
2   Salisbury to Selborne, 21 May 1918, Selborne Papers, vol. 7.
3   Wilson, 'Downfall of Liberal Party' (1966), Collins, pp. 112-21.
4   HC Deb., 20 November 1917, c. 1086.
5   Cities with two or more multi-member seats, and hence scope for
    dual voting would have been: London, Birmingham, Leeds, Liver-
    pool, Sheffield, Manchester and Glasgow.
6   HC Deb., 17 October 1917, c. 183-221.
7   HC Deb., 28 November 1917, c. 2060-74.
8   HC Deb., 15 November 1917, c. 646-69.
9   HC Deb., 28 November 1917, c. 1469.
10 HC Deb., 28 November 1917, c. 1484.
11 NEC Minutes, 26 September 1917.
12 C.P. Scott's Diary, 11-12 December 1917.
13 Ibid.
14 Ibid.
15 NEC Minutes, 13 February 1918.
16 NEC Minutes, 27 February 1918.
17 HC Deb., 22 November 1917, c. 1517-20.
18 'Manchester Guardian', 27 November 1917.
19 HC Deb., 21 November 1917, c. 1135-1272.
20 John Rae, 'Conscience and Politics' (1971), Oxford University
    Press, pp. 221-3.
21 C.P. Scott's Diary, 3 April 1917.
22 HC Deb., 26 July 1916, c. 1759.
23 S.E. Koss, 'Nonconformity in Modern British Politics' (1975),
    Batsford, p. 134.
24 HC Deb., 21 November 1917, c. 230.
25 Rae, op. cit., pp. 234-5.
26 Barnes, Brace, Goldstone, Hancock, Hodge, Parker, Roberts,
    Walsh, Wardle, Stanton.
27 Richard Holt's Diary, 3 December 1917.
28 HC Deb., 5 November 1917, c. 1935.
29 HC Deb., 7 November 1917, c. 2169.
30 Ibid., c. 2273-5.
31 HC Deb., 8 November 1917, c. 2379.
32 C.P. Scott's Diary, 19-21 April 1917.
33 R.B. McDowell, 'The Irish Convention 1917-1918' (1970), Rout-
    ledge & Kegan Paul, pp. 73-7.
34 CAB 1/25/2, 26 June 1917.
35 Lord Beaverbrook, 'Politicians and the War' (1928), Thornton
    Butterworth, chapter V.
36 Long to Mr Harris (copy), 28 June 1917, Long Papers.
37 R.A. Sanders' Diary, 9 December 1917.
38 Roscommon North, 3 February 1917;   Longford South, 10 May 1917;
    Clare East, 10 July 1917;   Kilkenny City, 10 August 1917.
39 McDowell, op. cit., chapter III.
40 J.R.P. Newman to J.H. Humphries, 17 September 1917, ERS.
41 Selborne to Bonar Law, 28 January 1918, BLP, 82/8/8.
42 Bonar Law to Selborne (copy), 30 January 1918, BLP, 84/7/2.

43   HC Deb., 17 October 1917, c. 103.
44   HC Deb., 18 October 1917, c. 303.
45   R.A. Sanders' Diary, 20 October 1917.
46   HC Deb., 6 December 1917, c. 784.
47   F.E. Guest to Lloyd George, 7 December 1917, LGP, F/21/2/9.
48   J. McVeagh and J. Clancy (Nationalists); W. Coote and D. Henry (Unionists).
49   Jerred to Long, 19 January 1918, Long Papers; Report of the Boundary Commission for Ireland, Cd 8830, 1917-18 (14).
50   J.W. Lowther, 'A Speaker's Commentaries' (1925), p. 222.
51   Dr C. Addison, A.C.T. Beck, Sir G. Hewart, F.G. Kellaway, J.H. Lewis, R.L. Harmsworth, H.A.L. Fisher, Sir A. Mond, J.W. Pratt, J.M. Roberts.
52   William Clough, Joseph Bliss, Sir C.H. Seely, Sir T.P. Whittaker, H.J. Glanville.
53   E.I. David, The Liberal Party during the First World War, Cambridge MLitt thesis, 1968.
54   Frances Stevenson's Diary, 18 April 1916.
55   Thornton's Diary, 31 August 1917, Milner Papers, vol. 301; Riddell's 'War Diary', 21 October 1917.
56   Thornton's Diary, 31 August 1917, Milner Papers, vol. 301.
57   Addison's Diary, 12 April 1917, Addison Papers, vol. 98.
58   Lists drawn up by F.E. Guest, 20 July 1918, LGP, F/21/2/28.
59   McKenna to Runciman, 15 January 1917, Runciman to Asquith, 29 January 1917, Runciman Papers, vol. 161.
60   McCallum Scott's Diary, 19 February 1917.
61   Richard Holt's Diary, 18 February 1917.
62   MacCallum Scott's Diary, 29 June 1917.
63   Richard Holt's Diary, 3 December 1917.
64   Richard Holt's Diary, 17 December 1917.
65   HC Deb., 19 December 1917, c. 1993.
66   Richard Holt's Diary, 27 June 1918.
67   Richard Holt's Diary, 3 December 1917.
68   Cabinet Minutes, 23/4, 27 September 1917.
69   Letter to Lord Edmund Talbot (copy), 10 August 1917, Asquith Papers, vol. 26.
70   Richard Holt's Diary, 22 April 1917.
71   Lloyd George to Bonar Law (copy), 10 April 1918, LGP, F/30/2.
72   MacCallum Scott's Diary, 23 May 1915.
73   MacCallum Scott's Diary, 19 February 1917.
74   C.P. Scott's Diary, 11-12 December 1917.

CHAPTER 10   THE REGIMENT OF WOMEN

1   Lord Riddell's 'War Diary' (1933), Nicholson & Watson, pp. 7-8.
2   Note on the Amnesty, 26 August 1914, Suffragette Fellowship Papers, Z6067; HC Deb., 7 August 1914; 'Votes For Women', VIII, no. 336, 14 August 1914.
3   HC Deb., 10 August 1914, c. 2265.
4   Speech at Plymouth, 17 November 1914.
5   'Britannia', 15 October 1915, 12 November 1915.
6   Annie Kenney, 'Memories of a Militant' (1924), Hutchinson, p. 271

7 Cecil to Mrs Fawcett, 5 August 1914, FLP.
8 'Common Cause', VI, no. 278, 7 August 1914.
9 Reports of the London Society For Woman Suffrage.
10 'Common Cause', VI, no. 282, 4 September 1914.
11 Mrs Fawcett to Mrs Chapman Catt, 15 December 1914, FLP.
12 WFL Executive Minutes, 29 November 1917.
13 John Grigg, 'The Young Lloyd George' (1973), Eyre Methuen, p. 284.
14 'Anti-Suffrage Review', no. 77, March 1915.
15 WFL Conference Reports, 16 October 1915, p. 150.
16 WFL Executive Minutes, 16 December 1916, Political and Militant Department (WFL) Minutes, 15 January 1917.
17 Mrs Fawcett to Mrs Chapman Catt, 21 July 1915, FLP.
18 Mrs Fawcett to Miss E. Atkinson, undated, FLP.
19 Dated 13 December 1915, Labour Party Archives, WNC, 29/5.
20 M.G. Fawcett, 'What I Remember' (1924), Unwin, pp. 232-3.
21 Asquith to Mrs Fawcett, 7 May 1916, FLP.
22 'Common Cause', VIII, no. 375, 16 June 1916; circular letter by the London Society For Woman Suffrage, 7 June 1917.
23 Mrs Fawcett to Miss E. Atkinson, 9 July 1916, FLP; 'Common Cause', VIII, no. 375; letters from the 'United Suffragists' and the WSPU in the Dickinson Papers.
24 Mrs Fawcett to Miss E. Atkinson, 9 July 1916, FLP.
25 Northcliffe to Lady Betty Balfour, 20 December 1916, FLP.
26 Mrs Fawcett to Miss P. Strachey, 23 December 1916, FLP.
27 Northcliffe to Mrs Fawcett, 25 December 1916, FLP.
28 Mrs Fawcett to Miss E. Atkinson, 21 December 1916, FLP.
29 Dickinson to Mrs Fawcett, 19 January 1917, FLP.
30 Ibid.
31 Mrs Fawcett's copy of the Speaker's Report, FLP.
32 WFL Political and Militant Department Minutes, 12, 19, 26 February 1917.
33 CAB 24/6/1, 13 February 1917.
34 The 1917 Deputation to Lloyd George (copy), Suffragette Fellowship Papers, Z6065.
35 A. Marwick, 'The Deluge' (1967), Penguin Books, pp. 100-11.
36 Women's International League Circular, 1 June 1916, Labour Party Archives, WNC, 29/5.
37 E.S. Pankhurst, 'The Suffragette Movement' (1931), Longmans Green & Co., p. 601.
38 HC Deb., 16 August 1916, c. 1959-60.
39 A Memorandum on Franchise Reform, Grey Papers, 236/3.
40 'Observer', 13 August 1916.
41 'Anti-Suffrage Review', no. 370, 24 November 1916.
42 Northcliffe to Mrs Fawcett, 27 December 1916, FLP.
43 HC Deb., 19 June 1917, c. 1724.
44 Long to H.A. Morton (copy), 14 June 1917, Long Papers; C. Petrie, 'Walter Long and His Times' (1936), Hutchinson, pp. 210-11.
45 CAB 24/6/1, 13 February 1917.
46 Asquith to Mrs Fawcett, 7 May 1916, FLP.
47 HC Deb., 14 August 1916, c. 1451-2.
48 HC Deb., 28 March 1917, c. 469-70.
49 R. Jenkins, 'Asquith' (1964), Collins, pp. 60-1.

50 Asquith Papers, vol. 89 for transcripts of deputations from Mrs
    Fawcett, pp. 47-84, and Sylvia Pankhurst, pp. 127-52.
51 'Letters From Lord Oxford to a Friend' (1933), Geoffrey Bles,
    pp. 125-6.
52 Jenkins, op. cit., pp. 56-7.
53 'Conservative Agents' Journal', no. 40, April 1916.
54 Joseph Lawrence to Earl Grey, 2 April 1917, Grey Papers, 236/7.
55 Notes on the Report of the Speaker's Committee, 3 February 1917,
    Steel-Maitland Papers, vol. 202.
56 MacCallum Scott's Diary, 19 June 1917.
57 Geoffrey Mitchell (ed.), 'The Hard Way UP: the Autobiography of
    Hannah Mitchell' (1968), Faber & Faber, p. 189.
58 Pankhurst, op. cit., p. 605.
59 HC Deb., 20 June 1917, c. 1812-54.
60 Mrs Fawcett to Dickinson, 22 June 1917, Dickinson Papers.
61 Salisbury to Selborne, 23 August 1916, Selborne Papers, vol. 6.
62 Bryce to Dicey, 11 April 1917, Bryce Papers, English Part I,
    vol. 4; also HL Deb., 11 December 1917, c. 176.
63 Lady Frances Balfour to Mrs Fawcett, 3 January 1917, FLP.
64 Correspondence in the Curzon Papers, D/1/12 for 1916-17.
65 E.A. Mitchell Innes to Curzon, 6 April 1917, Curzon Papers,
    D/1/12.
66 Curzon to Mrs Ward (copy), 26 December 1917, Curzon Papers,
    D/1/12.
67 Curzon to Mrs Ward (copy), 20 December 1917, Curzon Papers,
    D/1/12.
68 Ward to Curzon, 27 March 1917, Curzon Papers, D/1/12.
69 Ward to Curzon, 26 June 1917, Curzon Papers, D/1/12.
70 Mrs Ward to Curzon, 23 December 1917, Curzon Papers, D/1/12.
71 Curzon to Mrs Ward (copy), 7 November 1917, Curzon Papers,
    D/1/12.
72 Curzon to Mrs Ward (copy), 30 December 1917, Curzon Papers,
    D/1/12.
73 Mrs Ward to Curzon, 9 January 1918, Curzon Papers, D/1/12.
74 HL Deb., 9 January 1918, c. 508-25.
75 HC Deb., 23 October 1918, c. 813-22.
76 Ibid., c. 857-62.
77 Mrs Fawcett to Lloyd George (copy), undated, FLP.

CHAPTER 11 THE PEERS AND PROPORTIONAL REPRESENTATION

1 David Butler, 'The Electoral System in Britain 1918-51' (1953),
   Clarendon Press, p. 11.
2 Peers: Balfour of Burleigh, Beauchamp, Burnham, Archbishop of
   Canterbury, Crewe, Denman, Donoughmore, Dunraven, Durham, Lans-
   downe, Loreburn, Rutland, Selborne, Stuart of Wortley, Sydenham,
   Bryce.   MPs: Evelyn Cecil, Lord Hugh Cecil, Austin Chamber-
   lain, Ellis Davies, Sir Charles Hobhouse, Walter Hudson, J.A.
   Murray MacDonald, J.A.R. Marriott, Sir Henry Norman, T.P.
   O'Connor, J.M. Robertson, Clavell Salter, Thomas Scanlan, Sir
   T.P. Whittaker, Sir George Younger, R.A. Sanders.
3 Selborne to Huch Cecil (copy), 18 August 1917, Selborne Papers,
   vol. 85.

4   R.A. Sanders' Diary, 9 December 1917.
5   Memorandum dated 12 December 1917, Selborne Papers, vol. 85.
6   Selborne to Crewe (copy), 31 December 1917, Selborne Papers, vol. 85;   Rutland to Selborne, 22 December 1917, Selborne Papers, vol. 85.
7   Report on the Machinery of Government, Cd 9038 (1918).
8   Report, dated 17 July 1918, Selborne Papers, vol. 85.
9   Bonar Law to Selborne (copy), 30 January 1918, BLP, 84/7/2.
10 C.P. Scott's Diary, 28 January 1917.
11 C.P. Scott's Diary, 3 April 1917.
12 E.T. John to J.H. Humphries, 17 May 1917, ERS.
13 HC Deb., 28 March 1917, c. 492.
14 Minutes of the Parliamentary Committee, 15 February 1917.
15 Limited material exists in the Electoral Reform Society Records, the Long Papers, and the Papers of Sir William Bull.   Members of the Committee were: Unionists: W. Burdett-Coutts (Chairman), J.D. Gilbert, Lord Claud Hamilton, Herbert Jessel, Francis Lowe, De Fonblanque Pennefather, Samuel Roberts, Albert Spicer, E.A. Strauss, James Boyton; Liberals: Rowland Barran, W. Howell Davies, J.C. Wason, Sir T.P. Whittaker.
16 'Conservative Agents' Journal', no. 44, April 1917.
17 Salvidge to Derby, 2 June 1917, Derby Papers, 1/29.
18 The antis included 22 Unionists, 13 Liberals, 1 Labour, 1 Independent; the pros, 2 Unionists and 6 Liberals.
19 Minutes of the London Unionist Members Committee, 24 April 1917 and 19 June 1917.
20 Lord Chaplin to J.H. Humphries, 7 May 1917, ERS.
21 Grey to Hamilton (copy), 2 June 1917, Grey Papers, 236/7.
22 PR Pamphlet no. 31, March 1917.
23 'Liberal Agent', XIX, no. 88, April 1917.
24 'Edinburgh Review', vol. 226, July 1917.
25 Minutes of the Parliamentary Committee, 19 June 1917.
26 Minutes of the PR Society Executive Committee, 22 June 1917.
27 PR Pamphlet no. 32, by J.R.P. Newman, reproduced as Memo no. 1 by the House of Lords Committee for PR, 28 July 1917.
28 Ibid.
29 Memo no. 2, House of Lords Committee for PR, 20 October 1917; PR Pamphlet no. 32.
30 Grey to Wilson-Fox (copy), 26 March 1917, Grey Papers, 236/7.
31 Williams to Earl Grey, 2 April 1917, Grey Papers, 236/7.
32 HC Deb., 4 July 1917, c. 1168 and 1233.
33 HC Deb., 12 June 1917, c. 836-41.
34 'Westminster Gazette', 16 June 1917.
35 HC Deb., 22 May 1917, c. 2220-33.
36 The members were: Lansdowne, Salisbury, Londonderry, Grey, Mayo, Beauchamp, Selborne, Bryce, Chaplin, Balfour of Burleigh, Avebury, Burnham, Courtney, MacDonnell, Sydenham, Northbourne, Muir Mackenzie, Onslow, Stuart of Wortley - Minutes of the Parliamentary Committee, 10 July 1917.
37 Minutes of the Parliamentary Committee, 22 October 1917.
38 Minutes of the House of Lords Committee, 23 October 1917.
39 Lord Wolmer to Williams (copy), 4 October 1917, ERS.
40 Chancellor to Humphries, 26 November 1917, ERS.
41 'Manchester Guardian', 4 January 1918.

42   HL Deb., 21 January 1918, c. 824-44.
43   Humphries to Wolmer, 13 July 1917, ERS.
44   Ibid.
45   'Manchester Guardian', 4 January 1918.
46   Report on the National Union Special Conference, 30 November 1917.
47   Minutes of the House of Lords Committee, 11 December 1917.
48   Selborne to Humphries, 18 February 1918, ERS.
49   Cabinet Minutes, 23/5, 24 January 1918.
50   Selborne to Lloyd George (copy), 26 January 1918, Selborne Papers, vol. 87.
51   Cabinet Minutes, 23/5, 24 January 1918.
52   Cabinet Minutes, 23/5, 28 January 1918.
53   HC Deb., 30 January 1918, c. 1602-19.
54   MacCallum Scott's Diary, 6 July 1917.
55   Cabinet Minutes, 23/4, 27 September 1917.
56   R.A. Sanders' Diary, 2 February 1918.
57   R.A. Sanders' Diary, 10 February 1918.
58   'The Times', 24 January 1918.
59   Selborne to Lloyd George (copy), 26 January 1918, Selborne Papers, vol. 87.
60   Courtney to Simon (copy), 24 January 1918, Courtney Papers, vol. 12.
61   Cabinet Minutes, 23/5, 1 February 1918.
62   HL Deb., 4 February 1918, c. 321-31.
63   Cecil to Lloyd George, 5 February 1918, LGP, F/6/5/18.
64   Cabinet Minutes, 23/5, 5 February 1918; Addison's Diary, 5 February 1918, Addison Papers, vol. 96.
65   R.L. Harmsworth and A.C.T. Beck (Liberal); John Hodge and C.B. Stanton (Labour); William O'Malley (Nationalist).
66   HL Deb., 6 February 1918, c. 403-8.
67   Report of the Royal Commission on a Scheme for Proportional Representation, Cd 9044 (1918).
68   HC Deb., 6 February 1918, c. 2249-54.
69   Sir Clifford Cory, T.J. Williams, R.L. Harmsworth and Sir T.C. Warner (Liberal); C.B. Stanton (Labour); William O'Malley (Nationalist).
70   Dr C. Addison, J.H. Lewis, Robert Munro, Sir J.H. Roberts, Sir A. Mond, Sir E.A. Cornwall, Colonel J.W. Greig, Sir M. Levy, H.A.L. Fisher, J.W. Pratt, F.E. Guest, Sir W.H. Cowan, A.C.T. Beck.

CHAPTER 12   REFORM AND THE COUPON ELECTION

1   Roy Douglas, The Background to the Coupon Election Arrangements, 'English Historical Review', April 1971.
2   CAB 24/42, 20 February 1918.
3   CAB 24/51, 11 May 1918; Cabinet Minutes, 23/6/411, 14 May 1918.
4   CAB 24/51, 15 May 1918.
5   Absent Voters, Cd 9156 (1918).
6   HC Deb., 7 April 1919, c. 1653-4.
7   CAB 24/54, 15 June 1918.
8   Robert Blake, 'The Unknown Prime Minister' (1955), Eyre & Spottiswoode, pp. 381-3.

9 'The Times', 21 November 1918.
10 Percy Woodhouse to Derby, 17 May 1917, Derby Papers, 2/21.

CHAPTER 13 WAR, REFORM AND THE DECLINE OF PARLIAMENT

1 S. Andreski, 'Military Organisation and Society' (1954), Routledge & Kegan Paul.
2 R. Titmuss, 'Essays On The Welfare State' (1958), Allen & Unwin.
3 A. Marwick, 'War And Social Change in the Twentieth Century'
(1974), Macmillan.
4 H. Pelling, 'Britain and the Second World War' (1970), Macmillan, p. 299.
5 P. Abrams, The Failure of Social Reform 1918-1920, 'Past and
Present', no. 24, 1963.
6 R.H. Tawney, The Abolition of Economic Controls 1918-1921,
'Economic History Review', 1943.
7 W.H. Dickinson, The Greatest Reform Act, 'Contemporary Review',
113, March 1918.
8 'Manchester Guardian', 21 June 1917.

A NOTE ON SOURCES

It is obvious that the collections of private papers listed below
provide the largest single source for this book, though the records
of certain societies bulk large on some aspects of it.   It is, however, easy to exaggerate the importance of private papers as a
source of history, and a number of the collections consulted for
this study have yielded very little of relevance.   In general the
volumes of correspondence collectively underline the point that
during the First World War electoral reform did not dominate the
minds of politicians as it had done in earlier times.   A particular
difficulty arises from the tendency of the correspondence of leading
Liberals to drop off sharply in December 1916 and never fully to recover.   The Lloyd George Papers, for example, despite their size,
are not a source of great strength for domestic history in this
period.   Together with the Papers of Asquith and Bonar Law they
provide fitful insights of direct relevance to this study.   Some
collections have proved useful on limited aspects; for example
Curzon on the anti-suffrage campaign, Dickinson on the Speaker's
Conference, Gainford on pre-1914 reform, Selborne on Conservative
ideas on reform and Steel-Maitland on Central Office reactions to
reform.   The new collection of Walter Long's Papers help to substantiate evidence from elsewhere of his crucial role in promoting
reform.   Backbench diaries by Richard Holt, MacCallum Scott and
Arthur Murray give some life to one's picture of the Liberal Party
during the war, as does Colonel Sanders for the Conservatives.   But
major collections like the Papers of Haldane, Crewe, Runciman,
Samuel and Harcourt are somewhat disappointing, as are those of Balfour and Chamberlain.   The diaries of C.P. Scott and Dr Addison,
examined in the original versions, have been found to contain some
useful material not included in the published volumes.   Another
helpful diarist was Sir Hugh Thornton, private secretary to Lord
Milner, who suggests the muddle and inefficiency that characterised
Lloyd George's supposedly improved Cabinet system.
   A few omissions should be noted.   Two of these may be signifi-
cant, particularly the Papers of Sir George Cave which are in the
British Museum but will not become available until 1982.   Sir
Charles Mallet was given access to them when writing 'Lord Cave: a
Memoir' (1931) but not much emerges from the book.   Another gap is

the Papers of Sir John Simon, which might have been useful on the
Speaker's Conference, but which have been closed by the present Lord
Simon.   Similarly Sir William Bull, who was a member of the Conference and private secretary to Long, may have left useful material
apart from what is in the House of Lords Record Office and the Ham-
mersmith Public Library, but this is in the possession of Sir George
Bull and not available.   The diary of J.A. Pease was closed for
many years at Nuffield College awaiting publication.

The records of the Electoral Reform Society have been of major
importance and are supplemented by those of the Fourth Earl Grey at
Durham;   the Papers of Courtney and Avebury are, however, disappointing.   For the women's movement the Fawcett Library collections and the Papers of Catherine Marshall at Carlisle proved inval-
uable;   those at the London Museum and the John Rylands Library are
less helpful for the war years.

Among the political parties the minutes of both the National Executive of the Labour Party and the Conservative and Unionist Association's Council and Executive proved of direct use, though the
abundance of Liberal politicians' papers does not entirely compen-
sate for the failure of the Liberal Party to hold on to its records.
Comparatively little use has been found for the national press,
though journals have been found very rewarding.   In particular the
scarce copies of the 'Liberal Agent' at the National Liberal Club
and the 'Conservative Agents' Journal' at Conservative Central
Office provide a candid view of politics which was intended only for
a small group of people;   the copies were not on sale and were generally destroyed when no longer in use in case they should fall into
enemy hands.

LIST OF PRIMARY SOURCES

1 Official papers

Cabinet Papers: PRO CAB 23, 24, 37, 41
Parliamentary Debates, Fifth Series
Parliamentary Papers:
   Cd 3501, Misc. no. 3 (1907), Reports From His Majesty's Represen-
   tatives Abroad on the Application of Proportional Representation.
   Cd 3875, Misc. no. 2 (1908), Reports From His Majesty's Represen-
   tatives Abroad on the Second Ballot.
   Cd 5163 (1910), Report of the Royal Commission on Electoral Sys-
   tems.
   Cd 5352 (1910), Minutes of Evidence of the Royal Commission on
   Electoral Systems.
   Cd 8463 (1917), Letter From the Speaker to the Prime Minister.
   Representation of the People Bill, 1918 (7 & 8, Geo. V), Parlia-
   mentary Papers, 1917-18, vol. 2.
   Cd 8756-8 (1917-18), Reports of the Boundary Commissioners for
   England and Wales.
   Cd 8759 (1917-18), Report of the Boundary Commissioners for Scot-
   land.
   Cd 8830 (1917-18), Report of the Boundary Commissioners for Ire-
   land.

Cd 9038 (1918), Report on the Machinery of Government.
Cd 9044 (1918), Report of the Royal Commission on Proportional
Representation.
Cd 9156 (1918), Absent Voters.
Parliamentary Papers 1918 (138), XIX, 925, Return showing the
number of Parliamentary electors in 1918.

2   Records of societies and institutions

Conservative Party: Minutes of the National Union of Conservative
and Unionist Associations and the London Unionist Members.
Electoral Reform Society: Minute Books, Correspondence, Press Cut-
tings, Pamphlets and Periodicals.
Fawcett Library: Minute Books, Correspondence, Journals and Pamph-
lets.
Labour Party: Transport House Archives.
National Liberal Club: Election Addresses and Journals.
Suffragette Fellowship Papers (London Museum).

3   Private papers

At the Bodleian Library:
Dr C. Addison;   H.H. Asquith;   Viscount Bryce;   H.A.L. Fisher;
Lewis Harcourt;   Viscount Milner;   the Earl of Selborne.

At the British Museum:
Lord Avebury;   A.J. Balfour;   John Burns;   Lord Robert Cecil;   Herbert Gladstone;   C.P. Scott;   J.A. Spender.

At the Birmingham University Library:
Austen Chamberlain.

At the British Library of Political and Economic Science:
Lord Courtney.

At the Cambridge University Library:
Lord Crewe.

At Carlisle Record Office:
Catherine Marshall.

At Churchill College, Cambridge:
Reginald McKenna;   Sir Henry Page-Croft.

At Durham University, Department of Diplomatic and Paleography:
Earl Grey.

At the Greater London Record Office:
W.H. Dickinson.

At the House of Lords Record Office:
A. Bonar Law;   Sir W. Bull;   J.C.C. Davidson;   David Lloyd George;
Herbert Samuel;   John St Loe Strachey.

At the India Office Library:
Lord Curzon.

At the Liverpool Record Office:
Earl of Derby; R.D. Holt.

At the National Library of Scotland:
Master of Elibank; R.B. Haldane.

In the possession of Mr John MacCallum Scott:
Alexander MacCallum Scott.

At the Newcastle University Library:
Walter Runciman; Charles Trevelyan.

At Nuffield College, Oxford:
Lord Gainford (J.A. Pease).

At the Scottish Record Office:
Sir Arthur Steel-Maitland.

At the Wiltshire County Record Office:
Walter Long.

At the Conservative Research Centre:
Sir Robert A. Sanders.

4 Newspapers and journals

Anti-Suffrage Review
Common Cuase
Conservative Agents Journal
Conservative and Unionist Women's Suffrage Review
Contemporary Review
Edinburgh Review
Fortnightly Review
Labour Leader
Liberal Agent
Liberal Magazine
Manchester Guardian
Morning Post
The Nation
National Review
National Union Notes and Gleanings
Nineteenth Century and After
Punch
Quarterly Review
Representation
Suffragette
The Times
The Vote
Votes for Women
Westminster Gazette

INDEX